MARIE'S HOME IMPROVEMENT GUIDE

MARIE L. LEONARD

SEAL PRESS

Marie's Home Improvement Guide

Copyright © 2009 by Marie L. Leonard

Published by
Seal Press
A Member of the Perseus Books Group
1700 Fourth Street
Berkeley, California 94710

Library of Congress Cataloging-in-Publication Data

Leonard, Marie, 1959-
 Marie's home improvement guide / by Marie Leonard.
    p. cm.
 ISBN 978-1-58005-292-4
1. Dwellings--Maintenance and repair--Amateurs' manuals. 2.
Do-it-yourself work. 3. Women construction workers. I. Title. II. Title:
Home improvement guide.
 TH4817.3.L45 2009
 643'.7--dc22

                        2009010284

Cover design by Tim McGrath
Interior design by Tabitha Lahr
Illustrations by Tim McGrath
Printed in the United States of America
Distributed by Publishers Group West
9 8 7 6 5 4 3 2 1

To my parents, Romeo and Florence Levesque:
It all started with you.

To my husband, Bill Leonard:
I couldn't do what I do without you.

To my daughters, Renee and Keely Craig:
You are my inspiration and my joy.

CONTENTS

INTRODUCTION

After the events of September 11, 2001, many people stopped to reevaluate some aspect of their lives. I was one of the many that finally admitted to myself the hard truth about how dissatisfied I was with my career and how I was spending each day of my life during the week. I did something I had never done before—I asked myself the question, "What would I do if I could do anything I wanted?" I was shocked when the answer immediately popped into my head: "I would teach women how to do home improvement projects." I had spent the previous eight years doing projects on my own home: I had painted every inch of my house inside and out, installed new faucets, moved a few walls, tiled a floor and a countertop, put a new roof on my shed, and built a small porch. And I did most of these projects on my own (although my father and I worked together on some of the more complex ones).

The feeling of satisfaction and accomplishment I felt when I finished each project was unlike anything I had ever experienced professionally. That's what really made an impact on me. And I knew that other women would love to have similar experiences. Who doesn't want to feel like they can do just about anything? It feels good.

Over the next few months, I took the necessary steps to close down my corporate training business and start Marie's Home Improvement. I loaded my tools in the back of my minivan, and I started working as a handywoman; my business had a unique focus, however, because instead of simply completing each client's home project for her, I taught her how to complete it herself. In those first few months, I taught many women how to remove wallpaper, prepare and paint walls, tile a kitchen backsplash, replace a faucet, hang pictures, and much more.

Initially, I marketed myself through mother's groups I belonged to, or through women I met when my children had playdates. Friends of friends heard about me, and demand for my services slowly grew until November of 2002, when I was featured in *The Boston Globe*. I was stunned by the number of women who responded—women who were eager to complete the projects that had been on their to-do lists for years.

In order to reach even more women, I started teaching a class for women at the local adult education center. The class was called "I Can Fix It, You Can Too!", which is the motto of my business. In the first half of the three-hour-long class, I would go through all the basic tools in my toolbox, explaining the purpose of each tool and the different projects they could be used to complete. In the second half of the class, I would show my students how to fix a hole in the wall on a small wall I had constructed and brought with me, and how to make basic repairs to the moving parts in a toilet tank that I had created out of a trash can. I also demonstrated how to fix minor faucet leaks, replace a door handle, and hang a shelf.

This book, *Marie's Home Improvement Guide*, is the next step in my journey. My passion is teaching women how to do home improvement projects so that they can experience the immense satisfaction and self-esteem boost that comes from taking on a project you don't think you can do and successfully completing it. Not to mention that you can have fun and save lots of money by not paying someone else to do basic home repairs and improvements that can maintain or increase the value of your home, as well as improve its looks and functionality.

This book is written for all the women who weren't blessed, as I was, with a father who could not only fix anything around the house, but who was willing to teach me how as well. This book is for all the women who are tired of asking fathers, husbands, boyfriends, partners, and neighbors to come help them out with a project. It's for all the women who are tired of hiring a handyman, plumber, or electrician to do a simple job, and who have watched said handyman, plumber, or electrician, only to say to themself, "That wasn't very hard. I could have done that." It's for all the women who have been tempted to try a project but were afraid they would screw it up. And, lastly, this book is for all the women who have had the courage to start a project but didn't have the knowledge to see it through to a successful completion.

Since I cannot travel to every one of your homes to give you personal instruction, I wrote this book. I hope that, when you read this book, you'll hear my voice talking to you, just as I have talked to the women in my classes and to the women I have worked with one-on-one in the privacy of their own homes over the years.

I start the book with a very basic introduction to tools, all the tools you will need to complete the projects I cover in the book. The right tools make every job easier. After you're familiar with the tools, I go over how to go shopping for materials and supplies. This can be an overwhelming and frustrating process, and I hope that I have answered any questions you might have, which will make shopping easier and more fun for you. Once you have the tools and materials you need, I jump right into all the different projects women have asked me to teach them how to do since I started my business. You will learn how to hang things like pictures, curtains, and shades, and how to repair damaged walls. I will explain how to fix the many problems that can come up with the doors in your home, and how to paint a room successfully.

Then we'll move into the bathroom and take on the many water- and non-water-related projects that present themselves there. We'll finish up with a group of carpentry projects designed to introduce you to my favorite power tools, and a lesson on basic electrical repairs. By the time you have worked your way through the projects that interest you in this book, I hope you will have acquired several things: comfort and familiarity with hand and power tools, an understanding of how to assess and plan for a project, the freedom to say "no" to projects that you don't feel comfortable with, and the realization that you can say "yes" to an unlimited list of projects to improve your home.

DEGREE OF CHALLENGE

Assigning a degree of challenge rating for the projects you'll find in the book was tricky. The difficulty level of each project really varies by individual depending on previous home improvement experience, comfort level with the tools and materials, and basic personality type. Keeping all of that in mind, I have rated the challenge level of each project in this book. The ratings are on a scale of 1 to 5 and this is what each rating means to me:

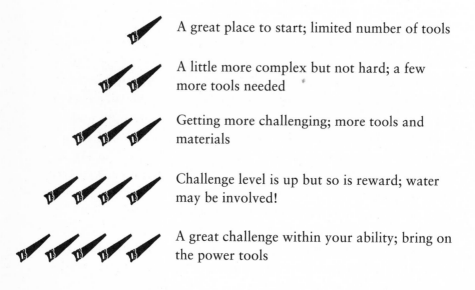

A great place to start; limited number of tools

A little more complex but not hard; a few more tools needed

Getting more challenging; more tools and materials

Challenge level is up but so is reward; water may be involved!

A great challenge within your ability; bring on the power tools

1. GETTING STARTED

One of the reasons that professionals can do jobs better than amateurs is the greater quantity and superior quality of their tools. Having the right tool and knowing how to use it really does make any job easier to do well. Every woman should have her own toolbox. In this chapter, I'll provide you with a list of basic tools that will give you what you need to do most any job on your to-do list. You do not need to rush out and purchase every tool on the list at once; you can pick them up when you find you need a specific tool for the job at hand. Tools are also great gifts to ask for on your birthday.

Shopping for tools can be a bit overwhelming. There is no such thing as just a hammer or screwdriver. Every tool comes in more than one variety, and many tools come in different sizes. Armed with a basic list and a little knowledge, you can shop for tools confidently.

I would rather wander through a good hardware store than a department store any day. Only a hardware store can make me exclaim, "Wow, I didn't know they made a tool that did *that*!"

My father, Romeo, has been and continues to be one of my best teachers in all things related to tools and home improvement projects. Throughout this book I will be passing on his knowledge to you. Romeo's mantra regarding tools is: "Buy the best tools you can afford. A good tool will work better and last longer than a cheap one." Besides buying good quality tools, it is also very important to choose tools that feel good in your hands. The old saying "Looking good is all that really matters" does not apply to tools. I try and avoid all the pink tools marketed to women and instead look for good brands of tools that are well made and seem to fit my hands.

The Toolbox

I have been on the quest for the perfect toolbox for many years and have yet to find it. I currently use a collection of tool bags, boxes, and buckets to lug my tools around, and I spend more time than I would like trying to find each individual tool. But, like handbags, toolboxes are suited to the individual's style and needs. You need to determine whether your toolbox will be just for carrying tools, or whether you will also use it to carry a small assortment of hardware, such as screws and nails.

Two small toolboxes are easier to carry around than one large one. I like ones that are 16 inches wide by 8 inches high by 8 inches deep.

I keep my small hand tools like screwdrivers and nail punches in one box, and larger hand tools like hammers and pry bars in a different box. I keep most of my power tools in the carrying case they come in when purchased. These cases protect the tools and make it easier for me to carry and identify them.

If you're lucky enough to have a small workshop area in your home, then it can be fun to set up a pegboard area where you can hang your tools. When they're all visible at once, they're much easier to find. My dad helped me set a pegboard up when I first moved into my house, and he outlined each tool with magic marker so I could always tell what tool was missing!

Hand Tools

Screwdrivers are designed to drive screws into something and come in two basic styles:

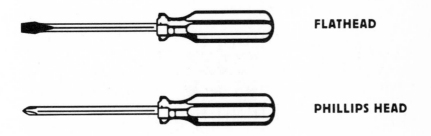

FLATHEAD

PHILLIPS HEAD

Screwdrivers come in more than one variety because screws come in more than one variety, and the screwdriver must match the screw both in shape and size. You will want to purchase at least three of both types of screwdrivers, in small, medium, and large. These sizes are all relative. Your best bet is to buy either a kit containing a collection of six to eight screwdrivers or a screwdriver with a wide variety of interchangeable bits that are stored in the handle.

A **STEEL MEASURING TAPE** is a very important tool. In order to hang pictures, order blinds correctly, or complete successful carpentry projects, you will need a good steel tape. You *cannot* use your flexible sewing tape, your child's 12-inch ruler, or a yardstick if you want consistent, reliable measurements. I suggest a 16-foot-long tape with a ¾-inch-wide blade.

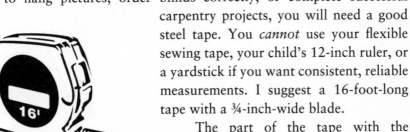

The part of the tape with the measurements marked on it is called the blade. I like this size tape because it will serve me in most of my projects, it's comfortable to hold in my hand, and it fits well in my tool belt. I also have a 25-foot by 1-inch tape that I use for longer projects.

I was standing at the service desk of a window replacement company recently and overheard a woman say, "My window is 30 inches and three of those little stripes" wide. Counting those "little stripes" can be challenging, and translating them into accurate measurements can be even harder. The littlest stripes measure ¹⁄₁₆ of an inch, every fourth stripe equals ¼ of an inch, every eighth stripe equals ½ of an inch, and every twelfth stripe equals ¾ of an inch.

If you find that you are "stripe challenged," have no fear: You

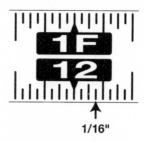

1/16"

can purchase a steel measuring tape that has the measurements of the individual stripes marked so that you don't have to add them up and convert them into parts of inches.

If I had a **HAMMER** . . . I wouldn't have to look at the variety offered at the store and be completely overwhelmed! I used to think that a hammer was a hammer, but I have since learned about the wide variety of hammers on the market. Hammers are sold in different styles; each kind serves a different purpose, ranging from framing a building to hanging a picture. They also come in different weights. If you already own a hammer, it's probably a 16-oz. claw hammer.

This is a good, basic hammer that will be useful in most situations, but it is quite heavy. I suggest you buy a 7-oz. claw hammer for your toolbox, and keep the heavier hammer around for bigger projects.

Are you on the **LEVEL**? Without a level, houses and most everything in them would be crooked or uneven. Levels allow us to hang a group of pictures in a straight line, make sure a storm/screen door is hanging correctly, and put a shelf up that nothing will slide off of. Levels are available in lengths from 10 inches to multiple feet. Most household projects can be handled with a 10-inch, 2-foot, or 4-foot level.

Objects are level (horizontally) or plumb (vertically) when the bubble on the level is framed by two black lines.

A laser level is a great tool to have when you need a longer

line than you can get with a 4-foot spirit level. When you attach it to a wall, a laser level shoots out a beam of red light that's perfectly straight. I use my laser level when I hang long pieces of shelving or when I hang up a group of pictures that all need to be at the same height. Laser levels are wonderful additions to any toolbox, but they won't replace an old fashioned spirit level in many situations.

My workshop is full of power saws, but I still carry and use my **HANDSAW** regularly. Saws are made in many shapes, sizes, and lengths, and they're designed for very specific uses. What you need is a small saw designed to cut wood cleanly (if not quickly).

Saws that have very small teeth set very close together are designed for finer, cleaner cuts. Saws with large teeth set far apart are designed for rough, fast cuts—like for cutting down a tree, for example. I don't cut down many trees, so I carry a handsaw that's

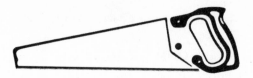

about 14 inches long. Find yourself any lightweight saw that fits comfortably in your hands, and you'll be all set.

Whereas the handsaw is designed to cut wood, the **HACKSAW** is designed to cut through metal and plastic. The blade on a hacksaw is only about a ½-inch wide and 12 inches long. It has lots and lots of tiny teeth put very close together. You need a hacksaw to cut through a metal threshold, to make cuts when installing a metal screen/storm door, or to cut rusted bolts off of your toilet. It is also handy for cutting PVC (polyvinyl chloride) plumbing pipes. Hacksaws are inexpensive and come in various shapes and sizes.

Some of the projects you will take on around the house will require the removal of existing wood or nails. In those situations, you'll need a good **FLAT BAR, PRY BAR,** or **CAT'S PAW.**

Flat bars and pry bars provide leverage, which allows you to lift or move something that you otherwise couldn't with your bare hands. The longer they are, the more leverage you can get. More leverage equals less effort on your part. A cat's paw is a small pry bar with an end that is shaped—you guessed it—like a cat's paw. Just as a cat can dig things up with its paw, this pry bar can dig nailheads out of wood when helped by a good whack with a hammer.

When I get in my car at the end of a day's work, the tool I always find in my back pocket is my **UTILITY KNIFE.** There are very few jobs that I do without the help of my utility knife, which is why it lives in my pocket. I keep another one in my kitchen drawer for everyday uses around the house, like cutting open those annoying plastic packages that encase almost everything I buy.

A utility knife contains a blade shaped like a trapezoid.

When you depress the button on top of the knife and push it forward, half of the blade is exposed for use. The blades are very sharp and can be used to cut wallboard, vinyl flooring, cardboard, carpeting, plastic, and much more. To change the blade or flip it over to use its other end, you have to open the utility knife up. Inexpensive knives come with a screw on one side that holds the two side shells of the knife together. You must remove the screw and take the entire knife apart in order to change the blade. Because it is such a hassle to change the blade in these knives, people don't change them often enough and end up using a dull blade, which is actually far more dangerous than using a sharp blade. A cheap knife costs between three and five dollars. I strongly urge you to splurge and buy a really good knife for between ten and fifteen dollars. The better knives are designed to open up very easily, making changing the blade a breeze (which will encourage you to do it more often). It will last forever, and you may come to love it as much as I love mine!

Many women I meet are afraid to make holes in the walls of their homes, because they don't know how to fix the holes once they exist. With the right **PUTTY KNIVES** and a little know-how, you will soon be filling up every hole, nick, or scratch in your walls. Putty knives come in metal and plastic versions, and they're sold in varying widths, from 1½ inches up to 6 inches.

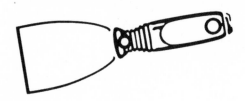

I suggest you get a 1½-inch, a 3-inch, and a 6-inch knife to start. You can add a 12-inch knife later, when you graduate to fixing larger holes. This is another case where spending just a little bit more money up front will buy you a much better tool that will feel really good in your hands, do the job required of it more effectively, and last forever if you take good care of it.

ELECTRONIC STUD FINDERS are a wonderful invention, and (just like your computer) when they work, they're marvelous. What is a stud? Behind the painted, plastered, or wallpapered rooms in your home is a wooden skeleton: the frame upon which your home was built. Just like the bones of a human skeleton, the frame of a home—which includes the walls, floors, and ceilings—is designed to support all the weight of the home, including the roof. Studs are vertical boards, spaced about 16 inches apart, that run from the floor to the ceiling throughout your walls; they measure 1½ inches wide by 3½ or 5½ inches deep.

If you want to hang something like a shelf or heavy mirror on your wall, you will get the most support for that object if you can find a stud to hang the object upon. Since most of us don't have x-ray vision, we can't just look into the wall to locate studs. My father used to use a hammer to locate studs. He would work across the wall, tapping the wall lightly with the hammer every inch or so. It would go something like this: "Tap, tap, tap, tap, tap, tap, tip, 'Oh, there it is!'" I would stand there looking at him with a bewildered look on my face. Being tone deaf, I couldn't hear the different sound the hammer apparently made when he tapped the part of the wall covering the stud after having repeatedly tapped the hollow part of the wall.

Enter the stud finder! The original stud finder looked like a small compass, and its needle would react when it passed over one of the screws or nailheads that hold the wallboard to the studs. Today's modern electronic stud finders can sense the difference in density between wood and wallboard.

You gently slide the stud finder across a wall, and when it locates a stud, it beeps and/or lights up. Once you locate one stud in the wall, you can assume there will be another one roughly 15 to 16 inches away in each direction. When they work, electronic stud finders are more accurate than the hammer method, but false positives are common.

If you live in a home that was built before 1940, your walls may be covered in plaster and lathe instead of wallboard. An electronic stud finder will not work in these older homes. In order to find the studs in those old walls, you must act like a detective and look for nailheads in the baseboard, chair rail, or crown molding. The nailheads indicate the location of the studs that they are nailed into.

PLIERS come in huge variety of shapes and sizes designed for a multitude of uses. I have about nine pairs of pliers in my toolbox, but they represent three basic types.

First are **CHANNELLOCK PLIERS** (also called water pump), which have adjustable jaws for large and small objects and are used for plumbing and anything involving nuts (the kind found on bicycles and plumbing fixtures, not the kind you eat).

Second, you need **NEEDLE-NOSE PLIERS**, which are used for bending and shaping wires during electrical work and for holding small nails while hammering.

Third, **ELECTRICIAN'S PLIERS** (also called a Linesman's Tool), which have a flat tip and an area for cutting wires. While one hammer can be used to hammer a variety of types and sizes of nails, you will find that pliers cannot be used interchangeably, and you will really struggle if you try and do a job with the wrong kind.

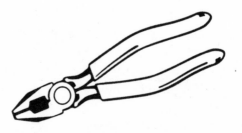

CRESCENT WRENCHES are used in situations where pliers don't work, so it's important to have a couple on hand. I suggest a small- and medium-size wrench. Each one is adjustable to fit several sizes of nuts. I find crescent wrenches a little hard to use; they slip off the nut you're trying to tighten too easily. In their place, I often reach for a fixed wrench or a ratchet (or socket) wrench, both of which come in nice kits.

In order to complete many of the projects you're going to take on around your house, you'll need to finish the job with a nice bead of caulk. In order to lay a nice bead of caulk, you will need to own (and master) a **CAULKING GUN.** I have met many women who are frightened of or intimidated by caulking guns. During one of my classes, for instance, when I brought out a tube of caulk and a caulking gun to demonstrate how they fit together, a woman in the class let out a sort of frustrated groaning sound and said, "I didn't know you needed a *gun.*" She clearly had never tried to squeeze caulk out of a tube with her bare hands (it's next to impossible, I promise). After we all had a good laugh with her (not at her), we talked about how many tools are not self-explanatory. It often

helps to have tools explained (like I'm doing here) or demonstrated; otherwise, it can be difficult to get a sense of how they really work. When shopping for a good caulking gun, avoid the ones that cost less than five dollars—the trigger mechanism is rough, and it's hard to get the caulk to stop squirting out when you want it to. Instead, I have found that it is worth investing ten to fifteen dollars on a better-designed gun: It will have a smoother operation, an easier-to-pull trigger, and a pointy thing to poke holes in new tubes of caulk. Also, if you really need some help pulling the trigger on the gun, there are electric caulking guns (even more expensive, but they require less muscle).

When I discovered the **SIX-IN-ONE PAINTER'S TOOL,** I thought I had died and gone to heaven. It quickly became the favorite tool in my toolbox, and one I reach for daily because it is so versatile. I still cannot believe how much painting and other miscellaneous jobs I had to do without this tool before I found it. Its unique shape, with a beveled end for paint scraping and putty application, its curved edged for removing paint from rollers, and its sharp tip for digging stuff out of tight places make it the best tool for its price. You will also see ten-in-one and even fourteen-in-one painter's tools. In these cases, more is not better. The basic six-in-one—which costs about seven dollars—is all you need.

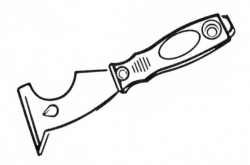

No toolbox is complete without good **SAFETY GLASSES** to protect your eyes. They're available in a wide variety of styles, so finding one that fits your head shouldn't be difficult.

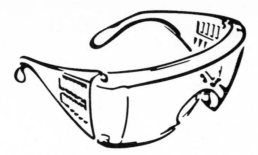

The biggest lesson I have learned regarding safety glasses is a simple one: If I take good care of them and keep them from getting scratched and dirty, I am more likely to wear them, and if I wear them, I am less likely to get injured. It's kind of like using a diaphragm for birth control: How many women have gotten pregnant because their diaphragm was still in its box in the bathroom while they were in the bedroom? Lots! And how many people have injured their eyes while their glasses lay snugly in the bottom of the toolbox? Lots!

Because they are made of plastic, glasses scratch easily, and when they get scratched, they are very difficult to see through. If you are going to keep your glasses in your toolbox, find a case to put them in to protect them. Put them on at the beginning of every job, no matter what you are doing; it's a great habit to get into.

Power Tools

When we had been dating about one year, my then-boyfriend (now my husband) gave me a **DEWALT 18-VOLT CORDLESS DRILL** for my birthday. It was the best present ever! It was my first introduction to cordless tools, and I fell in love. Of all my power tools, I still use my cordless drill the most.

What I love most about cordless drills is their versatility. Many jobs require the use of both a drill and a screwdriver, and the cordless drill becomes a power screwdriver when you take out the drill bit and replace it with a screwdriver bit.

The weight of a cordless drill is mostly determined by the size of its battery. The 18-volt battery is big and heavy, and now, six years later, I feel that weight more than I originally did. I suggest that most women purchase a drill with a battery in the 9- to 12-volt range. The most important thing to do is to try out how it feels. If it's too heavy, you won't be comfortable using it, and it will never see the light of day.

I have lost count of the number of women I've watched sheepishly bring their cordless drill, which has been sitting unused for who knows how long, out of the closet. In many cases it was a gift given to them when they first moved into their own home, and it sat collecting dust for years because they never learned how to use it properly. Ladies: It's time to bring the drills out in the open and get to know them. This tool (and its little sister, the **RECHARGEABLE SCREWDRIVER**) can make jobs that a handheld screwdriver can't do downright easy.

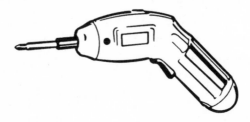

All of the jobs I will discuss in this book (with the exception of the minor carpentry projects detailed in Chapter 9) can be handled successfully without any additional power tools, with the possible exception of a **HANDHELD RANDOM ORBITAL PALM SANDER.** I know it sounds like it belongs at NASA, but it is actually a small electric sander that is fun and easy to use.

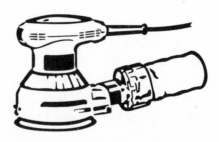

Even though I have a degree in Business Administration, I hate doing my taxes; my accountant describes himself as someone who should never have been allowed to own a house! So, every year, we do a little bartering. I have done many jobs over the years at his home, and I've gotten to know his wife in the process. I saw her recently, and she was excited to tell me about her success with a palm sander. Her outdoor picnic table was a little the worse for wear, and she had decided to buy a new one, because she thought that fixing it up would be too big a job for her to tackle. Her landscaper told her it would be easy: All she needed, he said, was a palm sander and some linseed oil. She purchased a sander, followed the directions on it, and succeeded in freshening up the surface of her picnic table. She was so thrilled with her victory that she also decided to replace the hardware on her kitchen cabinets. If she keeps it up, I'll be out of a job!

Now That I Have Them, How Do I Use Them?

Having the right tools easily accessible in your toolbox is only half the battle; learning how to use them correctly will make the biggest impact on your success in taking on home improvement projects. Let's go back through the list, and I will cover the most important points about some of the tools and give you tips on using them correctly. Any tools not touched upon here will be explained later, in the context of a project.

1. SCREWDRIVER: The head of the screwdriver must fit snugly into the slot or cross on the head of the screw. Flathead screwdrivers are for slotted screws, and Philips head screwdrivers are for screws with a little cross on the top. Set the tip of the screwdriver into the head of the screw and push to make a tight connection. While you are pushing into the head of the screw, turn the screwdriver to the right to drive a screw in, or to the left to remove a screw (some people remember this with the saying, "righty tighty, lefty loosey").

If the screwdriver is slipping when you try to turn it, check to make sure it is not too small. A screwdriver that is too small will not work well and can strip the head of the screw, making it impossible to turn. A screwdriver that is too big will not sit snugly in the head of the screw, and you won't be able to turn the screw. Make sure the screwdriver fits the screw!

2. STEEL MEASURING TAPE: The little metal tab at the end of the tape can be hooked over the end of a piece of wood you need to cut or the outside trim on a window. Once the tab is firmly in place, pull the tape toward you; when you're done, push the button on the tape case, and the tape will retract. Be careful when you do this—the tape can come back quickly and pinch your finger. When marking off your measurement, use a sharp pencil, and make one fine line (don't go back over the line several times and end up with a fat mark that will distort your measurement). Precision in measuring is important. As Norm Abram from *This Old House* always says, "Measure twice and cut once."

3. HAMMER: Grasp the hammer firmly on the thicker part of the handle, closer to the end of the hammer, away from the head. Many women hold the hammer just under the head and tap nailheads very tentatively. The weight of the hammer moving through space is what drives the nail into the wood—let gravity be your friend. Grasp the hammer and then, using your forearm as a fulcrum (bending only at the elbow), drop the center of the round head of the hammer onto the nail. You can tap the nail gently until it's started, but after that, move the hand holding the nail in place away and don't be afraid to swing the hammer with more force.

It will take some practice to get good at this, and you will occasionally miss the nailhead. Get a piece of scrap wood and some nails, and practice hammering until you feel comfortable. Even after you become skilled with a hammer, you'll still miss the nailhead on occasion. If you're scared of hitting your finger while starting the nail, you can hold the nail with your needle-nose pliers and keep your fingers out of harm's way. I even do this myself on occasion, mostly when I'm dealing with very small nails.

4. HANDSAW AND HACKSAW: The trick with both of these tools is the same and is the opposite of what I just said about using a hammer. In this situation, a light, gentle touch works best. First, you need to make sure that whatever you are trying to cut is held firmly in place by a set of clamps, your knee, or a friend. Set the saw on the line you have made and pull it lightly towards you and then push it lightly away, repeating this motion until a groove begins to form in the wood, metal, or plastic. Once a groove forms, you can pull and push with long, smooth strokes. The weight of the saw moving back and forth is enough to make the cut. If your saw is snagging, sticking, or jumping, it means you are pressing down too hard and need a lighter hand. Try and make a practice cut on some waste material to get used to the saw before you make your first final cut.

5. UTILITY KNIFE: A great invention when used correctly, and a very dangerous tool when used incorrectly. I have cut myself more with this tool than any other tool in my bag, but I also use it more than any other tool. The challenge with this tool is keeping miscellaneous body parts out of its path, which is easier said than done. In order to use this tool to cut wallboard, linoleum, or even plastic sheeting, you need to press down on the button on top of the knife and push it forward, which will expose half of the blade. Then set the blade up against a guide or on the line you want to cut, and move it toward you while simultaneously pushing down.

That last part right there is the problem: In order to exert proper force on the blade, you usually have to be moving it toward yourself. Whenever you do this, think ahead about where the knife might end up if it slips or if you lose control of it. If your other hand or leg lies in the potential path, rearrange your body. Most of my injuries have occurred when I have ignored the little voice inside that says, "I'm not sure this is a good idea." That voice is there to protect you, and I have learned to listen to it. As soon as you complete one cut, close the knife, even if you intend to use it again in thirty seconds—a closed knife causes no injuries.

6. CAULKING GUN: The end of a tube of caulk has a nozzle on it that's a little over two inches in length. In order to access the caulk in the tube, you have to cut off the end of the nozzle. The cut you make is a unique one. If you look very closely at the tip of the nozzle, you should see a set of two or three diagonal lines. Using your utility knife, make a small diagonal cut across the tip of the nozzle on one of the lines. The steeper the angle of the cut, the more caulk will be released. When it comes to caulk, in most cases, less is more. You can always come back and make the cut bigger, but you *can't* make it smaller.

Once you have made your cut, stick the pointy thing on the caulking gun (or a long ñail) down into the nozzle to break the seal at the base of the nozzle (not all tubes have a seal, but many do). Once that's done, insert the tube of caulk into the gun and pull the trigger until some caulk comes out of the tip. Press on the release button (located somewhere behind the trigger) to take the pressure off the caulk until you are ready to proceed. Keep lots of rags or paper towels handy when doing any caulking job, as it is messy work. We'll talk more about laying a bead of caulk in the painting and bathroom chapters.

Caring for Your Tools

I see tool abuse firsthand on a regular basis, and it is not pretty! Stiff and crunchy paintbrushes, knives encrusted with dried putty, rusted tools, and dead batteries are just some of the horrors I've witnessed. When you start a new project and reach for a tool, you want the tool to be ready to use. If the tools you need are not clean, charged, and easy to locate, starting your project will go from easy to frustrating. Get in the habit of cleaning your tools off before you return them to the toolbox. Many of the tools you use will never need cleaning anyway, unless they unexpectedly come in contact with an unusual substance (if your pliers fall into the joint compound or your hammer lands in the paint bucket, for example).

Putty knives can be scraped clean and then rinsed with water and dried. Never scrape the remnants from the blade back in to the putty container—doing that contaminates the putty with lumps. The basic rule is to check to see if any tools need cleaning before you put them away, and always dry any tools that will rust. I'll explain how to clean a paintbrush in Chapter 6.

Safety First (and Always)

I can tell you from personal experience that nothing spoils a project faster than a trip to the emergency room. What I find most interesting is that I have never injured myself with the tools that make the most noise and are capable of doing an amazing amount of damage to the human body, like my circular saw, wet saw, reciprocating saw, or jigsaw. Instead, my injuries have come while using a hammer, utility knife, and wallpaper scraper, among others! I think the reason for this is that when I work with the big, loud power tools, I'm hypervigilant, but when I work with the smaller, less frightening tools, I relax and sometimes forget to pay attention to where the tool is in relation to the rest of my body (especially my other hand).

When I was a teenager, my family lived in northern Vermont. For a short time, my father ran a business buying and reselling the contents of people's attics, barns, or basements at auction. At one auction, a large number of antique carpentry tools were for sale. I was there helping my dad, and I noticed that the front-row seats at the auction were filled with antiques as well: All of the men there must have been over seventy and had probably spent their entire lives working as carpenters. Upon closer inspection, I saw that most, if not all, of these men were missing a small piece of at least one finger. This story isn't meant to frighten you but rather to impart the same lesson I learned from the experience: A healthy respect for all tools—especially power tools—is crucial.

I will discuss how to use specific power tools to ensure your safety in later chapters. For starters, though, make sure that you read and understand all the written directions that come with any new tool you purchase. If you have inherited tools from someone else and you don't have the operating manual, try looking online for directions.

Here are a few specific safety tips:

✔ Keep the area where you are working clear and easy to walk through. It's tempting when you're in the thick of a project to set materials and tools down on the floor around you without thinking about how having them there will impact you later. If you're lucky, these mishaps are just funny; if you're one of the

IT HAPPENED TO ME ONCE: A mistake I once made happened while I was tiling the walls around the tub in a bathroom my clients were remodeling. There had been a leak in the old tub, so my client's husband had installed the new tub with new plumbing. There were still holes in the floor, under the tub, which we were waiting to close until the bathroom project was complete and we were sure the leak was fixed. I backed up to admire my tile job, and I knocked over a bucket containing about three gallons of water! Fortunately, since tiling is a very wet job, I had a lot of towels on hand. Some water did run under the tub, but it continued down through the open holes in the ceiling, so no new damage was created.

unlucky, you could end up seriously hurt or, at the very least, stuck with a big mess to clean up. I have learned to pick up debris as I go along when doing demolition, and to keep tools I am not currently using tucked over to one side. And when I use a ladder, I make sure that the base is stable and there is nothing blocking my path to and from the ladder.

✔ Always wear your safety glasses no matter how silly you think you look in them or how small the job. Make it a habit to put on your glasses when you reach into your toolbox for the first tool you'll be using. Clean them and put them away at the end of the project.

✔ Keep all your power tools unplugged and out of the reach of small children when not in use. Most power tools you buy come in a protective case. I store my tools in those cases, and that keeps them nicely tucked away.

✔ Dispose of any paints, thinner, solvents, or other hazardous materials in accordance with your city or town's guidelines. My town has a hazardous-waste-removal day once each year. Until that day, I keep the nasty stuff stored safely in an appropriate container in my garage or shed.

Picking Your Battles

One of the biggest challenges you face when starting to take on home improvement projects is determining which ones you feel you can complete successfully. It's important to give yourself permission to both take on projects and walk away from projects.

I suggest you make a list of all the projects you want and need to do around your house. Once you're done, go back through the list and assess each project based on the following criteria:

1. TOOLS
a. What tools are needed?
b. Do I own them?
c. Can I borrow or rent them?
d. Do I want to buy them and add to my collection?

2. TIME
a. How much time is involved?
b. Can the job be done in small pieces, or does it all have to happen at once?
c. Do I want to spend my time that way?
d. Is it worth it to me compared to what I would have to pay a professional?

3. COMPLEXITY
a. After a little research, does it sound like something I could do?
b. Is my first reaction a strong positive, a hesitant maybe or a strong no?
c. Does it involve plumbing or electrical work and the inherent risks that go along with those kinds of projects?
d. Am I ready to take on those risks?

4. PHYSICAL AND EMOTIONAL DEMANDS
a. Can I physically do what is required?
b. Do I have the patience?

c. Does it sound like fun?

d. How will I feel if I am successful?

e. How will I feel if I fail?

Asking for Help

You may discover that you do not always have the necessary information to answer the above questions. If you are thinking about replacing your storm/screen door, how do you know if it is a project you can complete successfully? If the project is covered in this book, read that chapter, and see how you feel about the project at the end.

If the project is not covered here, there are other places you can go to get a sense of what the project will entail and if it is right for you:

1. FAMILY AND FRIENDS: Is there anyone you know who is the handy type and can tell you what is involved in the projects you are considering? I'm fortunate that I've had my father at the other end of the telephone to answer my questions and give me perspective over the years. I have also developed a network of professionals who are happy to answer questions and help me determine if a job is right for me.

 **IT HAPPENED TO ME ONCE:** Once I told a client that I would be able to finish a project her husband had started, which involved turning their bathtub into a large-stall shower with a tiled floor and seat. Several aspects of this job I had done before, in previous jobs in my own home and for other clients. However, when I went to talk about the specifics of the job with Tom the tile guy, he talked me out of the job by explaining just how difficult it was to tile the floor of a shower stall and do it well. I felt bad having to tell the client I was unable to do the job, but at the same time I felt an intense feeling of relief. I realized then that I had been scared of the job and afraid I wouldn't be able to do it well enough. What happens more frequently, though, is that the people I turn to with questions reassure me that I can in fact do the job and do it successfully.

2. THOSE GUYS AT THE HARDWARE STORE: Whether male or female, most of the staff members at the local hardware store have a rich history in home improvement projects. Each guy at my local store has a different background. Some have done a lot of plumbing; others are skilled carpenters or do their own electrical repairs. In my experience, these people love to share what they know in order to help you become successful.

3. THE INTERNET: A bedazzling and sometimes overwhelming array of information is available at your fingertips. Type in your "How to fix [blank]" question, and then be prepared to sort through the answers. I use the Internet often when faced with something new, and I can almost always find some piece of useful information.

4. BOOKS: One book I have strongly recommended to all the women taking my seminars over the years was produced by The Home Depot and is available at all their stores. It is called *Home Improvement 1-2-3*, and it covers a multitude of projects not covered in this book. It has great photographs and simple, step-by-step instructions.

5. MAGAZINES: I get two magazines every month that I really love and that have taught me a great deal over the years. *This Old House* and *The Family Handyman* each talk about different aspects of home repair and have great tips on projects and tools.

6. ETCETERA, ETCETERA: I'm sure there are other resources out there that I don't even know exist. Don't be afraid to do whatever it takes to get the answers you need to proceed with a project and complete it successfully, or to realize it's not right for you, walk away, and take on something else.

I can't stress strongly enough how my life changed when I gave myself full permission to ask for help when taking on any home improvement project, be it large or small. I grew up believing that I was supposed to know how to do things even before I had learned how to do them. Asking for help is a skill I have had to acquire. At first, I was a little embarrassed and a little shy; I felt uncomfortable asking complete strangers for input on projects. Now, I'll ask just about anyone just about anywhere just about anything. I figure I can learn from their mistakes and experience, and then go on to add my own. The fact that you are reading this book tells me that you want to learn and are willing to ask for help. It's a great place to start!

FINAL THOUGHTS ON GETTING STARTED

It's impossible to finish a project if you never start it. You will never have all the right tools or enough time or money, and you're never going to feel completely ready to take on every project you want to do. It's okay to start a project, even if you're not sure you're ready for it; I personally have completed many projects I didn't think I was ready for at the time I started them. And you know what? They weren't executed perfectly. But they did get done, I learned a lot from doing them, and I took that learning and applied it to the next project I did. I wouldn't know what I know now if I hadn't been willing to start those first few projects when I didn't know much at all. So give yourself the chance to start from where you currently are, and trust that you will grow (both in skills and in confidence) with each new project you take on.

2. SHOPPING FOR MATERIALS AND SUPPLIES

One of the reasons professionals make jobs look easy is that, in addition to having all the right tools, they have the right materials and supplies. If you have ever gone to the home center looking for a nail, a tube of caulk, or some wall anchors, you know how overwhelming all the choices can be. Some questions you might find yourself asking are:

✔ What's the difference between common nails and finish nails?
✔ What does "galvanized" mean? Do I need that?
✔ I just need a tube of caulk, and there are eight shelves with ten different kinds on each shelf. What's the difference between silicone and latex, anyway? Does it really matter?
✔ Why are there so many different kinds of wall anchors? Can't there just be one?
✔ Why can't this just be *simple*?

The truth is, it can't be simple because there are just too many varieties of each item. Once you get past the confusion, you'll realize we are blessed to have so much to choose from; it means we can get exactly the right thing to do a job in the best possible way. I can't dedicate this entire book to the contents of the home center, but I will try to cover the items you will most commonly use in your projects and the ones that my women clients have found the most confusing.

Wall Anchors

One of the most confusing parts of hanging something other than a picture on a wall is determining what type of wall anchor to use. However, you have to know what an anchor is and why you need it before you can begin to figure out what kind of anchor to use. In the first chapter, when I explained what a stud finder was, I talked about how a wall is formed out of studs and wallboard. Studs are made of wood, and they're the strongest part of the wall; it's always best to hang at least one part of your item on the stud.

A wall anchor is what you have to use when you can't locate a stud, or when the location of the stud does not line up with the holes in your shelf bracket after you have decided where you want to hang it. You need to use an anchor because wallboard was designed to give walls a nice, flat, interior surface and give rigidity to the wall itself, but it has no inherent strength to hold things up on its own.

HOW DO I KNOW WHICH ANCHOR TO CHOOSE FOR MY PROJECT?

That's a great question! I wish I could give a simple answer. Unfortunately, it's complicated: The weight of the object to be hung, the condition of the wall it will be hung on, and the way that the object is going to be used all have bearing on which anchor you should choose. There are many different anchors, clearly, but I am only going to cover the three kinds that I use when I do jobs. For each project I cover in this book, I will suggest a specific kind of anchor. After you have used each kind of anchor several times, you will be much more capable of determining for yourself which anchor you will need for your future projects.

1. PLASTIC ANCHORS come in a variety of styles, shapes, colors, and sizes. They are usually sold in a package with the screws you'll use to

attach them. Plastic anchors are ¾
of an inch to 1¼ inches in length
and are either cone-shaped or
cylindrical. They are hollow inside
and split down the sides. Once a
plastic anchor has been inserted
into a predrilled hole in the wall
and a screw has been screwed into

the anchor, the "legs" of the anchor are spread apart so that they can
press up against the back of the wallboard. It is this pressure from
the legs of the anchor that hold the anchor (and the object you have
attached to it) to the wall.

2. SELF-DRILLING DRYWALL ANCHORS also come
in various sizes, but—unlike plastic anchors—
these anchors are rated for specific weights,
similar to OOK-brand picture hooks. As the name
implies, these anchors are specifically designed
for use in drywall/wallboard walls; they will not
be successful in walls made of plaster and lathe.
The plastic anchors that were described above

can be used in both kinds of walls, but are better used in drywall/
wallboard construction.

Self-drilling drywall anchors also come with their own screws.
Unlike plastic anchors, these anchors do not split open when the
screw is inserted. Instead, the large threads behind the head of
the anchor are designed to hold firmly in drywall and they do a
reasonably good job—until excessive force is exerted on the object
that has been hung on them. For instance, if you were to hang a
towel bar in your bathroom using either plastic or self-drilling
drywall anchors, and a small child tried to use the towel bar to do
chin-ups (Outrageous, right? Your child would never do that!), or
an adult slipped and grabbed the towel bar for support, the anchors
would probably give way, and the bar would come out of the wall.
I can't count the number of times I have been hired to rehang towel
bars and toilet paper holders that had been pulled out of the wall
due to bad anchor choices.

3. TOGGLE BOLTS are the golden standard of wall anchors, as far as I'm concerned. They are comprised of a bolt and a toggle, both of which are made of metal; they come in various lengths (the bolt) and widths (the toggle). I have never seen one of these (properly installed) anchors come out before it was removed on purpose. They're the only kind of anchor I'll use in old plaster and lathe walls, which are usually found in buildings  constructed before 1940. I have used them to hang heavy shelving, heavy mirrors, medicine cabinets, towel bars, and toilet paper holders. When they are first introduced to them, most women are terrified of using toggle bolts because of the size of the hole they have to drill in the wall in order to use them. Personally, I hated toggle bolts and decided they were stupid when I first tried to use them, because I didn't understand how they worked and was too embarrassed to ask anyone for help. Once I (accidentally) discovered how they worked, I fell in love, and I've used them ever since. One thing: Make sure you only buy toggle bolts with a Phillips head bolt; they're much easier to use than the flathead bolt.

There are lots of other kinds of anchors for sale and use, but these are the three kinds I most commonly use. If someone tells you about another kind that they think is wonderful, feel free to try it out. The worst-case scenario is that you won't like it. Best-case, you'll love it, and then you can write to me and tell me all about it!

Caulk and Grout

If you're confused about the difference between caulk and grout and find yourself using the terms interchangeably, rest assured: You are not alone. I have often been asked to come to a house to "fix" the grout, only to find upon arrival that it was the caulk that needed replacing. The opposite is also true. Caulk and grout are confusing, because they are often used in very close proximity to one another, they are often the same color, and they are both used to seal joints.

Just as, in your body, a joint is where two bones come together, in your house, a joint is where two materials come together. Here are some examples of joints in houses:

✔ Kitchen counter meets wall
✔ Kitchen counter meets tiled backsplash
✔ Bathtub meets tiled tub surround
✔ One wall meets another
✔ Baseboard meets wall
✔ Tile meets tile
✔ Tile meets wood

The most basic difference between caulk and grout lies in their flexibility. Caulk is designed to be flexible and fill joints between two materials that expand and contract at different rates, like a granite countertop and a wall built out of plaster-coated wallboard. Grout is not flexible; it's designed to fill joints between two similar materials, and, in my experience, it's used exclusively to fill joints in tiled areas.

WHY ARE THERE SO MANY DIFFERENT KINDS OF CAULK?

Because caulk is used to seal the joints between so many different kinds of materials, there are many different kinds. Caulk is made from several materials, including latex, silicon, and vinyl. Traditionally, silicon caulk was designed for use in kitchens and baths, while latex was used in most other situations (because silicon caulk isn't paintable). Then somebody invented vinyl caulk, which theoretically can be used anywhere and is available in paintable varieties.

This can all be very confusing, so let me try to make this as simple for you as possible—if you're doing a project and you need to buy caulk, ask yourself these questions:

1. WHY AM I SEALING THIS JOINT? If the answer is to keep water out, then buy caulk made of silicon, and look for one that is pretreated to prevent mold and mildew growth.

2. WILL THIS JOINT EVER NEED TO BE PAINTED? If the answer is no, then you can use any kind of caulk. If the answer is yes, then make sure the container of caulk you purchase says "paintable" on it.

3. WHAT COLOR SHOULD I GET? Get the color that most closely matches the material you are sealing if you are not going to paint it. If you are going to paint over the caulk, I usually recommend white or translucent.

4. I'VE ANSWERED THESE QUESTIONS, BUT I'M STILL NOT SURE WHAT KIND OF CAULK TO BUY. NOW WHAT DO I DO? Ask for help. Go to a good hardware store and describe your project in detail. You will get great advice on which product is best for your situation.

5. IS IT OKAY TO BUY THE CHEAP STUFF? It is okay but not recommended. My dad taught me to buy the most expensive caulk available, because it's usually the best. A caulking job done well will not have to be redone for many years, if ever, which makes it worth it to spend $7 instead of $3 for a better tube of caulk.

6. CAN I SAVE THE UNUSED CAULK IN THE TUBE TO USE AT A LATER DATE? You can try. I have tried several different methods of sealing tubes of caulk and had very little success. It may last for a day or two, but a couple of weeks or months later, the caulk in the nozzle will have dried out.

GETTING TO KNOW GROUT

Grout is either sanded or unsanded. Unsanded grout is designed for very small grout lines, usually less than $\frac{1}{8}$ of an inch wide. Sanded grout is designed for all grout lines greater than $\frac{1}{8}$ of an inch wide.

Grout is usually sold in a powdered form that you mix with water prior to use. It is possible to purchase the most common grouts in small, premixed containers, but I prefer working with grouts I have mixed myself.

When choosing which color grout to get, there are no right or wrong answers. People either choose a color that closely matches the tile they're working with, or they choose one quite different, to make a design statement with the grout. My only opinion on grout color is that on floors, darker is better than lighter. No matter how well grout is sealed, it eventually shows some staining or discoloration, and darker grout simply shows dirt less. White tile and grout might look great in a design magazine, but in the real world they look pretty awful unless they are constantly cleaned.

Recently, manufacturers have come out with some grouts that are resistant to staining, mold, and mildew growth. They are quite a bit more expensive than traditional grouts, but again, they are well worth the investment up front for the time they will save you later.

Filling Holes and Cracks

If caulk and grout are used to fill joints, what are you supposed to use to fill holes or cracks in walls, ceilings, and woodwork? Again, there are many different choices and no one right answer. When I first started doing projects, I heard the words "spackle," "putty," and "joint compound" used interchangeably, and I was very confused. Since then, I've learned that they are made of different materials, but they can often be used interchangeably, so it generally doesn't matter which one you choose.

Rather than keeping many different products on hand, I keep only three:

1. LIGHTWEIGHT SPACKLE: I keep this on hand to fill small holes. It dries quite fast, and it sands easily. It's great for nail holes and little dings in walls and woodwork.

2. JOINT COMPOUND: This is used by professional drywall hangers to cover the joints where two pieces of drywall meet. When applied correctly, the seam is invisible once the wall has been painted. I use joint compound in conjunction with self-adhesive drywall tape and self-adhesive drywall patches to repair holes of all sizes (see Chapter 4). I buy joint compound in the 1-gallon size.

When you use joint compound, once you're done with the project, you'll want to scrape down the sides of the bucket and remove the dry, flaky parts. Put a piece of plastic wrap down onto the surface of the compound and replace the lid, and the compound will last a very long time without drying out.

3. WOOD FILLER: This comes in very small containers and is used to fill nail holes or gouges in wood trim.

You can buy wood filler that can be painted or stained, or you can buy it to match already stained woodwork. In a pinch, I have used both lightweight spackle and joint compound to fill nail holes in wood. They work okay, but wood filler works best.

Nails and Screws

If you really want to be overwhelmed, check out the nail and screw aisle at your local home center. There are enough different kinds of nails and screws to make your head spin. The most basic difference between nails and screws is their shape: Nails usually have a smooth shank, while screws have a spiraled shank. In terms of use, nails are most commonly used to hold two pieces of wood together, and screws are most often used to hold two different materials together (a door hinge and a door, for instance).

A NAIL IS A NAIL IS A NAIL . . . ISN'T IT?

You probably already own a small collection of nails. Over time, all homeowners, and even apartment dwellers, eventually purchase a wide assortment. There are many situations in which it really doesn't matter what kind of nail you use, but for almost all situations, a nail has been created for that specific use.

These are some of the most common types of nails and their uses:

COMMON NAILS: Smooth nails with a relatively large round head; most commonly used in rough situations where it doesn't matter if the head of the nail is visible, like in framing.

FINISH NAILS: Smooth nails with a relatively small head, designed for finish work such as window and door trim. The head of the nail is small so that it can be buried in the wood and covered with wood putty. A good carpenter leaves no nails visible in finish work.

ROOFING NAILS: Short, common nails with a big, round head designed to hold down roofing tiles.

BRADS: Very small finish nails used in picture frames and window frames.

GALVANIZED NAILS: Can be common or finish nails, treated with a special finish that inhibits rust. These nails are designed for exterior use.

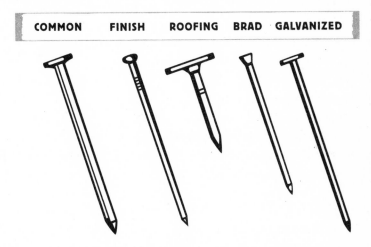

| COMMON | FINISH | ROOFING | BRAD | GALVANIZED |

When you buy nails, they will be sold as 6-penny (or "6d") or 10-penny (or "10d"), etc. Nail sizing goes by an old system that was based on how much it cost to buy 100 nails. 6-penny nails are 2 inches long, and at one time you could by 100 of them for six cents. 10-penny nails are 3 inches long and you used to be able to buy 100 of them for—you guessed it—ten cents. A simple rule of thumb to follow when purchasing nails for a project is that the nail should be at least three times longer than the wood it is intended for. So if you're nailing a piece of wood that is ¾ of an inch thick to a tree, you should use a nail that is at least 2¼ inches long.

Once again, a trip to the hardware store with a clear description of your project is a great place to start. The folks there will be able to guide you through the maze of nails and help you find exactly what you need to do the job right.

NAIL GUNS

Today, most professionals and even lots of homeowners use pneumatic nail guns for their carpentry projects. I was initially terrified of nail guns, because, well, I'm terrified of guns in general, and these guns shoot nails, which are almost as dangerous as bullets. However, I have grown to love my nail guns, because they allow me to complete projects I never could with a hammer. If you really get into your carpentry projects you may find yourself purchasing a small compressor and finish-nail gun. At that time, you'll discover that nails for nail guns are sold in a different manner than loose nails. Just ask for help, and you'll get what you need.

SCREWS

Screws come in at least as many variations as nails, if not more! Wood screws, machine screws, self-tapping screws, and drywall screws are just a few of the screw types available. The good news is that many things you will want to hang or install, such as hinges, towel bars, and doorknobs, all come with the proper type and size screws. For most other situations, I keep an assortment of coarse-thread drywall screws on hand.

If I have ⅝-, 1¼-, 2- and 3-inch-long drywall screws in my toolbox, I can solve almost any problem that requires a screw. I like drywall screws because they are designed to screw into studs, and they have a very hard head that's almost impossible to strip. One reminder: Drywall screws are meant to be installed with a battery-powered or electric screwdriver. Most other screws can be screwed in by hand if you predrill the hole for them.

Sandpaper

Shopping for sandpaper can be almost as confusing as shopping for nails. It comes in sheets, strips, circles, and blocks, and each of those come in different grits. Grits are a measurement of coarseness. The coarseness is measured with a number such as 40 grit, 100 grit, or 220 grit. A lower number indicates a rougher surface than a higher number.

When you are purchasing sandpaper, it's because you have a project that requires you to make something (like an unpainted wall or an unfinished piece of wood) smoother. Sandpaper with a lower grit number will remove more of the surface being sanded at a faster rate than sandpaper with a higher grit number. It's exactly like using an emery board that has two sides—you use the rougher side first to sand your fingernail down quickly, and then you switch to the smoother side of the emery board to finish the job.

I keep the following kinds of sandpaper on hand so I'm ready for almost any job that comes along:

1. SANDING SPONGES in fine, medium and coarse grit.

2. SHEETS OF SANDPAPER in 110 and 220 grit for use with my large sanding block.

3. CIRCLE SHEETS of sandpaper in 60, 100, and 220 grit for use with my random orbital electric sander.

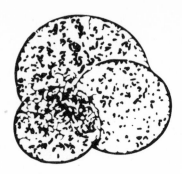

Again, if you're uncertain about which sandpaper to purchase for your project, describe the exact nature of your project to the folks at the hardware store and they'll help you buy what you need.

Adhesives and Glues

There are many projects around the house that will require the use of glue or tape as either a temporary or permanent measure.

GLUE

It's helpful to have the right materials on hand, but it is equally important to not have so many choices that you don't know which to use when. I keep it really simple in my own toolbox, and I only keep the following two glues on hand:

1. CARPENTER'S WOOD GLUE: This is water-based glue that comes in a bottle like good old Elmer's glue and is designed to stick wood to wood. I use wood glue when doing small projects with wood, or for minor repairs to things made of wood, like chairs, doors, railings, spindles, etc. It washes off your hands with soap and water.

2. GORILLA GLUE: This is a brand name for a polyurethane glue that is just amazing. You can use it for wood-on-wood situations and just about any other surface you can think of. It's waterproof and incredibly strong, and it can be used indoors and out. I use it everywhere I don't use carpenter's glue, and even sometimes in place of carpenter's glue. The only downside to this glue is that you have to wear gloves while using it, because it doesn't wash off your skin. If some does get on your skin, wait a few days and it will eventually wear off. Check out the company website (www.GorillaTough.com) for more product information and demonstrations.

IMPORTANT NOTE: When using glue, less is more! A small amount of glue spread evenly on one of the two surfaces involved is usually all that is required. Excess glue will ooze out and make a mess, and it won't contribute anything of value to the project.

DUCT TAPE

It's not just a myth: All of the jokes you may have heard over the years about the unlimited uses of duct tape are rooted in fact. Duct tape is a very strong, very sticky tape that comes in handy all around the house. The only thing it really isn't good for is repairing ducts! Believe it or not, although duct tape was commonly used on heating and air-conditioning ducts in the 1950s, it was later deemed ineffective in that application. Most commonly available in gray, it is now available in many colors, including clear.

I often use duct tape as a temporary fix to buy myself time to think up a more permanent solution to a problem.

Wood

It seems like it should be simple to buy a piece of wood for a project such as a shelf, a platform, or a window box. But unless you know the correct alphabet, your experience trying to buy wood at a home center might sound like the conversation below:

> **YOU:** "I'd like to buy some wood to build a box."
> **HOME CENTER GUY:** "Would you like dimension lumber or manufactured wood?"
> **YOU:** "I just want some wood, like from a tree."
> **HOME CENTER GUY:** "Listen lady, not all wood comes from trees. I can sell you dimension lumber, plywood, OSB, MDF, or particle board. What do you want?"
> **YOU:** "Um, well . . . maybe I'll come back tomorrow."

In order to prevent this conversation from happening to you, let's look at the many different kinds of wood available for your projects:

DIMENSION LUMBER is wood that has been cut directly from a tree and milled to a certain size. It is usually a solid piece, and it actually looks like wood. It is sold in dimensions, hence the name, but the measurements can be deceiving. For instance, if you wanted a piece of wood that was 6 inches wide, 1 inch thick, and 4 feet long, you would probably ask for a one-by-six-by-four piece of wood. When you got your piece of wood home and measured it, however, you would find that it was actually ¾ of an inch thick, 5½ inches wide and 4 feet long.

IT HAPPENED TO ME ONCE: I learned this lesson the hard way. I was building a new door for my backyard shed, and I wanted it to be 36 inches wide, so I purchased 6 "one-by-six" pieces of wood. After I had connected them all together with cross pieces and put the door in place, I discovered that I was short by 3 inches, because each of my "one-by-sixes" was actually only 5½ inches wide!

PLYWOOD is made from multiple thin layers (plies) of wood that have been glued together to make a larger, much stronger, sheet of wood. Most commonly used for roofs, subfloors, and the exterior sheathing of houses, plywood is also great for projects like shelves, window boxes, and all sorts of repairs. Plywood comes in various grades, which describe the quality of the exterior layer of wood:

AA plywood has two very smooth sides and would be used for furniture, cupboards, and nice shelving.

AC plywood has one good side and could be used for subfloor or simple projects.

CDX plywood is rough on both sides and is used in situations where the strength of plywood is needed but it's going to be covered with another material.

There are at least three other types of manufactured wood available for home projects:

MEDIUM DENSITY FIBERBOARD (MDF) is made from softwood fibers that have been glued together. MDF is very heavy and quite strong. You may have seen it used to build inexpensive furniture on the "let's-redo-your-house-in-ten-minutes-or-less" design shows on television.

ORIENTED STRANDS BOARD (OSB) is made of wood chips that have been glued together and pressed into large sheets. OSB is most often used for less-expensive exterior siding or subflooring. I rarely use OSB for anything.

PARTICLE BOARD is made from little pieces or particles of wood that have been glued together and pressed into large sheets. Particle board is most commonly used as a surface covered with veneer to protect it from water. Your kitchen countertop, for example, is probably made of particle board covered with veneer unless it's made of granite or a solid surface like Corian. Much of the "assemble-yourself" furniture kits and kitchen cabinets are also made from particle board, as is lots of ready-made shelving.

Wallboard

Most walls in homes built in the United States after 1945 are made from ½-inch-thick wallboard. Wallboard, also know as drywall or by a common brand name, Sheetrock, is made of paper and gypsum. Wallboard comes in several varieties designed for different installation situations:

BLUEBOARD is covered with a blue paper that is specially designed to hold a thin plaster veneer.

FIREBOARD is thicker, usually ⅝ of an inch thick, and is used on the walls and ceilings of garages or furnace rooms.

MOISTURE-RESISTANT BOARD is required for use in bathrooms, where water and moisture will be present. Newer versions of this board are also mildew-resistant.

STANDARD wallboard is usually grey and is used everywhere else.

 **SHOPPING TIP:** Wallboard is usually sold only in 4-foot by 8-foot sheets, which are great for large construction projects but way too big for small repairs. Sometimes home centers will sell precut 2-foot by 4-foot pieces, or you can ask if there are any broken sheets available. Worst-case, you can purchase a full sheet and have it cut into smaller pieces that will be easier to carry and to store.

FINAL THOUGHTS ON SHOPPING FOR MATERIALS AND SUPPLIES

I realize that it's not possible for me to answer every question you may have about everything you'll need to buy when you're shopping for projects. I'm always learning about new products, as well as discovering old ones. The real secret here is giving yourself permission to not know what you don't know, and letting yourself ask people who do know. There's a ton of information out there about everything you will need to complete these projects; the challenge is to get enough information without getting overwhelmed by too much. Ask enough questions to feel comfortable about what you're doing, and then go ahead and buy what you need. You can almost always return it if it turns out to be the wrong thing, or if you change your mind. Relax, and go shopping!

3. GETTING THE HANG OF THINGS

I n all the how-to classes I have taught, the one thing that women have repeatedly wanted to learn, more than anything else, is how to successfully hang things on their walls. They may have just moved into the house or just finished a repainting project, and they want to do some finishing touches by hanging pictures and mirrors, putting up shelves for practical use and for display, and hanging up curtains, valences, and drapes. But they are a bit apprehensive about actually doing it.

Hanging a picture, mirror, or shelf can be a little scary if you have never done it before. Think of all the things that could go wrong: You might make a bunch of holes in your wall; you might hang it crooked; you might hang it badly, and in the middle of the night you might be awakened by a loud crash as your picture or mirror falls to the floor!

So, instead of hanging anything, you let the pictures and mirrors lean against the walls for years, and the shelves are stuffed in the back of a closet. Fear no more! This chapter will give you everything you need to know to successfully hang almost anything.

You will learn to hang:

✔ Small- and medium-size pictures and mirrors
✔ Large pictures and heavy mirrors
✔ Shelves with brackets
✔ Shelves with keyholes instead of brackets
✔ Curtain or drapery rods
✔ Inside mount blinds and shades
✔ Outside mount blinds and shades

Hanging a Small- or Medium-Size Picture

Tools you will need:
✔ Hammer
✔ Steel measuring tape
✔ Sharp pencil
✔ Eraser
✔ 2-foot or 4-foot level

Materials you will need:
✔ Picture hooks

If you're hanging a picture that you have had professionally framed, it will usually come with a picture hook taped to the back that's appropriate to its size. If not, you will need to purchase picture hooks. I recommend OOK-brand hooks: They come rated for the weight they can hold, and they're designed so they can be removed from the wall at a later date without leaving a large hole.

Most small pictures can be hung using the hooks rated to carry 10 pounds, but larger pictures will need heavier ratings. You can usually purchase a kit that contains hooks with an assortment of ratings.

STEP ONE: MARKING THE HEIGHT

When you're hanging pictures, it's good to have a helper, someone who can hold the picture up and move it around until you say, "That's it, perfect, right there!"

✔ While they're still holding the picture in place, take your pencil and make a small mark on the wall while resting the pencil against the top of the picture frame.

✔ If you're working alone, you will need to hold the picture with one hand and make your pencil mark with the other hand.

STEP TWO: IS IT CENTERED?

If you're hanging your picture over a desk or sofa, you will probably want to center it horizontally over that item. If you are hanging it on a wall with nothing under it, you will usually want to center it on that wall. Finding center is relatively easy once you get the hang of it (no pun intended!).

1. USING YOUR STEEL MEASURING TAPE, measure the length of the desk or sofa. Let's say it's 39 inches: Divide that measurement in half, and you'll get 19½ inches.

2. HOLDING THE TAB of the measuring tape over the edge of the desk or sofa at 19½ inches, extend the tape to the wall and make a pencil mark there. The mark you just made is probably a lot lower than the mark you made for the height of the picture. You'll need to use your level so you can move the mark up the wall and not lose its centered position.

3. HOLD YOUR LEVEL LENGTHWISE up and down the wall (vertically) so that one edge of the level is against your pencil mark at 19½ inches. Watch the bubble at the top of the level and move the top of the level slightly in either direction, without moving the bottom part of the level off your pencil mark, until the bubble is floating between the two black lines. Make about a 2-inch-long pencil line along the side of the level at the approximate point of your original height mark.

4. NOW YOU NEED TO TRANSFER your height mark onto your center mark. Turn the level crosswise on the wall (horizontal), with the bottom of it resting on your height mark and the bubble in the middle of the level floating between the two black marks. Hold the level firmly and make a new height mark across your center line.

STEP THREE: HEIGHT ADJUSTMENT
Remember how you made the initial mark on the wall for the height of the picture? You made a pencil mark along the top of the frame. But if you nail the picture hook in at that height, the picture will be too high. Why? If you look at the back of the picture, you'll notice that the wire is strung across the back *a few inches down from the top*. Your picture hook needs to be on the wall at the location where the wire will rest so the picture hangs where you want it.

There's a simple way to figure out where the picture hook should be placed:

1. TURN THE PICTURE OVER and hold one finger under the wire, pulling it up toward the top of the frame and making sure that it's taut.

2. MEASURE THE DISTANCE from the top of the frame to the wire with your steel measuring tape while you're still holding it taut. It usually turns out to be somewhere between 2 and 5 inches. For this example, let's say it's 3 inches.

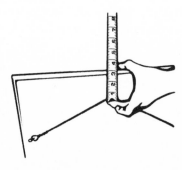

3. GO TO YOUR NEW HEIGHT MARK on the wall (the one that has been transferred onto your center line), and measure down from it 3 inches.

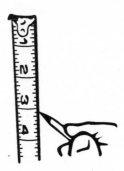

4. MAKE YOUR FINAL MARK. That's it—that's the spot where you will nail in the picture hanger.

STEP FOUR: NAIL IT IN

1. HOLD YOUR PICTURE HOOK in one hand, with the nail resting in the hole in the picture hook, and set the hook on the wall so that the bottom of the hook is resting on the final mark you made on the wall.

2. GENTLY TAP THE NAIL into the wall with the hammer until the hook is flush with the wall.

NOTE: If the nail, instead of the bottom of the hook, is on your mark, your picture will be slightly lower than planned, since the wire rests on the hook itself.

STEP FIVE: CLEAN UP YOUR MESS
Use your eraser to clean up all the lines and marks that you made. As you get better at this process, you will make smaller, lighter marks.

STEP SIX: HANG IT UP
This can be a very awkward process, since you're often working blind. You have to somehow get the wire you can't see on the back of the picture onto the hook you can no longer see on the wall. I try to put my hand on the wire, pulling it away from the back of the picture, and place it on the picture hook. It sometimes takes a few tries; don't get discouraged. It helps if you can squish your face up against the wall to try and get a look at the hook while you are hanging the picture.

STEP SEVEN: STAND BACK AND ENJOY
You may need to slightly lift one end or the other to make sure the picture is hanging level. Once you have done that, stand back and look with pride at the picture you have just hung.

Hanging a Very Large Picture or Heavy Mirror
Tools you will need:
- ✔ Hammer
- ✔ Steel measuring tape
- ✔ Sharp pencil
- ✔ Eraser
- ✔ 2-foot or 4-foot level

Materials you will need:
- ✔ Picture hooks

In order to safely hang a very large picture or heavy mirror, you'll need to use two picture hooks, both of which should be rated for 50 to 75 pounds. I always err on the side of safety—choosing bigger hooks than I think are necessary—since it is really difficult to figure out what a mirror or picture actually weighs. In addition to the larger hooks, the process of figuring out where to place the marks for the anchors will be slightly different and a bit more complicated. The goal is to get two marks that are level with one another and about twelve inches apart on the wall. Putting two hooks up distributes the weight of the larger picture and it makes it easier to keep the picture level.

STEP ONE: MARKING THE HEIGHT

Get someone, possibly even two people, to help with this step, so they can hold up the mirror while you mark the height. Mark the height using the same steps listed for a small or medium-size picture.

STEP TWO: IS IT CENTERED?

Find and mark center using the same procedure listed for a small or medium-size picture.

STEP THREE: HEIGHT ADJUSTMENT

This is the step that is slightly different for a larger, heavier, framed object, because using two hooks changes the final height of the wire on the back of the picture. A wire hung on one hook will be higher than a wire hung across two hooks. Just as you determined the center of the wall in the step above, now (using the same technique) you need to find the center of the large picture or mirror:

1. MEASURE THE WIDTH of the frame from one outside edge to the other and then divide that number by two to find the center. Make a mark at this location on the back of the picture near the top of the frame.

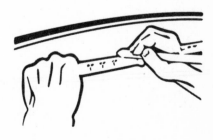

2. NOW MEASURE OUT 6 inches to the left and 6 inches to the right from this point, and make another mark on each side.

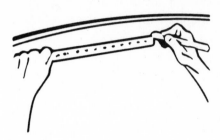

3. PLACE ONE FINGER from each hand under the wire and pull the wire up toward the two marks you just made. When the wire is taut and your fingers line up with the marks you made 6 inches from either side of center, mark the location of the wire.

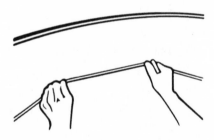

4. MEASURE THE DISTANCE from the top of the frame to your mark. For this example, let's say the distance is 8 inches.

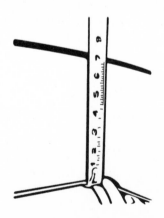

5. THIS DISTANCE IS THE HEIGHT adjustment from the initial height mark you made on the wall. Make a new height mark on the wall, 8 inches down from your original mark.

6. PLACE YOUR 2-FOOT LEVEL horizontally on the adjusted height mark, making sure that the bubble is floating between the two black lines. Trace a pencil line along the level on your height mark. Now, using your measuring tape, measure 6 inches out from the center in each direction, along the height line, and make two marks. These marks are where you will hammer in your two picture hooks.

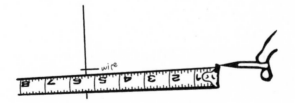

STEP FOUR: NAIL IT IN
Remember to put the bottom of the hook, not the nail, on your adjusted height line!

The larger picture hooks will usually have two or three nails. Hammer in the one in the center first, and then hammer in the other two nails. Repeat this process for the other hook.

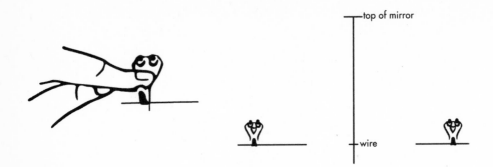

STEP FIVE: CLEAN UP YOUR MESS

Using your eraser, erase all your pencil lines.

STEP SIX: HANG IT UP

This part of the process is difficult because of the size and weight of the object you are trying to hang. It is made even more difficult if you are standing on a ladder or step stool. I was once hired to hang an 8-foot-tall by 4-foot-wide framed movie poster of King Kong in a client's stairwell. That was a challenge!

You need a helper for this step: Each of you needs to hold onto the picture and put one hand behind it on the wire and guide the wire onto the hook. Make sure that the wire is on the actual hook, not one the nailheads or the top of the hook.

STEP SEVEN: STAND BACK AND ENJOY

1. THE LARGE PICTURE OR MIRROR will always need some adjustments in this step to get it level. Have one person stand back and look at the picture while the second person slides the picture right or left to get it level. You can always set your 2-foot level on the top or bottom frame of the picture to see if what your eye sees as level really is level.

2. SOMETIMES, ONCE THE PICTURE is level, you will realize that the ceiling is not!

Hanging Shelves

There are many kinds of shelves available for you to hang. Here, I'm going to teach you how to hang two of them:

THE STANDARD WOODEN or melamine shelf that is 4 to 6 inches deep and around 3 feet long. This shelf might be used to hold books, spices, or knickknacks and often has metal brackets that are used to support the shelf.

THE PICTURE-DISPLAY SHELF. It is usually about 3 inches deep, has a small lip on the front, and is 2, 3, or 4 feet long. It often looks like it has been made out of the kind of wood trim that is used for crown moldings on ceilings.

The skills and methods used on these two types of shelves can be used to hang just about any shelf out there.

HANGING A SHELF WITH BRACKETS

Tools you will need:

✔ 2-foot or 4-foot level
✔ Drill
✔ Drill bits
✔ Screwdriver bits
✔ Steel measuring tape
✔ Pencil
✔ Stud finder

Materials you will need:
- ✔ ¼-inch toggle bolts
- ✔ Shelf and brackets
- ✔ 2-inch wood or drywall screws
- ✔ ½-inch wood screws to attach bracket to shelf

Usually you will purchase your shelf and shelf brackets separately. It's difficult to work with the shelf once the brackets are attached to it; it becomes too big and awkward to handle easily. Individual brackets, however, are easy to handle and hang. I find it easier in most situations to attach the brackets to the wall first, and then attach the brackets to the shelf.

STEP ONE: DETERMINING WHERE TO PUT THE SHELF

If you're planning to center the shelf over something like a couch or table, use the centering techniques describe earlier in the section on hanging pictures:

1. IF (FOR EXAMPLE) YOU WANT to center the shelf between a window and a door, start by measuring the distance between the two, and write it down on a piece of paper (not on the wall).

2. NOW MEASURE THE LENGTH of your shelf, and make a pencil mark on the top of the shelf, near the back edge, at the center-point. Remember that you find the center-point by measuring the length of the shelf and dividing by two. Once you've made the mark, you should always double-check to see if you are correct: Hold the tab over one end of the shelf near the back and measure to your mark, then measure from the other end of the shelf to your mark, and see if the distance is the same. If it's not, erase it and start over. It's easy to make a mistake in your math, or to make the mark in the wrong location on your measuring tape.

3. NOW HOLD THE SHELF up against the wall and move it around until you have it at the height that you want. Make a small pencil mark on the *underside* of the shelf.

4. DON'T WORRY ABOUT how level the line is; you'll fix that later. Put the shelf down.

5. TAKE THE MEASUREMENT for center that you wrote down and transfer that measurement to the wall. Measure over from either the window or door trim, and make a mark on your height line at the distance for center you had written down earlier.

6. GRAB YOUR 2-FOOT or 4-foot level and hold it horizontally so that the bottom of the level rests on your height mark. Adjust the level until the bubble is centered between the black lines, then press the level tightly against the wall and make a pencil mark along the bottom of the level.

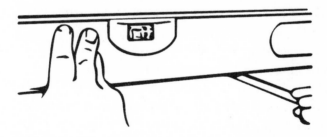

7. IF YOU DON'T HOLD the level firmly enough, it will slip and your shelf will end up tilted to one side. Get help if you can, and have someone else hold the level while you make the mark.

STEP TWO: HANGING THE SHELF BRACKETS

There is no absolute rule that says where you have to put shelf brackets. However, they are usually installed a few inches in from each end of the shelf. I suggest a minimum of 3 inches and no more than 5. Before making a final decision on the location of the brackets,

I check to see where the studs are in the area of the wall where I want to hang the shelf.

1. GRAB YOUR ELECTRONIC stud finder and hold it flat against the wall at eye level. Press the button that turns it on, and slide it slowly across the wall until it beeps. Make a pencil mark there.

2. CONTINUE SLIDING THE STUD finder across the area where the shelf will hang. If it beeps again, make another pencil mark. If your stud finder is designed to beep at the leading edge of a stud, your mark indicates the front edge of a 1½-inch-wide stud. If your stud finder is designed beep in the center of a stud, your mark indicates the center-point of a 1½-inch-wide stud.

NOTE: It's always best to hang things like shelf brackets on a stud if you can, because then you can skip wall anchors and just use a screw. You don't need to completely alter the planned location of the shelf in order to utilize the stud; it's just easier if you're able to. Remember, wall anchors are designed to replace the strength of studs.

3. LET'S PRETEND THAT in this situation one of the studs is located 4 inches in from the left side of the shelf, but there is no stud 4 inches in from the right side of the shelf. That's okay! We can use wood screws to hold up the left bracket and wall anchors to hold up the right bracket.

a. Hold the *left* bracket on the wall, center it on the stud mark with its flat top resting against the level line, and use a pencil to mark the screw holes.

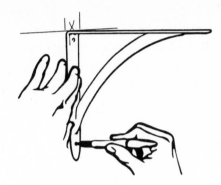

b. Hold the *right* bracket 4 inches in from the point on your line where the shelf ends, and mark those holes with a pencil. Most brackets have at least one hole near the top and one hole at the bottom. Some have more.

c. If the brackets you purchased came with screws, you will use those to hang the *left* bracket. If it did not come with screws, you will need 1½-inch-long wood screws or drywall screws. I like to predrill all my holes in order to make it easier to get the screw into the wall later. The only exception to this rule is if I am using drywall screws, which are designed to go into studs without predrilling.

d. Grab your battery-powered or electric drill and your drill bits. You will need to select a drill bit that is about half the diameter of the threaded part of your screw.

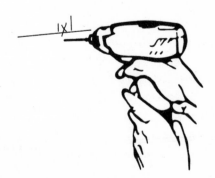

TIP: Predrilling removes some of the wood that the screw would have to travel through, which makes it easier for the screw to go in. If the drill bit you use for predrilling is too big, you will remove all the wood, and there will be no wood left for the screw to catch on. When it comes to selecting bits for predrilling, it's better to err on the side of too small than too big.

e. Once you have inserted the drill bit into the drill, drill a hole at each pencil mark you made for the *left* bracket.

f. Now replace the drill bit with the appropriate screwdriver bit. Hold the bracket up on the wall, lining up the holes in the bracket with the holes on the wall. Use your fingers to get the two screws started in their holes, and then use the drill with the screwdriver bit to drive the screws all the way into the wall. If you have trouble at any point with the drill, you can always finish the job with a handheld screwdriver.

g. To hang the bracket on the *right* side of the shelf, I suggest using toggle bolts. A ⅜-inch toggle with a 2- or 3-inch bolt will work fine. Using the same drill bit as you used on the left side, predrill your two holes, just to make sure there is no hidden stud behind the wall that the stud finder didn't find! Then change that drill bit for a ⅜-inch drill bit. I know it looks really big—don't be afraid, it has to be that big to make a hole big enough for the toggle to fit through. Drill the same two holes again, this time with the ⅜-inch bit.

h. Insert a bolt into each of the two holes on the bracket, then attach a toggle onto each bolt, making sure that the wings on the toggle close *toward* the bracket (not away from it!). This is vitally important. If the toggles are facing the wrong direction they won't work. Only screw the toggle about ¼ of an inch onto the bolt, just enough so that it is firmly attached to the bolt.

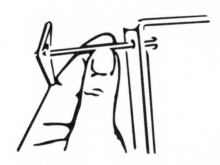

i. Now for the fun part! One at a time, pinch the wings of the toggle together and press the head of the toggle into the hole on the wall that aligns with the correct hole in the bracket. This may take a little force, and a lot of wiggling. You may even need to tap gently on the head of the bolt to get the toggle all the way in. It's important to make sure that the entire toggle is behind the wall. If you see that a wing is stuck in the hole, keep jiggling it in and out until the wing is behind the wall.

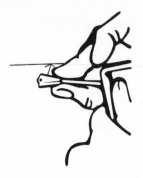

IT HAPPENED TO ME ONCE: Remember when I said I used to think toggle bolts were stupid? That's because no one had taught me how to use them, and I couldn't figure them out myself. This was back before I learned that it was okay to ask for help. So I didn't use toggle bolts for years, until one of my customers gave them to me to use to hang a shoe rack in a closet. I figured out how they worked accidentally—the weight of the shoe rack pulled the toggles against the back of the wall, and the bolts tightened perfectly. Now I know that the reason they hadn't worked for me before is that the toggle just spins around behind the wall and the bolt doesn't tighten if you don't make sure the wings are snug up against the back side of the wall. The moral of the story is that toggle bolts are worth the trouble it takes to learn how to use them correctly. Once they're tight, nothing will pull them out of the wall!

j. Once all the wings are firmly behind the wall, grab your drill and put the screwdriver bit in it. Hold onto the bracket and pull it gently away from the wall. Using the drill, move from one bolt to the next, screwing each one in a little bit at a time until they are all tight and the bracket is snug against the wall.

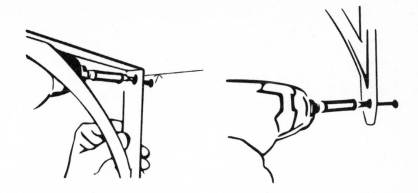

STEP THREE: IS IT LEVEL?

1. SET YOUR 2-FOOT LEVEL across the brackets and see if the middle bubble is resting between the lines in the center of the level. If it isn't, use a handheld screwdriver to loosen the toggle bolts a tiny bit. Adjust the right bracket up or down until the bubble is centered between the two black lines, and then retighten the toggle bolts.

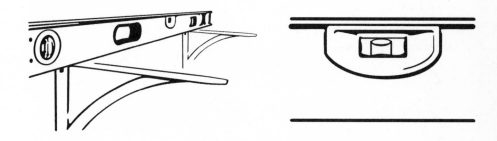

2. CHECK FOR LEVEL AGAIN; repeat this process until you are satisfied. You cannot adjust the left bracket (the one you attached with wood screws or drywall screws) without relocating the screws. With the right bracket, however, since you made such a large hole to push the toggles into the wall, you have quite a bit of room to adjust (which you almost always need to do when using toggle bolts).

STEP FOUR: ATTACHING THE SHELF TO THE BRACKETS

1. SET THE SHELF ON THE BRACKETS, matching the center-point mark on the shelf with the center line on the wall.

IMPORTANT NOTE: You need to drill starter holes for your screws, but you have to stop the drill before it goes all the way through the shelf and out the top. How do you do this when you can't see how much of the drill bit is in the shelf once you start drilling?

There are a couple tricks to help with this:

a. Measure up ⅜ of an inch from the tip of the drill bit (the base is the part inside the drill and the tip is the end that goes into the wood) and make a mark with a permanent marker. When you start drilling, make sure that mark does not go into the hole. This will ensure that the hole you drill is no more than ⅜ of an inch in depth.

b. You can wrap a 1-inch piece of blue painter's tape tightly around the drill at your mark. As you are drilling your holes, keep an eye on the bottom of the tape. When it bumps into the wood, stop drilling—your hole is the correct depth. The holes do not need to be the exact length of the screw; they're just starter holes to make it easier for the screw to go into the wood.

2. USE YOUR STEEL TAPE TO MEASURE the distance from the outside of each bracket to the outside edge of the shelf. It should be the same on both sides, but it will probably be off by a smidge. Adjust the shelf and measure again. Don't be too anal here—a tiny difference won't be noticeable once the shelf is loaded up.

3. ONCE YOU'RE HAPPY with your measurements, use your pencil to transfer the location of the holes in the top of the bracket onto the bottom of the shelf.

4. REMOVE THE SHELF and lay it down so that you are looking at its underside. You should have four to six marks on the shelf. These marks tell you where to predrill for the screws that will hold the shelf onto the brackets. The screws you use for this process are very small, only about a ½-inch long. If they were any longer, they would poke through the top of the shelf.

5. CHOOSE A DRILL BIT that is about half the diameter of the shaft of the screw (not the threading, the shaft itself). A $\frac{1}{16}$- or $\frac{1}{8}$-inch drill bit will probably work. Predrill each hole. See note on pg. 60.

6. ONCE YOU'VE COMPLETED predrilling the holes, set the shelf back on the brackets, lining up the holes you drilled with the holes in the brackets. Use a handheld or rechargeable screwdriver to screw the little screws into the shelf. When they're tight, the shelf should feel very sturdy.

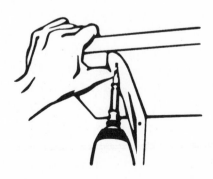

STEP FIVE: CLEAN UP YOUR MESS

Use your eraser to remove any pencil lines that are still visible once the shelf is in its final location. There will also be some wallboard dust on the floor (from the drilling you did for the toggle bolts) that you may want to sweep up.

STEP SIX: LOAD IT UP AND ENJOY!

You're done! You can load up your shelf with books, towels, or knickknacks and enjoy the fruits of your labor. Congratulations!

HANGING A SHELF WITHOUT BRACKETS

When you hang shelves on brackets, the brackets are meant to be both practical and aesthetically pleasing. Some shelves are designed to be hung without brackets: These are decorative shelves, and they're meant to display photographs or very small baubles. You'll find two or three small keyhole-shaped openings made of metal embedded in the back of the shelf.

These keyholes are designed to slide down over screw heads and hold the shelf snug against the wall. Whoever invented them was clearly more concerned with how the shelf looks than ease of installation! I used to dread hanging these kinds of shelves, but then I came across a brilliant trick in one of my handyman magazines (there is, as of now, no handy*woman* magazine!). I will pass this trick on to you here, and spare you the frustration I experienced for years.

HANGING A SHELF WITHOUT BRACKETS

Tools you will need:

✔ 2-foot or 4-foot level
✔ Drill
✔ Hammer
✔ Phillips head screwdriver
✔ 1 nail, 2 or 3 inches long
✔ Steel measuring tape
✔ Pencil
✔ Eraser
✔ Patience!

Materials you will need:

✔ Self-drilling drywall anchors with screws
✔ Masking or blue painters tape
✔ Shelf

IMPORTANT NOTE: Check to see that the heads on the screws that go with the self-drilling drywall anchors can fit into the large part of the keyhole and slide down into the small part. If they can't, you need to get a smaller-size anchor-and-screw pair.

STEP ONE: DETERMINE THE LOCATION OF THE SHELF ON THE WALL

Use the same exact process described for the shelf with brackets to determine height, center, and level for the location of this shelf. The only thing you have to do differently is make the pencil line the exact length of the shelf. So, if you have a 3-foot shelf, make a 3-foot-long level line that is centered in your desired location. Make sure you have a clear, sharp line indicating the center-point.

STEP TWO: THE TIP THAT CHANGED MY LIFE

This step will not seem earth-shattering to you unless you have already struggled to hang this type of shelf before. I found it almost impossible to get the exact measurement from the center of one keyhole opening to the center of the next in order to figure out where to put the screws into the wall. If there were three openings, I'd forget about even trying! I found the following tip in one of the monthly how-to magazines that I subscribe to:

1. GRAB YOUR 2-FOOT or 4-foot level (it just needs to be longer than the distance between the two keyholes on the back of the shelf). Put a piece of masking tape or blue painter's tape along the entire length of the top of the level. Don't put it on the edge that contains the bubbles.

2. LAY THE SHELF ON A TABLE or on the floor so that you have access to its backside. Put your level up against the back of the shelf so that the taped edge of the level rests just under or just above the keyholes.

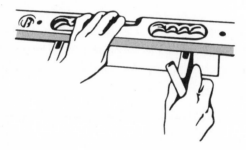

3. USE A SHARP PENCIL to make a single line on the tape at the center-point of each keyhole. Don't make multiple strokes with your pencil; you want a single sharp line.

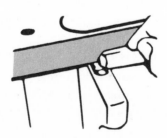

4. MEASURE THE EXACT DISTANCE between the two lines, divide it in half, and make a mark on the tape indicating the center-point.

5. HERE'S THE BEST PART (yes, I really do get this excited about this stuff!): Hold the level against the wall, resting it on your pencil line, and match up the center-points of the line on the wall with the center-point mark on the tape.

6. TRANSFER THE TWO MARKS indicating the location of the keyholes from the tape on the level onto the wall. You will place your anchors and screws (or just screws) at the points where the lines intersect.

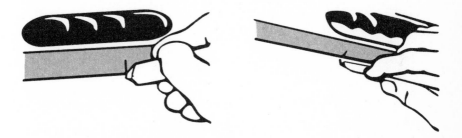

STEP THREE: ANCHORS AWAY

To hang this shelf you'll have to use self-drilling drywall anchors if your marks have not ended up over studs. If you've already determined where you are hanging something, besides using the electronic stud finder, you can also use a hammer and nail to test for studs:

1. GRAB YOUR HAMMER AND NAIL. Place the place the tip of the nail on one of the marks you transferred to the wall and begin to hammer it in. If it slides all the way in to the wall with ease, there's no stud there. If you meet solid resistance after two or three good whacks (not gentle taps, whacks!), then you have found a stud. *Do not* hammer the nail all the way into the wall—this is for test purposes only. After you have determined whether or not there is a stud at this location, remove the nail.

2. LET'S ASSUME THAT YOU FOUND a stud behind one mark, and found no stud behind the other mark. First, place the sharp, solid end of a self-drilling drywall anchor into the hole left by your hammer in the "non-stud" location.

3. PLACE A HANDHELD PHILLIPS head screwdriver into the open end of the anchor, push in, and start turning the screwdriver clockwise. The long, pointy part of the anchor should start making a larger hole where your test hole was, and then the large threads of the anchor will begin to grab the wallboard. Stop turning when the head of the anchor is flush with the wall.

4. PUT THE SCREW THAT CAME with the anchor into the hole in the anchor and screw it in using a handheld screwdriver, or put a Phillips head bit in your drill and use that. Stop when the head of the screw is about ¼ of an inch from the wall. You're doing this so that the keyhole in the back of the shelf will have something to slide over and rest on. We'll come back to this in a moment.

5. AT THE LOCATION OF THE SECOND mark, where you found a stud, place the screw only (without the anchor) into the hole made by the hammer. Using your drill (still with the Phillips head bit in it), gently and slowly insert the screw into the wall until the head is about ¼ of an inch from the wall.

STEP FOUR: HANG IT UP

You should now have two screws sticking out ¼-inch from the wall, and on a nice level line with one another.

1. TAKE YOUR SHELF AND SET IT against the wall, slightly above the screws. Match up the center line on the wall with the center line on the shelf. Your screws should match up perfectly with your keyholes.

2. GENTLY SLIDE THE SHELF DOWN over the screw heads until they catch in the keyholes. Continue gently pulling down on the shelf until both of the screws are caught in the narrow part of the keyholes.

3. TEST FOR TIGHTNESS by jiggling the shelf a little. If it doesn't move at all, you're done. If it wiggles a bit, slide the shelf up off of the screws and set it down. Using your handheld screwdriver, turn the screws until they are all a little bit closer to the wall, say ⅛ of an inch. Try sliding the shelf down over the screws again. If you have tightened them enough, the shelf will be very snug against the wall. If it's not, remove it and keep tightening the screws in small increments until you're satisfied with how the shelf fits against the wall. This may take a lot of patience. If the wall is not perfectly flat, one of the screws may need to be set at a different depth than the others. When you get the right fit, the shelf will sit snugly on the wall.

4. IF ONE OF YOUR SCREWS DOESN'T LINE UP with its keyhole and won't go in, see if you can figure out which direction it needs to move in so they fit together. Do this by looking at the back of the shelf while it is resting on the other screw. It may need to go left or right by just a smidge. Put the shelf on the floor and grab your hammer. Gently tap on the side of the screw that needs to move, nudging it just a bit in the desired direction, then set the shelf on the wall and slide it down over the screws until it fits snugly.

STEP FIVE: CLEAN UP YOUR MESS
Use your eraser to clean up any visible pencil lines. Clean up any mess down on the baseboard or floor.

STEP SIX: PAT YOURSELF ON THE BACK
Stand back, admire your work, and congratulate yourself. This was not an easy job, and you did it well. I always make time to give myself a lot of credit for a job well done. Each time you pass by that shelf or admire the pictures displayed on it, a piece of your enjoyment will be the knowledge that you did it yourself. You took it on and succeeded!

Hanging Curtain or Drapery Rods
The hardest part of hanging curtain and drapery rods is figuring out where they should go. Do you put them on the woodwork at the top of the window? Do you put them in the wall, just outside the woodwork? If you put them in the wall, how high do you put them? Do they hang even with the top of the woodwork, slightly above it, or slightly below it? If I had a foolproof answer to these questions, it would make my job a lot easier. Unfortunately, as usual, there is no one correct answer. I usually just go with what I think looks the best in each situation; I hang the curtain on the rod and then play around with different locations until I find the one I like best.

Curtain rods come with brackets that need to be screwed onto the wall or woodwork so that they can hold up the rod. Rods less than 3 feet in length usually have two brackets, and longer rods have at least three: one for each end and one for the middle. When you purchase curtain rods they usually come with plastic wall anchors and matching screws. If you've decided to hang your rod in the woodwork, you will not use the anchors, but you will use the screws. If you're hanging the brackets on the wall above or next to the woodwork, you may need to use some or all of the anchors.

HANGING CURTAIN OR DRAPERY RODS

Tools you will need:
- ✔ Steel measuring tape
- ✔ Pencil
- ✔ Drill
- ✔ Drill bits
- ✔ Hammer
- ✔ Eraser
- ✔ Screwdriver bit for your drill (or screwdriver)

Materials you will need:
- ✔ Curtain rod
- ✔ Brackets
- ✔ Anchors and screws

INSTALLING RODS IN WOODWORK

1. DETERMINE WHERE you want one bracket to go, and hold it up against the woodwork.

2. USE A PENCIL TO MARK the location of the holes in the bracket on the wood (I usually trace the circle rather than trying to make a dot or an **X** in the center.

3. REPEAT THIS PROCESS for each bracket, making sure they will all be level with one another.

4. CHOOSE A DRILL BIT that is about half the diameter of the shaft (the solid part, not the threading) of the screw. Probably a $\frac{1}{16}$-inch or $\frac{1}{8}$-inch drill bit will work. Insert the drill bit into the drill.

5. SET THE TIP OF THE DRILL bit in the center of each of the marks you made on the wall and drill a hole for each one. You don't need to worry about going in too far; in this case, you do want to make a hole that is at least as long as your screw.

6. PLACE THE BRACKET OVER the holes and use your fingers to start the screws in each hole.

7. FINISH SCREWING IN THE SCREWS with either a handheld screwdriver or your drill (fitted with the screwdriver bit). Sometimes you can't use your drill to screw them all the way in, because the bracket and the body of the drill bump into each other. If this happens, I use the drill to do as much of the job as possible and then finish with the handheld screwdriver.

8. REPEAT FOR EACH BRACKET until you are done.

9. SET THE CURTAIN ROD into the bracket.

10. IF IT LOOKS AND FEELS GOOD, go ahead and hang the curtain on it!

INSTALLING RODS IN THE WALL

1. DETERMINE THE LOCATION of your first bracket on the wall next to or above the window, and make a pencil mark along the top of the bracket.

2. MEASURE DOWN TO YOUR MARK from the ceiling and over from the window, and write these measurements down—you'll need to use them for the second bracket. If you can hang the hardware even with the window woodwork, it will be much easier, because you won't have to worry about measuring down from the ceiling.

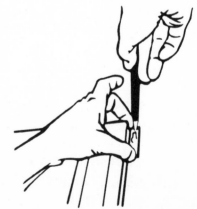

3. USE A PENCIL TO TRACE the holes in the bracket onto the wall.

4. IN ORDER TO DETERMINE whether or not you will need anchors or just screws, you need to find out if there is wood at the location where you are planning to hang your bracket. A stud finder usually won't work in this situation because of the way windows are framed, so you need to predrill to test for studs.

5. INSERT AN ⅛-INCH DRILL bit into your drill and use it to make a hole at each of your marks. If the drill penetrates easily, you'll need to use an anchor there. If the drill meets resistance, stop drilling—you've hit a stud, and you'll only need to use a screw there.

NOTE: If you install the hardware right next to the window frame, you increase your chances of hitting a stud and not needing to use anchors.

6. THE ANCHORS THAT USUALLY come packaged with curtain rods are plastic. They should be sufficient to hold up the rods, unless the curtains you are planning to hang are really heavy. If you're going to hang really heavy curtains, you should upgrade to self-drilling drywall anchors. I rarely use toggle bolts for curtain rods; the only case in which I do use them is if the original anchors that were used didn't hold up over time.

7. LET'S ASSUME THAT IN THIS situation none of your predrilling indicated wood behind the wall, so you will need to use the anchors that came with the rods. The directions that come with the brackets will usually tell you what size drill bit to use to predrill the hole for the anchor. If there are no directions, choose a drill bit that is slightly smaller in diameter than the diameter of the widest part of the anchor; that could be just below the top, the collar, or the large opening of the anchor.

8. USE THE APPROPRIATE-SIZE DRILL bit to drill a hole at each of your (predrilled) original marks.

9. USE YOUR HANDS TO START pushing the anchors into the holes. You shouldn't be able to push the anchor in all the way with your hands; use a hammer to tap it flush with the wall.

10. REPEAT FOR THE REMAINING anchors of the first bracket.

11. SET THE BRACKET OVER the anchors and insert the screws through the holes in the bracket; get them started into the anchors by hand with a couple turns.

12. USE A HANDHELD OR battery-powered screwdriver to finish tightening up the screws.

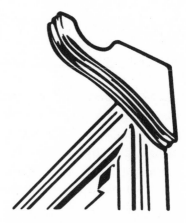

13. IN ORDER TO HANG THE SECOND and (if necessary) third brackets, you will need to use the measurements you wrote down way back at Step 2. Use these measurements to determine where the remaining brackets belong. After you have made your marks, double-check your measurements against the actual location of the first bracket.

14. ONCE YOU'RE SURE YOUR MARKS are in the right place, repeat everything you did for the first bracket until all your brackets are hung.

15. IF YOU ARE HANGING RODS on more than one window in a room, stay consistent with the location of your brackets from one window to the next. Even when all the windows in a room are not the same size, they are usually installed at a consistent distance down from the ceiling.

16. CLEAN UP YOUR MESS, and hang up your curtains!

FINAL THOUGHTS AND TIPS ON
HANGING CURTAIN OR DRAPERY RODS

Once the curtains, drapes, or valences are hanging in place, you may notice that one end seems slightly lower than the other, even though you're sure you measured everything twice and installed the brackets at a consistent height. Don't panic: You probably did do everything right.

The reason for this lopsidedness is that curtain rods are designed so that one half of the rod can fit inside the other half and slide in and out, which means that one half is smaller than the other. The solution to this problem is simple—you don't even have to adjust the height of the brackets: (1) Take a small piece of cardboard, or a piece of masking tape folded over several times, and place it under the smaller side of the rod where it rests in the bracket. (2) Stand back and see if the rod looks level. (3) If it doesn't, adjust the size of your shim until it gives your rod the height adjustment it needs to look level.

I have also had several experiences where the rods were hung correctly but the curtains were not uniform in length. In this case, you either have to return the curtains, hem them, or live with a slightly off-balance look. Either way, remember, you shouldn't always assume that you have made a mistake! The mistake is often in the materials, and you just have to figure out a way to work around it.

Installing Blinds

The first thing many women want to do when they move into a new home or apartment is install blinds in their windows. They're not just for privacy anymore; blinds are often used as a fashion statement now. For that reason (and a couple others), hanging blinds can seem like an intimidating job. The scariest part of putting up blinds, though, is measuring for them; if you measure incorrectly, the blinds won't fit inside the window frame, or there will be a large gap that looks awful.

 **IT HAPPENED TO ME ONCE:** I was hired to replace 10-foot-wide by 4-foot-high venetian blinds in an office building. First I had to measure and place a custom order for the blinds. After I placed the order, I became terrified that I might have measured incorrectly . . . even though I had made two trips to the building and measured twice on each trip! I was hugely relieved when the blinds fit perfectly upon installation.

The second issue you will be confronted with when ordering blinds is determining whether you want to mount them inside or on the window frame. This is mostly a matter of preference (though it is sometimes determined by the construction of the window, since there isn't always enough space in a window frame for the blinds).

Lastly, when you actually install the blinds, you have to be able to decipher the instructions and use a battery-powered or electric drill to get the job done.

I CAN'T GET MY OLD BLINDS OUT!

In order to correctly measure for your new blinds, you might need to remove any existing blinds or shades. This can often be much harder than you think it should be. I once got a call from a friend's husband who was having trouble removing shades from a bathroom window they were getting ready to paint. I talked him through it, and it turned out that he was doing it correctly, but he wasn't succeeding because he was afraid to push hard with the screwdriver. It takes more force than you might expect to pop the old blinds out of their brackets—don't worry, you won't break them! Here's how you do it:

1. CLOSE the blinds completely.

2. TAKE A MEDIUM-SIZE flathead screwdriver and look up near the top of the window, behind the blinds. You should see two small metal or plastic lips that the back of the blinds sits upon.

3. PUT THE SCREWDRIVER head between the back of the blinds and the lip of the bracket and use the screwdriver as a lever.

4. PUSH OR PULL HARD on the screwdriver until the blinds release from the bracket. Repeat on the other bracket.

5. USE A BATTERY-POWERED or manual screwdriver to remove the screws holding the bracket in place.

NOTE: You don't need to do this step if you are just measuring, since you may want to put the old blinds back up until the new ones arrive.

MEASURE THREE TIMES, ORDER ONCE

Whether you're buying inside- or outside-mount blinds, the most important part of this step is to be accurate (to $\frac{1}{16}$ of an inch). This is not a time when you can say, "I *think* it's about 52 inches wide and 37 inches high." You have to be able to say—*with certainty*—"My window is $52\frac{3}{16}$ inches wide and $37\frac{1}{4}$ inches high."

MEASURING FOR INSIDE-MOUNT BLINDS

The hardest part here is holding onto both ends of the measuring tape at the same time. You can hang most shades by yourself, but I strongly recommend getting another pair of hands to help with this step. Your helper does not have to be highly qualified; they just need to be able to hold the end of the measuring tape exactly where you tell them!

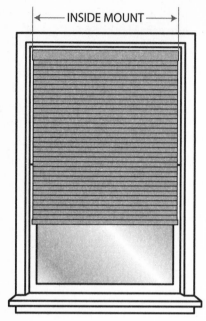

←— INSIDE MOUNT —→

NOTE: I suggest you draw a rough sketch of your window on a piece of paper. As you take your measurements, write them in the corresponding location on the sketch. That way, you won't mix up your height and width measurements.

MEASURING FOR WIDTH

1. HOLD THE TAB of the steel measuring tape against the inside left edge of the window near the bottom.

2. NOW PULL THE TAB toward you so it rests just against the front most edge of the window.

3. EXTEND THE TAPE straight across the window and past the edge of the right side.

4. READ THE MEASUREMENT where the tape crosses the inside edge of the window.

5. WRITE DOWN the measurement.

6. REPEAT THESE FIRST five steps twice more, once halfway up the window, and again near the top of the window.

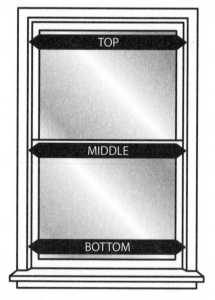

TOP

MIDDLE

BOTTOM

7. DOUBLE-CHECK YOUR MEASUREMENTS. If your numbers for the top, middle, and bottom vary, the smallest measurement is the one you'll use for your width measurement.

MEASURING FOR HEIGHT

1. HOLD THE TAB of the measuring tape on the inside front edge of the bottom of the window.

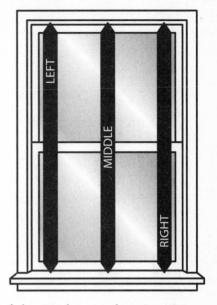

2. EXTEND THE TAPE past the top of the window and record where the tape crosses the inside edge of the window. You may need to stand on a step stool or ladder to read the measurement. Make sure you get high enough to look at the measurement straight on; if you look up at it from below, you will not get the correct measurement.

3. REPEAT THIS PROCESS at the center of the window, and again at the far edge.

4. DOUBLE-CHECK YOUR measurements. This time, the longest of the three will be your height measurement.

The reason you're doing so much measuring is that many windows—especially old ones—are not a perfect rectangle. Over time, one side can become slightly longer or shorter than another, which is why you have to find the longest and narrowest points of the window to use as your measurements when you order the blinds. If you use the largest measurement, or just take one measurement, the blinds probably won't fit.

MEASURING FOR OUTSIDE-MOUNT BLINDS

As the name implies, these blinds mount outside the window, on the window trim at the top edge of the window, or on the wall above the window (if there's no window trim). In this situation, we will use the *largest* of the three measurements, to ensure that the blinds or shades cover the entire window.

If your window does not have trim around it, you'll take your measurements for the outside mount the same way that you took them

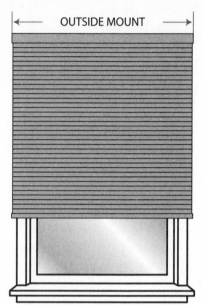

for the inside mount; the only difference is that you'll use the *largest,* not the smallest, of the three measurements for both the height and the width.

WINDOWS WITH WOOD TRIM
MEASURE FOR WIDTH:
1. HOLD THE TAB of the measuring tape against the outside left edge of the trim near the bottom of the window and pull it across to the outside right edge of the trim. Take your measurement where the tape crosses the outside edge of the window trim.

2. REPEAT THIS PROCESS at the center and top of the window, and write the measurements down on your sketch.

WINDOWS WITH WOOD TRIM
MEASURE FOR HEIGHT:
1. REST THE TAB of the steel tape on the left edge of the windowsill; measure up from there to the outside edge of the top trim.

2. REPEAT AT THE CENTER and right edge of the window.

3. DOUBLE-CHECK ALL your measurements, and use the largest of the three for both the height and the width when you order your shades or blinds.

MY BLINDS HAVE ARRIVED: NOW WHAT?

Be careful not to lose any of the parts, papers, or pieces that come with the package when you open it. You may not need everything they send you, but you'll determine that as you go along. Since all blinds come with unique hardware, I cannot give you specific instructions for yours. However, I have installed many different blinds from many different manufactures, and they are remarkably similar to one another. These are some general instructions based on what I've learned:

1. **THOROUGHLY READ** through the instructions and find the parts that apply to you. Circle those, and disregard the rest—they will only confuse you!

2. **SORT OUT THE HARDWARE** and be sure you understand and recognize what each piece is and what it's for before you begin installation.

3. **IF YOU ARE REALLY CONFUSED,** or think something is missing, don't hesitate to call the manufacturer. They can be quite useful over the phone.

4. **ONCE YOU UNDERSTAND** the directions and know what all the pieces are for, you are ready to begin.

INSTALLING INSIDE-MOUNT BLINDS
Tools you will need:
- ✔ Steel measuring tape
- ✔ Pencil
- ✔ Drill
- ✔ Drill bits
- ✔ Screwdriver bit for your drill (or screwdriver)

Materials you will need:
- ✔ All the materials you need should come with the product

Most inside-mount blinds are mounted to the top of the inside of the window frame or opening. Getting the brackets oriented correctly is the first, and most important, thing to do:

1. **CHECK THE ORIENTATION** of the brackets against the sketch provided in the directions until you think you have it right.

2. **I STRONGLY SUGGEST** that you play with mounting the shade on a bracket (they snap in and then snap out) until you figure out how they go together before you put the brackets up. It's much harder to figure this out while wrestling a shade over your head.

3. FOLLOW THE DIRECTIONS GIVEN to determine where to mount each bracket. They are usually mounted 2 to 3 inches in from either end so they don't interfere with the mechanical workings at the top of the shade. If the shade is wide enough, the directions will tell you to mount another bracket (or more) in between the other two. The most important part of placing each bracket is making sure they're all lined up with each other. Whether they are set back from the front by ¼ of an inch or placed tight against the back of the window, they all need to be at the same level, or the shade won't mount well.

4. ONCE YOU HAVE DETERMINED the location of the brackets, mark the holes with a pen or pencil.

5. PREDRILL EACH MARK using a drill bit that is smaller than the shaft (not including the threads) of your screw.

6. HOLD THE BRACKET in place and start (carefully) screwing in each screw with your battery powered screwdriver. (This job is difficult with a handheld screwdriver.) You usually need two or three for each bracket. Don't tighten any of them completely until you have all of them most of the way in.

7. DOUBLE-CHECK TO MAKE sure the bracket is where you want it and square to the front of the window, and then finish screwing in your screws.

8. REPEAT WITH THE remaining brackets.

9. HOLD THE SHADE UP on the brackets and snap it into place. This sometimes requires quite a bit of force, so don't be afraid to push really hard. You might want some help with this step. It also helps to be high enough up on a step ladder so that you can get some of your weight behind you. If the shade doesn't appear to be centered once you've snapped in into place, you may be able to slide it to where it belongs. If it won't slide, you will need to snap it out of its brackets, get it in the correct location, and then snap it in again.

10. IF YOUR SHADE COMES with a tie-down or safety bracket for the strings, follow the directions that came with the shade to install it.

11. CONGRATULATIONS! You have successfully taken on shade installation and succeeded.

INSTALLING OUTSIDE-MOUNT BLINDS

Tools you will need:
- ✔ Steel measuring tape
- ✔ Pencil or pen
- ✔ Drill
- ✔ Drill bits
- ✔ Screwdriver bit for your drill (or screwdriver)

Materials you will need:
- ✔ All the materials you need should come with the product

There are two possible major differences between installing outside-mount blinds versus inside-mount blinds. The first is the location of the brackets, and the second is that you may need to use wall anchors if you won't be mounting your brackets on wood. To install outside-mount blinds, follow the instructions for installing inside-mount blinds, with the following exceptions:

1. THE DIRECTIONS THAT come with the blinds will explain where to place your brackets. If the brackets are being installed on the wood trim that surrounds the window, mark, predrill the holes, and then follow the remaining steps for installing inside-mount blinds.

2. IF THEY ARE BEING MOUNTED on a window with no wood trim or above/outside of the wood trim, you may need to use the wall anchors that came with your product.

3. AFTER YOU HAVE MARKED the location of each bracket, making sure that they are level to and in alignment with each other, use a ⅛ -inch drill bit to predrill at each hole. If the bit goes in easily, you'll need to use an anchor there. If the bit meets resistance (indicating a wooden stud behind the wallboard), use the same process for marking and predrilling described above.

4. IF YOU NEED TO USE the plastic anchors, follow the directions that came with the blinds. The directions should tell you what drill bit size to use to make the hole for the anchor. Once the anchors are in place, the process for installing the brackets and hanging the blinds is the same as the process for inside-mount blinds.

5. CONGRATULATIONS! Now you can relax and enjoy your privacy.

FINAL THOUGHTS ON GETTING THE HANG OF THINGS

Hanging things up is one of the most satisfying of all home improvement projects, because the results are instantaneous. It wasn't there, and now it is! I hope that this chapter has helped you discover how much fun it is to get all those things up and onto your walls and windows. Don't wait for someone else to do this for you. It's just not necessary.

4. WHAT ABOUT WALLS?

Many of the women I have worked with over the years have shared some of their greatest fears with me, and I've learned that one of the biggest factors that hold women back from taking on home improvement projects is the fear of making holes in their walls.

I'm really not sure why holes are so scary, but in this chapter, we're going to learn how to slay our dragons. No more waiting for a white knight to come riding in on his trusted steed, toolbox in hand; I want you to become your own home improvement hero, so you can feel free to make all the holes in the walls you need to (on purpose or by accident), and so you can relax and have fun with these projects.

Size Is Relative

What I might call a little hole, you might think is huge. Different size holes require different solutions, so let's agree on some definitions:

A **SMALL HOLE** is anything under 1 inch in diameter. These holes are usually made when installing or removing wall anchors, moving furniture, or as a result of the everyday bumps and bruises a house is subject to.

A **MEDIUM HOLE** is larger than 1 inch but smaller than 4 inches in diameter. These holes are often made when doorknobs slam into walls, or by small children's feet.

A **LARGE HOLE** is anything larger than 4 inches in diameter. These holes can be made in a frightening variety of ways. For instance, my mother-in-law once tripped while she was carrying my young daughter down the stairs. All the humans involved survived intact, but the wall sustained a major injury from her shoulder.

Regardless of the size of the hole or how it came to be, there is a way to fix it and make it disappear forever. Let's start with the small holes and work our way up.

Patching Small Holes

Tools you will need:
- ✔ 1-inch and 3-inch putty knives
- ✔ Paintbrush
- ✔ Utility knife
- ✔ Safety goggles
- ✔ Breathing mask
- ✔ Damp cloth

Materials you will need:
- ✔ Patching compound (See Chapter 2)
- ✔ 150- and 220-grit sandpaper or sanding sponges
- ✔ Primer
- ✔ Paint

The goal when filling holes of any size is to fill them in such a way that, once they are painted, it's hard to tell a hole was ever there. In most cases, if you look closely enough, you can find evidence of repairs that have been made to walls. The goal here is for the repair not to be visible under normal observation; you'll always know there was a hole somewhere, but with this fix—unless you get your nose right up against the wall—you won't be able to figure out exactly where it was! Here's how to do it:

1. YOU CAN'T FILL THE HOLE well if it is messy and jagged, so use my old friend the utility knife to clean it up first. Make sure you have a new blade in the knife, then use it to gently cut away any wallboard paper or chunks of plaster that are hanging around the edge of the hole or sticking out of the hole past the surface of the wall.

2. USE YOUR 3-INCH PUTTY KNIFE to test for smoothness: Move it across the hole and see if it catches on anything. If it doesn't, you're ready to move on. If it does, try some more surgery with your utility knife.

3. MAKE SURE THE PATCHING compound you are using is smooth, fresh, and lump-free. If it is old, flaky, or lumpy, it won't work well. Put a small glob of compound on your 3-inch putty knife and smooth it into and over your hole.

4. IF YOU ARE FILLING A HOLE made by removing a nail, use your 1-inch putty knife to scrape away the excess compound, leaving none on the wall surrounding the hole. If your hole is larger than a nail hole, you need to leave a little extra compound on top of the hole, because joint compound shrinks as it dries.

5. STOP AND WAIT. The compound has to dry completely before you sand it.

6. SOMETIMES COMPOUND will dry in 10 to 15 minutes, especially if the hole is really small. Other times it will take several hours. It all

 TIP: If you are in a real rush to finish the repair in one day, you can use a blow-dryer to speed up the drying process; just aim the dryer at the wet joint compound until it dries out.

depends on the size of the hole and the amount of humidity in the air. There is one compound sold that turns from pink to white when it is dry, if you want to make it easy on yourself.

7. ONCE THE PATCHING COMPOUND is dry, sand it down, but leave just a tiny bit of extra compound on the hole ($\frac{1}{32}$ of an inch or so). You won't be able to see it and you'll barely be able to feel it, but it will save you from sanding away the entire amount of compound you put on.

8. SOMETIMES THE COMPOUND SHRINKS when it dries, and the hole isn't full. If this happens, you'll need to apply a second coat of compound, let it dry, and then sand it.

9. USE A DAMP CLOTH to wipe away any dust left after sanding.

10. ONCE THE REPAIR IS DUST FREE, apply a small amount of paint primer with a brush to cover the joint compound.

11. AFTER THE PRIMER ON YOUR patch has dried, you can repaint the area you have repaired with your existing wall paint, or you can repaint the whole wall.

12. CONGRATULATIONS! The small hole is gone, and you are ready to take on bigger, uglier holes.

Patching Medium-Size Holes

Tools you will need:
- ✔ Utility knife
- ✔ 6- and 12-inch putty knives
- ✔ Paintbrush
- ✔ Safety goggles
- ✔ Breathing mask

Materials you will need:
- ✔ Self-adhesive drywall repair patch
- ✔ Joint compound (See Chapter 2)

✔ 150- and 220-grit sandpaper or sanding sponges
✔ Primer
✔ Paint

Medium holes require a slightly different approach than small holes. If you try to fill a 3-inch hole with joint compound, the joint compound will just fall through the wall, into the great abyss inside. I know—I've tried it more than once.

Joint compound needs something to stick to in order to stay in place. Fortunately, someone came up with a great invention that I stumbled across a couple years ago while working on a renovation project. Another tradesman had been hired to repair holes in the ceiling that electricians had left behind (electricians are notorious for leaving holes behind when they are hired to snake new wire in old buildings). This handy guy was using self-adhesive drywall patches to make his repairs. Until I discovered these patches, I had to make my own patches out of scraps of drywall (I'll show you how to do that in the section on large holes).

A self-adhesive drywall patch is made of a thin, rigid piece of aluminum that has lots of little holes in it and adhesive on the back. The aluminum is covered by a square of self-adhesive drywall tape that extends past the aluminum by about an inch in every direction.

I've found these patches at the hardware store in 4-, 6-, and 8-inch squares. Always choose a patch that is slightly larger than your hole. For instance, I would suggest a 6-inch patch for a 4-inch hole.

Let's get started so you can see how cool these patches really are. They're so much fun, in fact, you might start making holes in your walls just so you can use them some more!

1. USE YOUR UTILITY KNIFE to cut away any ragged edges on your hole, including any chunks of plaster or big flaps of drywall paper. You want a clean, smooth edge around your hole.

2. WIPE OFF THE AREA around the hole to remove any dust or dirt so your patch will have a clean surface to adhere to.

3. REMOVE THE NONSTICK BACKING from your patch and place it over your hole, centering it if possible.

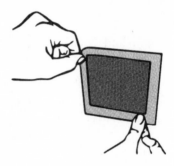

4. USE YOUR FINGERS TO SMOOTH down the adhesive. Make sure it's stuck onto the wall well. If any of the threads from the mesh part come loose or stick up, you can cut them away with your utility knife. You want the patch to be as smooth as possible on the wall.

5. WITH YOUR 6-INCH PUTTY KNIFE, spread a thin layer of joint compound over the entire patch and extend it 2 to 3 inches beyond the edges in every direction. You should end up with a circle of thinly spread joint compound about 8 to 10 inches in diameter.

6. USE A 12-INCH putty knife to smooth out the joint compound and remove any ridges left behind by the smaller putty knife.

IMPORTANT NOTE: Do not obsess here about getting this layer perfectly smooth. It is just the first layer; there will be two more. It should be very thin (think of spreading jelly on toast). You want to avoid big lumps and areas of uneven distribution, but you have to know when to stop. If you overwork joint compound, you'll get to a point where you're making it worse instead of better!

7. LET THE JOINT COMPOUND DRY. This will take several hours. You can speed it up a little by aiming a fan or a blow-dryer at the spot. Unless you're in a rush to get this patch done, it's best to walk away and let it dry in its own time (you'll usually have to leave it overnight).

8. WHEN THE JOINT COMPOUND has turned white and is hard to the touch, it's dry, and now it needs to be smoothed out. Scrape away any of the ridges with your small putty knife and then sand the whole area gently with a fine sanding sponge. As you sand with your right hand, run your left hand over the area, feeling for unevenness or small ridges (they're easier to feel than they are to see).

SAFETY NOTE: You should wear goggles and a breathing mask for this step, since it generates a very fine dust.

9. WIPE AWAY THE DUST and apply a second coat of joint compound, even slightly thinner than the first coat. Extend it 1 or 2 inches beyond the first coat in every direction. Let it dry.

10. REPEAT THE SANDING PROCESS, and run your hands over the patch. Look closely to see if you have covered all evidence of the patch material. If you can still see any pieces of the mesh covering, a third and final coat is necessary.

11. APPLY A VERY THIN THIRD (and final) coat of joint compound.

12. WHEN IT HAS DRIED, do a final sanding, paying special attention to the outermost edges of the joint compound. Sand until you can't feel a line where the joint compound ends.

13. WIPE AWAY ANY DUST on the patch area and surrounding wall.

14. PRIME and paint.

Repairing Cracks and Gouges

Tools you will need:
- ✔ Utility knife or 6-in-one painter's tool
- ✔ 3- and 6-inch putty knives
- ✔ Paintbrush
- ✔ Safety goggles
- ✔ Breathing mask
- ✔ Damp cloth

Materials you will need:
- ✔ Self-adhesive drywall tape
- ✔ Joint compound (See Chapter 2)
- ✔ 150- and 220-grit sandpaper or sanding sponges
- ✔ Primer
- ✔ Paint

Repairing cracks and gouges is very similar to repairing small holes in the walls. The smallest cracks and gouges can be filled with a small amount of joint compound. After sanding, a second coat is sometimes required, and that's about it. Larger cracks, however, require a bit more work.

The most common crack is one that occurs between the top of a door or window and the ceiling. Houses settle over time, and the settling can cause cracks in the wallboard and plaster. If you just lay joint compound over the crack and follow all the steps for medium hole repairs, the crack will initially disappear. Unfortunately, it will usually return within six months to a year, because you just covered the crack, you didn't actually fill it. Here's what I do to repair a crack above a door or window:

1. USE YOUR UTILITY KNIFE or painter's tool to make the crack wider by making a **V**-shape cut in the crack along its full length. You're doing this so you can get joint compound *into* the crack rather than on top of it. The **V**-cut should be at least $\frac{1}{8}$ of an inch deep at its center. It's not a problem if you accidentally cut a little deeper.

2. LAY SELF-ADHESIVE drywall tape over the crack.

 **TIP:** If the crack is not straight, cut several lengths of tape and overlap their ends, then cut through both layers with your utility knife and remove the overlapping pieces once they're laid over the crack. You should end up with one layer of tape and no overlap.

3. SPREAD A THIN LAYER of joint compound, covering the tape and extending beyond it about 1 inch on either side. The compound will go through the tape and into the crack.

4. LET IT dry completely.

5. SAND THE DRY COMPOUND smooth with a fine sanding sponge.

6. WIPE AWAY THE DUST with a damp cloth, then add a second layer of joint compound, extending it about an inch past the original layer on every side.

7. LET THE SECOND LAYER DRY completely, sand it, and repeat the process with one more layer if necessary. Do a final sanding and clean up any dust.

8. PRIME and paint.

Fixing Large Holes

Tools you will need:
- ✔ Utility knife
- ✔ Handsaw
- ✔ Speed square
- ✔ Keyhole saw or drywall saw
- ✔ Battery-powered or electric drill with a screwdriver bit in it
- ✔ Straight edge
- ✔ Measuring tape
- ✔ Pencil
- ✔ Safety goggles
- ✔ Breathing mask
- ✔ 6-inch and 12-inch putty knives
- ✔ Fine sanding sponge or sandpaper

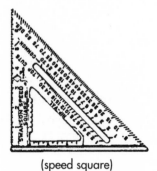

(speed square)

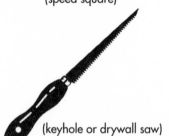

(keyhole or drywall saw)

Materials you will need:
- ✔ Small piece of wallboard that is larger than your hole

✔ Self-adhesive drywall tape
✔ 1⅝-inch drywall screws
✔ Scrap lumber (about 2 inches wide and 3 feet long)
✔ Joint compound

Large holes are too big to be covered by a self-adhesive drywall patch. The method used to repair them can also be used when you would like to be able to use the area of wall you're mending to mount something (you can't mount pictures or shelves on an area that has been patched with a self-adhesive drywall patch). Large holes are repaired by rebuilding the wall with a drywall patch, using some wood to hold it in place.

Drywall is sold in 4-foot by 8-foot sheets, which are way bigger than what you'll need for this job. Home centers, lumber yards, and hardware stores will often have broken pieces available for purchase, or they'll sell small pieces that are about 2 feet by 2 feet. Most drywall used in home construction is ½ of an inch thick, with the exception of the drywall in walls in attached garages or furnace rooms, which is ⅝ of an inch thick.

In this case, let's pretend that the hole you need to fix is approximately 10 inches in diameter:

STEP ONE: MAKING THE DRYWALL PATCH

1. USE YOUR UTILITY KNIFE to cut away the wallboard on the inside edge of the hole. Usually it's hanging by some paper, or it's pressed up against the insulation behind it. Once the center of the hole is gone, you can see if there is anything behind it (like a stud or an electrical wire).

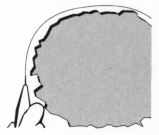

2. YOU NEED TO CUT A PIECE of wallboard to use as a patch. The patch should be approximately 1 square inch bigger than your hole. In this case, since you have a roughly 10-by-10-inch square, your patch needs to be about 11-by-11 inches.

3. USE YOUR MEASURING TAPE, straight edge, and pencil to mark an 11-by-11-inch square on the drywall piece you purchased.

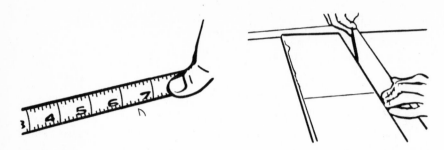

4. OPEN YOUR UTILITY KNIFE and hold the blade against the straight edge. Use the straight edge as a guide as you score (not cut through, *score*) the drywall along your pencil line with the blade of the utility knife.

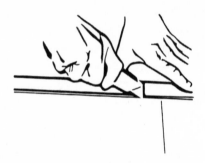

5. CUT ALL THE WAY ACROSS the piece of drywall a couple of times. You're not trying to cut through it; you're just scoring it so you can break it.

6. STAND THE DRYWALL UP and bend it along your score line. It should snap as its center breaks.

7. USE YOUR UTILITY KNIFE to cut through the paper on the back side of the drywall.

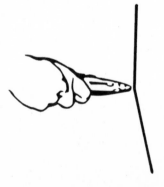

8. REPEAT THIS PROCESS ALONG the other pencil line. You should end up with a square piece of drywall. If the edges are a little rough, clean them up with your utility knife.

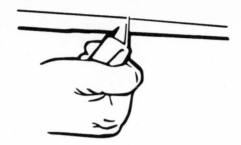

STEP TWO: PREPARING THE HOLE FOR THE PATCH

1. PLACE THE PATCH you just made over the hole in the wall, centering it as well as you can.

2. HOLD THE PATCH in place and trace around its entire perimeter with a pencil.

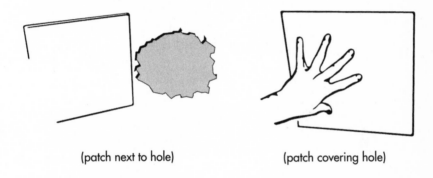

(patch next to hole)   (patch covering hole)

3. USE YOUR KEYHOLE saw and/or utility knife to cut neatly just outside your pencil lines and remove the excess drywall. You should end up with a hole in the wall that is just slightly larger than the patch you made.

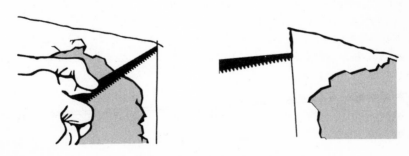

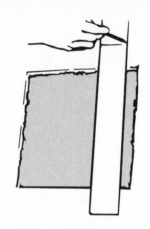

4. NOW YOU NEED something to attach your patch to so it doesn't just fall through the wall. You're going to cut two pieces of wood to put behind the hole in the wall. They need to be a couple of inches longer than the hole on both ends. Set a piece of scrap wood over the hole and mark the correct length.

5. SET THE WOOD on a bucket, counter, or table with the line you marked hanging over the edge. Use your handsaw to cut the piece of wood along the line. Remember, if the saw keeps catching, you're pressing down too hard. Also, this cut does not have to be perfect; it will be hidden inside the wall.

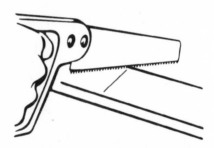

6. REPEAT WITH the second piece of wood.

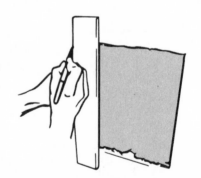

7. SET A PIECE OF WOOD over the hole, vertically, so that about the same length of wood is sitting on the wall above and below your hole. Make a mark on the wood even with the edges of the hole. This mark helps you know where to put the wood behind the wallboard.

8. ORIENT ONE PIECE OF WOOD so it's vertical and set it into the hole, being careful not to drop it. Place it so that half of its width is hidden under the right edge of your hole.

9. THE EXTRA COUPLE INCHES of length should be tucked up under the top and bottom of the hole so that you can just see the lines you made on the wood.

10. USE YOUR DRILL, fitted with a screw-driver bit, and a drywall screw. Screw through the drywall into the wood about an inch below the edge of the hole. You will need to hold onto the wood tightly and pull it toward you, because the screw will initially push it away. Once the screw really bites into the wood, it will pull it toward the drywall. Be careful not to bury the head of the drywall screw in the drywall. The head of the drywall screw should be just below the surface of the drywall.

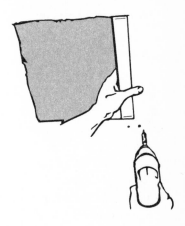

11. REPEAT WITH ANOTHER SCREW in the other end of the wood, 1 inch above the hole. Add a second screw in each end of the piece of wood, about an inch to the side of the first screws.

12. REPEAT THE WHOLE procedure with the other piece of wood, placing it so that only half of its width is hidden under the left edge of the hole.

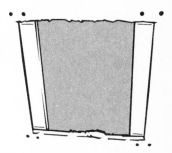

IMPORTANT NOTE: If you accidentally drive a screw too far into the drywall, just remove it and start it again in a new hole. It takes a lot of practice to get the hang of screwing drywall screws just the right distance in.

STEP THREE: PUTTING THE DRYWALL PATCH IN THE HOLE

1. PLACE YOUR DRYWALL PATCH in the hole. If it's too big, shave down the side of the patch or the hole until the patch will fit easily into the hole. It's okay if there is a gap of ¼- to ½-inch between the edge of the patch and the edge of the hole.

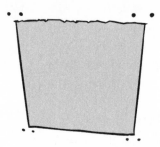

2. SCREW THE PATCH INTO both pieces of the wood you placed behind the hole with two or three drywall screws. Put one screw about an inch from each corner of the patch, and one in the middle on each side.

3. CUT FOUR PIECES of self-adhesive drywall tape about 4 inches longer than the patch. Our patch is a square, so they will all be the same length. If your patch is a rectangle, you will have two different lengths.

4. PRETEND THAT THE DRYWALL tape is a bandage and you are very carefully going to cover up the big "owie" in the wall. Place each piece of tape so that it straddles the gap, with half of its width on the wall, and half on the patch.

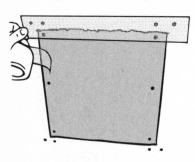

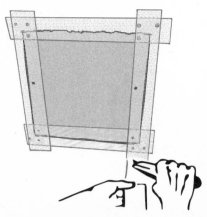

5. REPEAT UNTIL ALL FOUR SIDES ARE COVERED. You should have an overlap of drywall tape at the corners, and—if you're lucky—the drywall tape will now cover all of your screw heads.

6. USE THE FLAT EDGE OF A PUTTY KNIFE to make sure the drywall tape is stuck tight to the wall and that no pieces are lifted up or sticking out. If your putty knife catches on any screw heads, gently lift that piece of tape and screw the head of the screw farther into the wall. Put the drywall tape back where it was and test again for smoothness.

STEP FOUR: MAKING THE PATCH LOOK GOOD

1. ONCE YOU'RE SATISFIED with your patch, it's time to apply the joint compound. Put a glob of compound on your 6-inch knife and start spreading it over the tape and the entire patch. Your patch may be perfectly even with the wall, or it may be about ⅛ of an inch behind the wall. Don't worry; you'll make up the difference with the joint compound.

2. DON'T TRY TO COVER everything perfectly with the first coat. This fix is definitely going to require three coats. Your goal is to get a thin layer spread relatively smoothly over the entire patch and about 2 inches beyond it on every side.

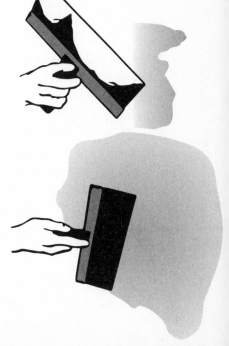

3. LET IT DRY COMPLETELY! This may take up to 24 hours. When it's dry, use a putty knife to scrape down any ridges, then sand it lightly. Remember to put on your dust mask! Do not try to sand it completely smooth at this point; just sand down any obvious ridges or bumps. Apply a second coat of joint compound with your 6-inch knife and then use your 12-inch knife to spread it out.

4. THIS COAT SHOULD EXTEND an inch or so beyond the first. After applying this coat of compound, you should no longer be able to see the mesh of the drywall tape.

5. LET THIS COAT DRY, and then sand it down until it's smooth (but not so much that you expose the drywall tape). Wipe off any dust, and then apply your final coat of joint compound. This coat should be very thin, and it should extend just beyond the boundaries of the previous coat.

6. LET THE COMPOUND DRY one last time and sand it with your finest sandpaper sponge, paying particular attention to the outermost edge. Run your fingers over the area as you sand until the outline of the joint compound disappears and it feels really smooth. If you are not satisfied with the look of your patch after three coats of joint compound, you can repeat the process with a fourth coat, but don't make yourself crazy here—it's not going to be perfect!

7. WIPE AWAY THE DUST with a damp rag, and you're ready to apply primer. When the primer is dry, you can paint it.

8. CONGRATULATIONS! You took on a very complex wall repair job and got it done well. It may not be perfect, but it's done, and the next time will be easier, because you'll know what you're doing.

FINAL THOUGHTS ON WALLS

Over time, we tend to cease to notice the walls that we live within— unless they have holes, cracks, and dings on them! You now have the ability to take care of just about any wall-related problem in your home. No hole is too big or too small for you and your joint compound and putty knife. Whether you choose to work your way through the house one room at a time, or take them all on at once, have fun with it. Don't wait until you're getting ready to sell your home to fix up the walls; do it now, and make each wall in your house something you like to look at.

5. ALL ABOUT DOORS

I get more calls to fix doors than just about anything else. I think that's because we all have so many doors in our homes, and doors get a lot of use. The range of problems I am called upon to fix is quite broad:

✔ My door won't close.
✔ My door won't open.
✔ My door closes but won't stay closed.
✔ My door opens but won't stay open.
✔ My door closes but the latch doesn't catch.
✔ My doorknob is broken.
✔ My doorknob works fine, but I want to replace it with a nicer one.
✔ I have bi-fold doors, and they're driving me crazy.
✔ My door is really drafty.

When a door is working properly, you should be able to close it with no effort. The latch should catch on the first try, and it should hold the door snug against its frame. Doors close poorly for two reasons:

the door was hung badly when it was originally installed, or it has shrunk, swollen, or dropped over time.

IT HAPPENED TO ME ONCE: I was working on a kitchen installation project recently. The new kitchen was part of a larger renovation project, and on the days I was there helping the cabinetmaker install the cabinets, there were many other carpenters on-site working on various tasks. One of the guys was installing new doors in the old door frames of the original part of the house. At the end of the day, the homeowner was chatting with me and said, "I'm getting new doors today. . . . I guess it takes a long time to install a door." She was referring to the fact that it had taken the guy the better part of a day to hang two doors. I explained to her that hanging doors—badly—takes no time at all; hanging a door properly, however, takes a lot of time.

It has taken me years to learn how to hang doors well, and in the process I have learned how to solve most door problems. If you have one of the door problems listed above, or even a different one, this chapter is intended to help you solve it. We will look at how doors are supposed to work, and we'll discuss a variety of tactics you can use to fix your doors so they work properly.

Diagnosing the Problem

Let's work our way through the list I made at the beginning of the chapter; we'll solve the problems one at a time. Some, like the faulty bi-folds and drafty doors, are obvious issues. For others, you'll need to figure out what's wrong. To start, in order to fix the problem, you have to have a specific description of the symptoms. Just like a doctor examining a patient, you need to examine your door from all angles to determine what is keeping it from closing.

First, close your door (or have someone else close it while you watch) slowly, and look closely at the top, bottom, and sides of the door as it slides (or tries to slide) into the door frame. Is there a part of the door that's actually hitting the frame?

If so, mark that spot on the door with a pencil. Next, open the door and examine the inside of the door frame. Are there any places where the paint or finish has been worn away by the door rubbing against it? If the area on the door that you marked with a pencil matches up with the worn area on the frame, you may have found your problem. If the door has swollen because of high humidity and it no longer fits into the frame easily, it will stick in one or more areas.

If the area that is sticking is within the first 10 inches down from the top of the door on the latch side, try **SOLUTION #1**. If the area that sticks or rubs is along the top or bottom of the door, try **SOLUTION #2**. Does the door close but not latch? Does your door close, but it jiggles in the frame? If so, try **SOLUTION #3**. If you want to repair or replace your door handle/lockset, **SOLUTION #4** provides the answer; **SOLUTION #5** will solve most bi-fold door issues. If you want to put an end to drafts coming in through the door, check out **SOLUTION #6**.

Solution #1: Replacing the Screws

Tools you will need:

✔ Medium flathead and Phillips head screwdriver
✔ Drill with a Phillips head screwdriver bit
✔ Stepladder

If the area of your door that appears to be sticking is in the lower half of the latch side (the area between the latch and the bottom of the door) you'll need to follow the steps in Solution #2. However, if your door is sticking on the top half of the latch side (especially the top quarter), it may mean that the door is sagging or dropping in its frame. This happens sometimes with solid wood doors: The weight of the door pulls on the frame, and the side of the door ends up rubbing against the latch side of the frame.

1. OPEN THE DOOR AND USE your screwdriver to remove the top screw from the half of the top hinge that is attached to the door frame (not the door itself!).

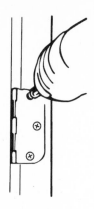 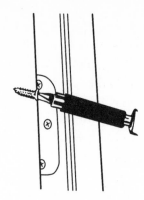

2. REPLACE THAT SMALL BRASS SCREW with a 2½- or 3-inch coarse-thread drywall screw. You will need to use an electric or battery-operated drill with a screwdriver bit installed for this step. You may need to stand on a small step stool or ladder so you're high up enough to get the leverage you need on the screwdriver.

3. TRY CLOSING THE DOOR. If it closes better, but not perfectly, repeat step 2 with another screw in the top hinge.

4. TRY CLOSING THE DOOR AGAIN. If it closes well, congratulations! If it still doesn't close, you'll have to try Solution #2.

Solution #2: Sand It Away

Tools you may need:

- ✔ Hand sanding block or electric sander
- ✔ Small flathead and Phillips head screwdrivers
- ✔ Six-in-one painter's tool
- ✔ Medium-size Phillips head screwdriver or drill with a Phillips head screwdriver bit
- ✔ Hammer
- ✔ Paintbrush
- ✔ Stepladder
- ✔ Safety glasses
- ✔ Another person, if you need to remove the door
- ✔ Something to set the door on, like sawhorses, a table, two chairs or a couple of trashcans

Materials you may need:
- ✔ 60-, 100-, and 150-grit sandpaper
- ✔ Primer and paint or stain and polyurethane.
- ✔ Masking tape
- ✔ Pencil

If the area that needs sanding is on the top or the latch side of the door, you can try and work on it with the door still hanging. If the area to be sanded is on the bottom of the door, or you don't feel comfortable working on a ladder to reach the top of the door, you'll have to remove the door from its hinges.

REMOVING THE DOOR

1. ONE PIECE OF THE DOOR HINGE is attached to the door with screws, another piece is attached to the door frame with screws, and those two pieces are attached to each other with hinge pins. Start by removing the hinge pins.

2. STAND ON THE SIDE of the door where you can see the hinges when the door is closed, then close the door.

3. PLACE THE TIP OF THE SMALL PHILLIPS head screwdriver at the bottom of the hinge pin and tap on the end of the screwdriver handle with the hammer. You are trying to drive the hinge pin up and out of the hinge. You can also place the tip of a small flathead screwdriver (or your 6-in-1 painter's tool) under the top of the hinge pin and tap

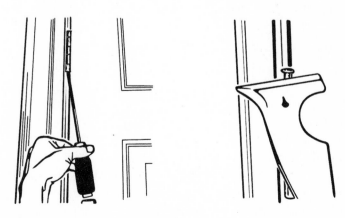

on the end of the screwdriver handle with the hammer. This part may take some work, but you need to find a way to get that pin out.

4. REPEAT THE PROCESS with the remaining hinge pins.

5. WHEN YOU HAVE REMOVED all the hinge pins, you can remove the door. Grasp the handle and turn it to the open position. Gently lift and pull on the door until the hinge pieces separate from one another. Be prepared for the weight of the door (you may want help with this step; if the door is solid wood, it will be quite heavy and awkward to deal with).

6. LIFT THE DOOR and lay it down on a level surface.

SANDING THE DOOR

1. IF YOU DIDN'T HAVE TO remove the door, this step can take place with the door still hanging in place. Having the door in place is convenient, because it allows you to check if you have removed enough material to allow the door to close properly as you go along. With 60-grit sandpaper on your sanding block, an electric palm sander, or a random orbital sander, you can start sanding the part of the door that you believe is sticking.

(sanding the edge of the door)   (sanding the top of the door)

In this case I would not use a sanding sponge—it's too soft. If you don't have a sanding block, you can fold sandpaper over on

TIP: Put masking tape on the door to indicate how much wood you think you need to sand off. When the wood is flush with the tape you can re-hang the door and see if you sanded off enough.

itself to form an about 2-inch by 4-inch rectangle, or you can wrap the sandpaper around a small piece of wood. If you're sanding by hand, you will need to put some force behind the sanding block and work on the area until you think you have removed enough of the door. If you're using an electric sander, you'll need to add a little force to the sander, but not much; the weight of the sander will do most of the work.

2. WITH THE HELP OF ELECTRICITY, you can remove a lot of wood very quickly, so go slowly. Stop when you think you have removed enough wood, and try closing the door.

3. IF YOU HAVE REMOVED the door from its hinges, you will have to put the door back in place to test your work.

REHANGING A DOOR
1. WITH THE HELP OF ANOTHER PERSON, lift the door upright and fit the two halves of one of the hinges back together. Don't worry about getting all of them in place right away—just try for one to start with.

2. WHEN ONE HINGE IS LINED UP, put the hinge pin back in place.

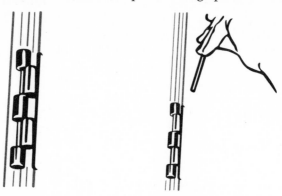

3. REPEAT THE PROCESS with the remaining hinges. Don't hammer the hinge pin all the way in; leave about ½ of an inch showing on the top.

FINISHING UP

1. NOW THAT THE DOOR IS BACK ON, test out your work by slowly closing the door. If it won't close yet, mark with a pencil where it's still sticking and repeat the sanding process, removing the door from its hinges again if necessary. If the door closes, but the gap between the door and the frame is less than ⅛ of an inch, you'll want to remove a little more wood. If the gap is about a ⅛ of an inch, you've removed enough.

2. SWITCH TO 150-GRIT sandpaper and smooth the area out by sanding it lightly.

3. IF THE DOOR WAS PAINTED, you need to prime and paint the area that you sanded. One coat of primer and two coats of paint are needed. If the door was sanded and sealed with polyurethane, it's a little trickier:

    a. If you sanded the top or bottom of the door: Just apply a couple coats of polyurethane to reseal the wood. No one will be able to see that the wood is not stained.

b. If you sanded a portion of the side of the door: Try to match the stain first, and then apply two coats of polyurethane. Don't worry about getting a perfect match on the stain color; close will be good enough in this situation, because the spot won't be highly visible.

IMPORTANT NOTE: It's essential that all six (yes, there are six, not just two!) sides of a door be sealed with either paint or polyurethane. It reduces the chances for swelling in the future.

Solution #3: Adjusting the Strike Plate

Tools you will need:

- ✔ Phillips head screwdriver
- ✔ Pencil
- ✔ Ruler
- ✔ Small chisel
- ✔ Hammer
- ✔ Utility knife
- ✔ Drill and drill bit

(chisel)

Materials you will need:

- ✔ Wood putty
- ✔ Wooden toothpicks, bamboo skewers, or wooden matches (see important tip)

The strike plate is the small metal plate, usually brass, located on the door frame where the latch from the door catches and rests when the door is in the closed position. It's hard to believe that something so small can cause big problems. Very small adjustments to the strike plate can solve problems with doors that drive people crazy. However, determining what the problem is and how to solve it will take some additional detective work.

The challenge here is that the problem occurs while the door is in the closed position, effectively covering up the strike plate and making it difficult to see the problem. Position yourself so your eyes are level with the latch, and watch it from both sides of the door as you close it (make sure no one comes bombing through the door while you're doing this;

it would be tricky to explain how you got your black eye!). Watch the latch carefully as you close the door. Is the latch missing the hole in the strike plate? If so, is it missing high or low? Open the door and examine the strike plate. Are there rubbing or wear marks on the plate above or below the hole?

Does it look like the latch is entering the hole in the strike plate but not staying there? Using a flashlight might help you see what's going

IMPORTANT TIP FOR ALL OF THESE SOLUTIONS: Whenever you move a strike plate a very small distance up, down, forward, or backward, you can run into a problem when you try to move the location of the screw. If the new screw location is right next to the old one, the screw is very likely to slide back into its original hole, making it impossible for you to move the strike plate. If you run into this problem, try this:

1. PLACE A WOOD GOLF TEE, a couple of wood toothpicks, a bamboo skewer, or a wood kitchen match (with the head removed!) in the old screw holes, and squirt in some wood glue (Elmer's white glue will do in a pinch).

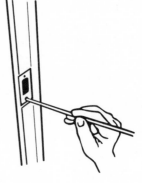

2. LET THE glue dry.

3. CUT OFF THE WOOD that sticks out of the hole with your utility knife.

4. SAND SMOOTH if necessary.

You are now ready to mark, pre-drill, and screw your screws into their new locations. This trick also works great when you have loose screws in door hinges and don't want to move the hinge.

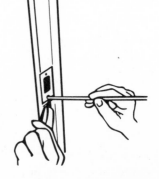

on. In doors that close correctly, you'll see that the latch is centered on the opening in the strike plate; this allows the entire latch to get into the hole in the plate. When the door is closed, the flat side of the latch is tight against the leading edge of the hole in the strike plate.

By watching the latch move over the strike plate, you can usually determine whether the latch is missing the hole on the strike plate on the high side or the low side. If it is missing the hole on the high side, you'll need to raise the strike plate; if it's missing on the low side, you'll need to lower the strike plate.

MOVING THE STRIKE PLATE UP OR DOWN

1. USING YOUR PENCIL, mark the door frame above or below the strike plate by the amount you think it needs to move. It's usually only ⅛ to ¼ of an inch.

2. USE YOUR RULER TO EXTEND your mark into a straight line across the door frame, just above or below the strike plate.

3. REMOVE THE STRIKE PLATE with your screwdriver.

4. SET THE SHARP EDGE of your chisel on your pencil line and strike the end of the chisel with your hammer a few times. Move the chisel and repeat until you've covered the entire pencil line.

5. TURN YOUR CHISEL VERTICALLY to clean out the corner that needs to be removed. The back corner of the latch plate is either square or curved. If you have difficulty making a curved cut with the chisel, just make a square one; the extra space can be filled with wood putty later.

6. USE YOUR CHISEL'S SHARP EDGE to scrape away the wood above (if you're shifting the strike plate down) or below (if you're shifting it up) your chisel line.

7. IN ORDER TO MOVE THE STRIKE PLATE up or down, you may have to use your chisel to enlarge the hole where the lip of the strike plate rests.

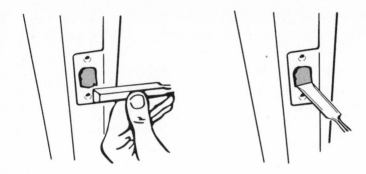

8. SET THE STRIKE PLATE BACK on the opening in its new position (above or below its original position).

9. MARK THE CENTER of the strike plate's two holes with a pencil.

10. REMOVE THE STRIKE PLATE and predrill one of the marks for the screws, using a drill bit that is smaller than $\frac{1}{8}$ of an inch.

11. REPLACE THE STRIKE PLATE and screw in one screw.

12. CLOSE THE DOOR AND SEE if the latch catches completely in the strike plate. If it doesn't, repeat steps 1 through 10.

13. IF THE LATCH CATCHES PROPERLY in the strike plate, predrill the second mark and screw in the remaining strike plate screw.

14. TO FINISH THE JOB PROPERLY, take a little wood putty and fill in the area around the strike plate that you uncovered when you moved it.

MOVING THE STRIKE PLATE FORWARD

When the latch enters the hole in the strike plate but doesn't stay there, it means that the strike plate needs to be moved forward a little. This small adjustment will allow the latch to catch behind the edge of the strike plate:

1. REMOVE THE strike plate with a screwdriver.

2. POSITION THE STRIKE PLATE forward about ¼ of an inch. In this situation, forward means toward the room, or in the direction the door opens.

3. IF THE WOOD BEHIND the strike plate will not allow you to move it forward, you will need to remove some wood. If this is your situation, proceed to step 4. If you can easily move the strike plate forward, proceed to step 6.

4. USE YOUR PENCIL TO MARK a line on the wood to indicate how much wood you want to remove.

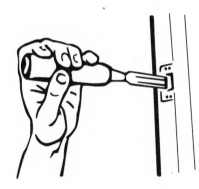 **5. PLACE YOUR CHISEL** on the line and tap your hammer against the head of the chisel to remove small chunks of wood. You don't need to remove all the wood with one blow of the hammer; take your time, removing a little wood at a time, continually checking to see if you have removed enough to place the strike plate in a new position. Stop chiseling when you have removed enough wood.

6. PLACE THE STRIKE plate in its new position.

7. MARK THE CENTER of the two holes with a pencil.

8. REMOVE THE STRIKE plate and use a drill bit smaller than $\frac{1}{8}$ of an inch to predrill one of the marks for the screws.

9. REPLACE THE STRIKE plate and screw in one screw.

10. CLOSE THE DOOR and see if the latch catches completely in the strike plate. If it doesn't, repeat steps 5 through 9.

11. IF THE LATCH CATCHES properly in the strike plate, predrill and screw in the remaining strike plate screw.

12. TO FINISH THE JOB properly, take a little wood putty and fill in the area behind the strike plate that you uncovered when you moved it.

MOVING THE STRIKE PLATE BACKWARD

If your door closes and stays closed, but it kind of rattles a bit in the frame (and it's driving you nuts), you can fix it with a small adjustment of the strike plate. We've already moved it up, down, and forward, so the only direction left is backward! In this situation, "backward" means in the direction the door closes, or more toward the frame.

To start, follow all the steps from "Moving the Strike Plate Forward," with the following change to step 2:

SLIDE THE STRIKE PLATE about ⅛ of an inch back. Don't move it back too far; that may make it impossible for the latch to get all the way into the hole in the strike plate. Small adjustments are all that is usually necessary.

We have (hopefully) solved the first five problems you might have with your door. Now that it closes correctly, let's move on to the door handle.

Solution #4: Replacing a Broken or Ugly Lockset

If your doorknob is broken, you will probably need to replace it with a new one. If you are tired of your old doorknobs and want to change their style, you can replace them all. I did this recently when I updated the first floor of my house with a new paint job.

There are two basic types of locksets found in most modern homes ("lockset" is the technical term for a doorknob and all its moving parts—both visible and hidden— within the door):

passage
locksets

1. PASSAGE LOCKSETS: You usually find these on interior and exterior doors. They may or may not have a locking mechanism.

2. SECURITY LOCKSETS: We typically call these deadbolts. They are used *in addition to* the passage lockset on an exterior door.

security locksets

In order to replace a lockset with a new one, you must first remove the existing one. Let's look at a picture of a lockset so you can become familiar with the names of the various parts I will be referring to in this section:

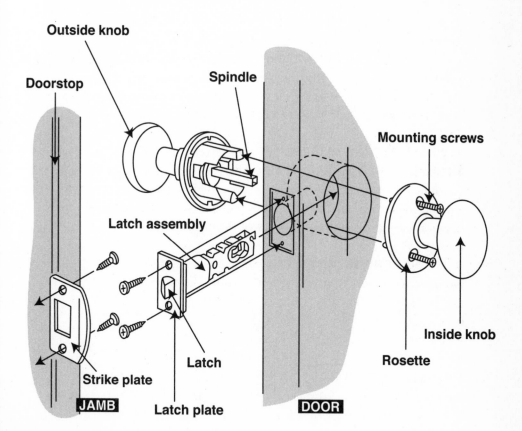

SHOPPING TIP: I was tired of the old, worn, round brass doorknobs I had, so I replaced them with the brushed-nickel lever-style handles that are currently in style. The new handles not only look much better, but they are easier to open and are easier for people with arthritis or young kids who can't grasp and turn a round doorknob. Of course, if you don't want those little kids opening doors, you'll probably want to stick with round knobs.

REMOVING THE OLD LOCKSET

Tools you will need:

✔ Medium-size Phillips head screwdriver
✔ Small flathead screwdriver

Ninety-nine percent of the time, you'll be able to replace your existing lockset with a new one without running into any problems. Very rarely, you'll find something unusual. If this happens to you, take all the parts of the lockset to your nearest hardware store and ask for help. If they can't help you, you can always call a locksmith.

1. TO REMOVE THE OLD LOCKSET you have to remove the knob or handle portion of the lockset first, because it passes through the latching mechanism. On the majority of doors, you'll find two mounting screws on the inside rosette. Use the Phillips head screwdriver to remove them, then pull apart the two sides of the doorknob.

2. IF YOU DON'T SEE ANY SCREWS on the rosette, look for a small slit on the column that runs between the knob and the rosette.

3. PRESS THE TIP OF YOUR FLATHEAD screwdriver into the slit. You should feel a release that allows the knobs to come off, leaving a round metal plate attached to the door with two screws. Remove those screws, and the metal plate should come off.

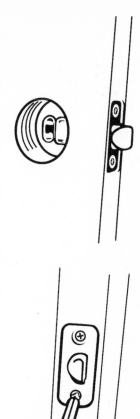

4. YOU WILL SEE TWO SCREWS in the latch plate surrounding the latch. Remove both of them with your Philips head screwdriver.

5. PULL OUT THE LATCH and attached latch assembly. If it doesn't pop out easily, use one of your screwdrivers in the large hole where the doorknobs were to apply some leverage from behind.

INSTALLING THE NEW LOCKSET
Tools you will need:
- ✔ Medium-size Phillips head screwdriver
- ✔ Small flathead screwdriver

Materials you will need:
- ✔ New lockset

1. A NEW LOCKSET COMES with one latch plate attached, and another optional one in the package. The latch plate will have round or square corners.

2. YOU WANT THE LATCH PLATE on your new latch to match shape of the one you removed. If the latch plate that comes on the latch from the factory is a different shape than the one on your old latch, you can pop it off with the tip of your flathead screwdriver.

3. ONCE IT'S OFF, put on the latch plate that's the right shape and snap it into place. Don't worry if it doesn't exactly snap; you'll be screwing it in anyway.

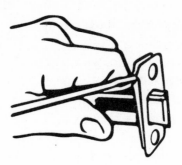

4. SET THE LATCH ASSEMBLY into the hole on the edge of the door, making sure that the sloping edge of the latch is facing the front of the door. It has to be positioned that way so it will slide over the strike plate. I have made this mistake several times, and every time it's embarrassing—when you try to close the door, the latch just bounces off of the strike plate.

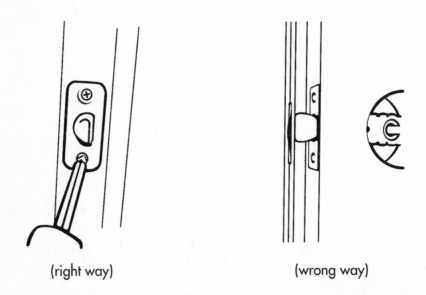

(right way)   (wrong way)

5. ONCE YOU'RE SURE THE LATCH is facing in the correct direction, screw it into place using two of the four 1-inch wood screws provided with your new lockset.

6. NOW YOU'RE READY TO INSERT the new handle into the door. Make sure that the half with the visible screws goes in from the back of the door. If you are putting in lever-style handles, they can only be oriented in one direction. The spindle on one of the door handles passes through the small, square opening in the latch assembly.

7. THE OTHER HALF OF THE LOCKSET slides onto the first so that the two openings for the screws that will hold the two parts together line up.

8. WHEN YOU HAVE THE TWO halves of the new lockset correctly in place, they'll fit snugly against the door, leaving no gaps. You may need to take them out and put them back in a couple of times before you get it right.

9. NOW IT'S TIME TO INSERT the two mounting screws that hold the door handles in place. These screws are the two longer machine screws (they have a flat bottom and small, even threads). This can be the trickiest part of the installation, or it can be really easy. Use your fingers to insert one of the screws into the upper hole on the doorknob, and start turning it clockwise until you feel the threads grab. You're trying to line the end of it up with a hole inside the doorknob that you can't see, so you have to work by feel in this situation. It may get frustrating, but just keep at it. If you're having trouble, make sure that the screw is not going in at an angle. It has to go in straight or it won't work.

10. DON'T TIGHTEN THE FIRST screw all the way. Once you have the first screw started, move on to the second screw. After both screws are started by hand, go back and tighten them all the way with the Phillips head screwdriver.

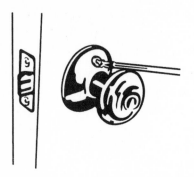

11. CONGRATULATIONS! You have successfully replaced your lockset. If you experienced any difficulties, take it apart and start over. I have had to do this many times. For a relatively simple job, it can be quite frustrating; just be patient, and you will be successful.

Solution #5: Fixing Bi-Fold Doors

I know I shouldn't hate the person who invented bi-fold doors. I'm sure he had really good intentions when he created doors that fold in the middle and take less room to open than conventional doors. They were probably heralded as a great invention in their day. But, as the law of moving parts states, the more moving parts something has, the more ways that it can break and be really annoying. (Okay, I just made that law up. Doesn't mean it's not true!)

The real problem with most bi-fold doors is not their essential design. Installed correctly, high-quality bi-fold doors probably work very well for a long time. Unfortunately, no one ever hires me to fix those doors. The only ones I ever see are the cheap ones that have (usually) been installed badly. The good news about bi-fold door problems is that most of them are relatively easy to fix. The bad news is that the fix doesn't always last, and it may have to be repeated at some time in the future. There are two very common problems with bi-fold doors that you may be dealing with in your home:

1. The door doesn't open smoothly.
2. The door pops off its track when you close it.

MY BI-FOLD DOOR DOESN'T OPEN SMOOTHLY

Tools you will need:
- ✔ Phillips head screwdriver
- ✔ Drill
- ✔ ⅛-inch drill bit
- ✔ Steel measuring tape
- ✔ Pencil
- ✔ Safety glasses
- ✔ Paintbrush

Materials you will need:
- ✔ Wood putty
- ✔ Paint

The most common reason for this problem is the position of the doorknob. The doorknob should be placed in the center of the lead door (the door farthest from the pivot edge). People frequently put the knob in the other door, which means physics are working against the door's functioning properly. In order to fix the problem, you have to relocate the doorknob:

1. USE A PHILLIPS HEAD screwdriver to unscrew the knob.

2. MEASURE 36 INCHES UP from the floor, and mark that height on the lead door.

3. MEASURE FROM ONE side to the other to find the horizontal center point, and mark it at the same level as the 36-inch height mark.

4. DRILL A HOLE with a ⅛-inch drill bit.

5. REPLACE THE SCREW in your new hole and attach the knob. I find that holding the tip of the screwdriver in the screw head and turning the knob with my hands works best. It's an awkward situation at best; a second pair of hands can be really useful.

6. FILL THE ORIGINAL HOLE with a little wood putty. Let it dry, then paint or stain the area to match the door.

MY BI-FOLD DOOR POPS OFF THE TRACK WHEN I CLOSE IT
Tools you may need:
- ✔ Phillips head screwdriver
- ✔ Channel lock pliers

At the top of the lead door, you'll find a piece of hardware that usually looks like a plastic disc.

This disc pops out of the track if the door is leaning toward the opening. In order to fix it, you have to move the pivot edge of the door closer to the door frame at the top of the door.

(the gap between the pivot edge of the door and the door frame is too big)

1. A BI-FOLD DOOR PIVOTS on two pins. Both are located on the side of the door nearest the frame. One is on the top of the door; the other is on the bottom. They are each held in place by a metal bracket. The top bracket is held in place by a screw.

2. LOCATE THE SCREW and unscrew it slightly with a Phillips head screwdriver.

3. ONCE IT'S LOOSE, you can push the entire bracket closer to the frame. Just slide it over a little bit, then retighten the screw.

4. FIND THE SMALL PLASTIC DISC that's on the top of the lead door. Press it down as you move the lead door back into position. When the disc is back within the limits of the track, let it go. It should pop back into the track.

5. NOW TRY CLOSING THE DOOR. If the wheel stays in the track, you're done. If it still comes out, repeat steps 1 through 4 until you succeed (or until you are completely frustrated and have to stop).

6. IF YOU HAVE MOVED THE UPPER bracket as close to the frame as you can and still have room for the door to open and the lead door is still popping out, there's another fix you can try:

    a. While the door is in the open position, try to get your hand underneath the bottom of the door right next to the bottom pivot pin. Lift up on the door and move it about ¼ of an inch away from the frame. Lower it back into place.

    b. Try closing the door again. If it stays in the track, congratulations!

7. IF THE DOOR STILL DOESN'T STAY in the track, there is one more fix you can attempt:

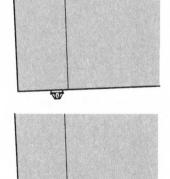

    a. You can try raising the door's height. In order to do this, you need to get access to the pivot pin on the bottom of the door. Having someone help makes it easier to do this.

    b. Have someone lift the door up toward the top of the door frame, exposing the lower pivot pin. With your fingers or a pair of pliers, turn the pivot pin counterclockwise. Keep turning it until you have made it between ⅛ and ¼ of an inch longer.

    c. Lower the door and try closing it. I really hope that at this point the door stays in the tracks when it's closed, but I have to tell you—sometimes, none of the fixes are going to work. Like I said: They're the doors I love to hate!

IMPORTANT NOTE: Sometimes, in order to really get at the lower pivot pin and adjust its height, you'll need to remove the door completely. Do this by lifting the door up into the upper track and then pulling the bottom out and away. Once you have adjusted the pivot pin, replace the door by pushing the upper hardware into its position on the track, lifting the door, and setting the pivot pin back into its spot in the hardware resting on the floor. You may have to do this a couple of times to get the height of the door correct.

Solution #6: Drafty Doors

Your home's exterior doors are important for many reasons: They provide security, can make an attractive welcoming statement, and are on the front lines protecting you from weather of all kinds. Exterior doors take a great deal of abuse from sun, rain, wind, and snow. The door that serves as your main entry and exit point gets opened and closed thousands of times each year. If you have an older door, or a door that no longer fits snugly against its weather stripping, then it's time for you to get off the couch and do something about it. You're losing precious heat in the winter and air-conditioned air in the summer through that drafty door.

Doors get drafty because wood closing against wood can never make a tight enough seal to prevent air from moving in or out. Most exterior doors are made of wood, metal, or fiberglass. These materials are extremely rigid, and they need a softer material to squish up against to make a tight seal. Felted wool strips were used for many years, before the development of different kinds of foam. Today the options for weather stripping can be a bit overwhelming. Even I am not always sure what the best material is for an individual situation! If you're not sure where you need weather stripping, try one of these options:

1. ON A SUNNY DAY, STAND on the inside of your closed door. Look all around the edges of the door: If you can see sunlight anywhere but through the glass window in your door, you need weather stripping.

2. TAKE A LIT CANDLE AND slowly move it around the edges of a closed door. Anywhere there's a big draft, the candle flame will move wildly.

3. THERE ARE COMPANIES AVAILABLE that will come and do an energy audit on your house. Many local electric companies offer this as a free service: You'll get a report with specific recommendations of what to do to reduce your energy losses (which will probably include something about weather stripping).

Start by checking to see if your door already has some type of weather stripping. It should. All prefabricated doors installed in this country in the last twenty-five years have come with it. However, weather stripping can lose its effectiveness because the door has begun to warp a little, or because the stripping itself has become condensed and is no longer squishy enough.

You have two options: Remove your existing weather stripping and replace it, or attach additional weather stripping to supplement the original. Removing weather stripping that came as an integral part of a prefabricated door can be tricky, so I usually opt for supplementing it. Since the choices for weather stripping can be overwhelming, this is a good time to ask the folks at the local hardware store for input.

Regardless of what type of weather stripping you end up installing, there are a couple of important things to know. For one, if you're using weather stripping that comes with a self-adhesive strip, make sure you do a great job of cleaning the area that the adhesive will be sticking to; you'll be surprised by how much dust, dirt, and greasy fingerprints have accumulated over time. Once the area is clean, be sure to press down firmly on the weather stripping to make sure the adhesive makes good contact. Also, weather stripping can be installed between the face of the door and the doorjamb, or up against the face of the door. If you're installing your stripping up against the face of your door, it's very important that you close the door tightly before you nail the weather stripping into place.

The goal is for the door to compress the material it comes to rest against, creating a tight seal. If the material presses too hard against the door, the door will be very difficult to close. Be patient, and be willing to move the weather stripping a couple of times to get it in the right place. It will be worth the effort.

If you're installing weather stripping that the door closes against, there's only one really important thing to know: The weather stripping material needs to be thick enough to fill the gap between the door and the door frame, but not so thick that the door can't close.

FINAL THOUGHTS ON DOORS

Door problems can be very annoying to live with, which makes them especially satisfying to solve. In this chapter we have covered many of the most common problems that homeowners have with their doors. You should now feel comfortable to take on and solve just about any door-related problem. The little trick with the screw in Solution #1 will impress your friends; everyone will want to have you over to their house to see if you can fix their door problems. If you're not careful, you'll become the "door detective" of the neighborhood before you know it!

6. PAINTING: IT'S ALL ABOUT THE PREP

Painting walls, ceilings, wood trim, and doors is the easiest job to do badly. I have been in hundreds of homes, and, whether I'm there for my work or simply socializing with friends, I always notice the paint job. Kind of like a dental hygienist always notices people's teeth. If you've watched any of the many home-design, quick-fix-it, or flip-it reality programs on television in recent years, then you've seen painting presented as a job anyone can do well, quickly, and easily. Unfortunately, that's not quite true. Anyone can paint, and anyone can paint well—it's just not a quick and easy job. It is simple and straightforward, however, and it can be done well if you are patient and focused, and if you follow all the necessary steps.

We are a culture of people who want instant gratification, and many of the home repair shows on television have depicted painting as something that can give you just that. So it's not unusual for a homeowner to go buy some paint, bring it home, and start applying it to the walls with no further thought to what they're doing. If you do this, you'll be disappointed in the final results, and the paint job will not stand the test of time.

I love to paint. In my opinion, if you are going to go to the trouble of painting some part of your home, you might as well do it right. I wouldn't want to do it every day, but I welcome the days that I have painting jobs. Painting well requires focus, but not a great deal of thinking. So, once I get all my tools and supplies together and turn on my radio, I can focus the part of my brain I use to paint and then let the rest of it wander.

Painting is one of the least expensive ways to make a dramatic impact on your home. Paint is also necessary to protect surfaces in our homes from water, dirt, and the daily wear and tear of living. You can expect to pay anywhere from $30 to $70 per hour for a skilled interior painter; it takes me (a skilled interior painter) two to three days to prep and paint the walls and woodwork in an average-size room. Quality paint costs about $30 per gallon, and most rooms can be painted with less than two gallons of paint. Even if you need a gallon of primer, your materials will cost you less than $100. Do the math: If you learn to paint well, you can save yourself hundreds of dollars on each painting project, and you can experience the satisfaction of knowing that you did the job yourself, and that you did it right.

In this chapter, you'll learn how to paint interior walls, ceilings, wood trim, and doors.

Tools of the Trade

A painter is only as good as the quality of her paintbrush, and I'm a firm believer that you cannot get excellent results with cheap tools. You will probably paint more than one room in your lifetime, so it will be worth it to invest in some good tools up front. If money is an issue, get together with a friend and share the costs; you can share the tools and help each other paint. The job always goes faster with two sets of hands!

As a general rule of thumb, natural-bristle brushes work best for oil-based paints, while synthetic brushes are recommended for latex paints.

A painter's tool kit should include the following:

✔ **2-INCH SASH BRUSH:**
This is my absolute favorite brush, and I use it for all my

interior work. A good brush should cost you about $15. If you clean it properly (I'll tell you how later) after every job, it will last you many, many years.

✔ **1- OR 1½-INCH SASH BRUSH:** This brush is for smaller jobs, like windows and touch-ups.

✔ **SIX-IN-ONE PAINTER'S TOOL:** This is a wonderful tool with multiple purposes.

✔ **SMALL PAINT HOLDER:** This is for woodwork and cutting in. You can use a cottage cheese container if you want, or you can purchase a container that looks like a large coffee mug and comes with replaceable plastic liners. I prefer this model, because it's easier to hold, which means it won't tire your hands out.

✔ **PAINT TRAY** (for use with a roller) **OR 5-GALLON BUCKET** (for use with a paint screen, for larger jobs).

✔ **PAINT ROLLER FRAME:** This is another tool it pays to spend more for. The cheap ones do not roll smoothly, and they apply paint unevenly. Try to find one that has five metal supports for the roller.

✔ **ROLLER COVERS:** These come in different length naps, and the texture of the surface you are painting will determine which length you get. For most smooth walls and ceilings, you need a ⅜-inch nap roller. For rougher surfaces or popcorn ceilings, you need a longer (about a ½-inch-long) nap. The professionals at a good paint store can guide you to exactly what you need if you describe your job to them in detail.

✔ **ROLLER EXTENSION HANDLE:** This is essential for painting ceilings, but I have begun using a 2-foot extension for painting all walls: It eases the strain on my hands, and it makes it easier to control a roller that's heavy with paint. Instead of buying an extension, I use a cut-off broomstick with duct tape on the end.

✔ **MASKING TAPE** (specifically, blue painter's masking tape): This is useful in moderation. Most amateur painters think that if they use enough masking tape, it will make them better painters. The opposite is true. The time spent applying yards of masking tape could be better spent painting slowly and carefully. I will suggest when and where to mask later on.

✔ **UTILITY KNIFE:** I use this tool on every job I do!

✔ **RAZOR BLADE PAINT SCRAPER:** It's easier to scrape paint off of windows than it is to try to avoid getting paint on them in the first place.

✔ **RAGS:** No matter how good a painter you become, some paint will end up in places where you don't want it. Old T-shirts, cut into 1-square-foot pieces, make good rags. If you can't imagine parting with an old shirt, you can buy bags of rags at the paint store, but I don't like them as much as the ones I make myself at home.

✔ **MAGIC ERASER:** This is a great invention. It's a sponge unlike any other sponge in existence. It's made by Mr. Clean, and it should be available at your supermarket. The Magic Eraser is amazing at removing dirt and marks from painted surfaces. I use the heavy-duty version, because it holds up better.

✔ **TRISODIUM PHOSPHATE (TSP):** You can use this or a non-phosphate cleaner.

✔ **DROP CLOTHS:** If you think you'll be painting several rooms, it may be worth it to invest in a quality canvas drop cloth. The 4-foot by 16-foot drop cloth is a great size; it's perfect for doing the walls of a room. Before I bought canvas, I used old sheets. Plastic is good to put over furniture but too slippery to use on the floor.

✔ **SANDPAPER AND SANDING SPONGES:**
150-grit sandpaper (the higher the
number, the smoother the paper) is
good for most paint preparation. For
walls, I prefer to put the paper on a
sanding block that gets attached to an
extension handle (or you can use a cut-
off broomstick, like me). For woodwork
and doors, I prefer sanding sponges, which come in a variety of
shapes and sizes. They're lightweight, and they're comfortable
in your hand.

✔ **STEP STOOL OR LADDER:** It's important
that this tool be sturdy and easy for
you to move. I have a great two-step
Rubbermaid stool that I can move around
with my foot; that way, I don't have to
put the paint down every time I need to
move my stool. I love to be efficient!

✔ **PUTTY KNIFE:** For most small holes, a
simple 1½-inch knife will do. You can also
use your six-in-one painter's tool instead.

✔ **LIGHTWEIGHT SPACKLE:** For filling holes in
wallboard or plaster.

✔ **WOOD FILLER:** For filling holes in woodwork
and doors.

✔ **CLEANING TOOL OR WIRE BRUSH:** For cleaning
brushes.

✔ **PAINT CAN OPENER:** A flathead screwdriver—
or even a quarter—will do in a pinch, but these
work better, and they cost less than a dollar.

✔ **RADIO OR CD PLAYER:** Painting gives you a great opportunity to listen to your favorite music.

Buying the Paint

Choosing the right color paint is hard enough, but when you go to purchase the paint, the paint professional is going to ask what finish you want too. "A nice one" isn't going to cut it. What the professional is asking is if you would like your paint with a gloss, semigloss, satin, or flat finish. The choices can be overwhelming. It reminds me of when I was sixteen years old, and my mother took my eighteen-year-old sister and me to New York City for a week's vacation. We went shopping at Macy's; I was so excited, because I had grown up watching the parade on Thanksgiving Day, and I wanted to see what the store was really like. There were more people in Macy's than lived in my entire town in Vermont. I wanted to buy a half-slip (yes, we still wore them in those days), but there were more slips in the lingerie department than there were cows in Vermont. Okay, that's a slight exaggeration, but I *was* completely overwhelmed, and I ended up not buying anything. I don't want you to have this experience when you go to buy paint.

SHOPPING TIP: For woodwork I use a semigloss, because it has a nice sheen and is easy to clean. For walls I use flat, satin, or pearl, depending on how the room will be used, and what condition the walls are in. Flatter-sheen paints are more forgiving. They bring less attention to the imperfections in the walls.

NOTE: This is one of the best possible times to take advantage of a paint store professional's experience. When I first started working on my own home, I knew just enough to be dangerous. I went to the bigger home centers and picked out my own paints, and I made a lot of mistakes. I finally learned that it's okay to ask for help, and that the man who'd owned my local paint store for more than twenty years knew all the stuff I didn't know—not to mention all the stuff I didn't even know I didn't know!

HOW YOU CAN HELP THEM HELP YOU

The professionals at the paint store need accurate information from you so that they can recommend the correct amounts of the right products for your project. Take the answers to the following questions with you when you go consult with the paint professional:

1. HOW BIG IS THE AREA I PLAN TO PAINT?

In order to buy enough paint for your project, you need to make a rough calculation of the square footage of the walls (or ceiling) you intend to paint. For example, if your room is 10 feet wide by 12 feet long with 8-foot-high ceilings, then your math should look like this:

Wall 1: 10ft. x 8ft. = 80ft.
Wall 2: 10ft. x 8ft. = 80ft.
Wall 3: 12ft. x 8ft. = 96ft.
Wall 4: 12ft. x 8ft. = 96ft.

80ft. + 80ft. + 96ft. + 96ft. = 352 sq ft

Don't get anal and try to subtract out for windows and doors. You're better off with too much paint than too little.

2. WHAT KIND OF CONDITION ARE THE WALLS IN?

Are they really smooth and mostly in good condition? Are they slightly damaged in several areas? Are they old plaster walls with lots of character?

TIP: These are all important questions to ask. Go to a local paint store at a time that's not super busy. If you go early in the morning or late in the afternoon, the professional painters will be there buying supplies for their jobs, and the store will be busy. If you go late morning or early afternoon, the store personnel will have the time to talk with you, ask you questions (and answer yours), and help you figure out the best paint for your job. You'll pay more for the paint than you would at a large home center, but you will save in the long run.

3. HOW WILL THE ROOM BE USED, AND BY WHOM?

Is it a kid's bedroom or playroom? Is it a bathroom or kitchen? Is it a great room or den used only by adults?

4. IS THERE EXCESS MOISTURE IN THIS ROOM, SUCH AS IN A BATHROOM OR DAMP BASEMENT?

PRIMER

Primer is a specially formulated paint that's designed to cover up problems on the existing painted surface, and to prepare it for the new paint. It allows the top coats to spread evenly and adhere well, ensuring a long-lasting, beautiful paint job.

You need to use a primer if:

1. IT'S BEEN MORE than ten years since your walls were last painted.

2. YOU'RE MAKING A DRAMATIC color change (in either direction).

3. YOU HAVE WATER STAINS, crayon marks, or damaged walls that need lots of repair work with spackling compound.

It can never hurt you if you prime your walls, but it can often hurt you if you don't. This is another great conversation to have with the paint store personnel. They will recommend the correct primer for your job, and they may even suggest a tinted primer. Nobody wants to use primer, because it's yet another coat of paint you have to apply, but all the time and money you put into this job will be wasted if you don't prepare the walls correctly for the final coat.

A coat of primer and two top coats are required for most paint jobs. However, several manufacturers are now making paints guaranteed to cover in one coat. This doesn't mean you won't need a primer coat, just that you'll only need one top coat. You will pay more per gallon, but if you really hate to paint, this may be a great solution for you.

Doing the Prep Work

You're probably thinking: I have all my tools, and I bought the paint; can I start painting now? The answer, unfortunately, is no. Before you start painting, you need to prepare the walls. This is the step most people enjoy the least and tend to skimp on (or skip altogether). The result is a paint job that looks lousy and won't last.

I'll quote my refrigerator magnet: "Put on your big girl panties and deal with it." The final results will make you glad that you put in the hours up front.

PREPARING THE ROOM

You need to be able to move freely around the room and have easy access to your paint bucket or tray.

1. REMOVE AS MUCH FURNITURE, art work, knickknacks, rugs, lamps, etc., from the room as possible. It's impossible to do a good job painting if you're always stepping around or over something. Learn from my mistakes!

 **IT HAPPENED TO ME ONCE:** I was painting a client's great room, which had cathedral ceilings and very high end walls. The accent wall was a deep red. I came down off the ladder and stepped back to admire my work (something I suggest you do on a regular basis). I stepped into another ladder that I had left lying on the floor. The next thirty seconds looked like a slapstick routine, as I danced around trying to keep my balance and not send the container of red paint I was clutching in one hand flying across the room. I got lucky that day and made the save, but I did (re)learn my own lesson above.

---

2. PUSH WHATEVER FURNITURE REMAINING into the center of the room, and cover it with a sheet, plastic, or drop cloth. After you have finished painting the room, you may decide to rearrange the furniture and not put everything back where it started.

3. ONCE THE ROOM IS AS EMPTY AS POSSIBLE, put drop cloths or sheets down on the floor around the whole room, or just in front of the walls you will paint first. Using a small flathead screwdriver, remove all cover plates from light switches, electrical outlets, and cable box hookups. Cover the outlet faces with blue painter's tape.

PREPARING THE WALLS

1. IF YOU HAVE MILDEW on the walls, it will need to be removed with a mixture of bleach and water (about a 1:1 ratio).

2. WASH THE WALLS AND WOODWORK with a mixture of TSP (trisodium phosphate)—or a phosphate-free substitute—and hot water. Be sure to wear rubber gloves and eye protection. I use rags or sponges, and I recently had success using a sponge mop in an attempt to find a more efficient way to clean the walls.

3. RINSE THE WALLS with clean water to remove the TSP.

4. START INSPECTING THE WALLS for damage, either with the help of bright sunlight or a really powerful lamp. Walk around the room and look at every square inch of the walls. You're looking for cracks, bumps, holes, marks, wall anchors that may need to be removed, tape from old posters, mold, mildew, and water stains. Use a small piece of blue painter's tape to mark each one that you need to come back and fix later. Pre-existing damage that has been previously painted over is usually not worth trying to fix.

5. REMOVE NAILS, picture hangers, towel bars, or anything else affixed to the wall that will get in the way of a paintbrush or roller.

6. REMOVE ANY WALL ANCHORS that will not be reused. If you're going to hang things back on the walls exactly where they were before painting, it's okay to leave picture hooks and anchors on the walls. When you paint those areas, you will need to cut in around anything left on the walls. I usually remove everything except wall anchors that I know will be reused; it's much easier to paint walls well when you're not swerving around picture hooks. Some anchors will come out when you pull on them with a pair of needle-nose pliers, others need to be cut out with a utility knife (I told you I could find a use for it on every job), and others will need to be pushed through the wall and allowed to drop behind it. When in doubt, take it out!

Fix the problems one at a time. Your goal is to end up with clean, smooth, stain-free walls. You have dealt with the cleaning part—now it's time to work on smoothing.

FILLING THE GAPS

1. SCRAPE AWAY ANY PEELING PAINT with your six-in-one painter's tool, and fill in any ridges left with spackle and a putty knife (or 6-inch flexible wallboard knife).

2. FILL ALL HOLES WITH SPACKLE and a small putty knife. Apply just enough to cover the hole and leave a small bump. You'll sand it smooth later. Fix all holes that are larger than 1 inch in diameter in accordance with the directions in Chapter 4.

SANDING

The final step in getting the walls nice and smooth is sanding. I like to use a sanding block: It's a plastic contraption about 3 inches wide by 8 inches long that looks like a Swiffer head.

1. WRAP A PIECE OF 150-GRIT sandpaper around the sanding block and attach it to a handle extension or a shortened broom or mop handle. This tool allows you to quickly sand large sections of the wall.

2. SAND THE AREAS THAT YOU patched with spackle with a sanding sponge. After sanding the patched areas, you'll be able to tell if a second coat of spackle is needed. If it is, apply, let it dry, and sand the area again (it takes time to do this, which is one of the reasons it's necessary to plan on prepping on one day and painting on the next).

3. WHEN YOU HAVE FINISHED sanding, you must get rid of the dust you created: Dust is the enemy of smooth walls. I use a vacuum cleaner along the tops of doors, windows, and baseboards, and a slightly damp rag for the walls.

TO CAULK OR NOT TO CAULK

Caulk is the painter's best friend. A trip around the room with a caulking gun and a tube of (paintable) caulk will make your paint job look like it was done by a professional. For more information about caulk and how to use a caulking gun, see Chapters 1, 2 and 7. In this case, you're looking for gaps between where the woodwork meets the walls and where wood has pulled away from other wood around windows and doors. Use as little caulk as possible to fill the gaps, and then let the caulk dry before you start painting.

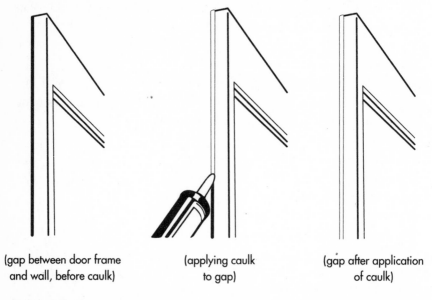

(gap between door frame   (applying caulk   (gap after application
and wall, before caulk)   to gap)   of caulk)

NOW CAN I PAINT?

Almost! There's only one last step to complete before you can begin applying primer or paint to the walls: determining where to apply your masking tape.

IMPORTANT NOTE: When I say "masking tape" I really mean "blue painter's tape." Masking tape comes in different degrees of tackiness (which in this case means "stickiness," not "unfortunate fashion choices"!). Traditional cream-colored masking tape is too sticky for painting projects. Blue masking tape (painter's tape) is designed to be just sticky enough to stick, but not sticky enough to damage what it is stuck to. That said, even blue painter's tape is not meant to be left in place for weeks or months. Make sure you remove it all when your project is completed.

IT HAPPENED TO ME ONCE: I have been hired multiple times to complete stalled painting projects where the painter's tape had been on the walls so long that it believed· that it belonged there—and it decided to take something with it when it was removed! Before I could finish the paint job, I had to repair the damage done when the tape was removed, either by sanding the damaged area or by applying small amounts of spackle and then sanding the area.

WHERE NOT TO MASK

I believe it never makes sense to mask a ceiling (before you paint the wall), or to mask window glass (before you paint the wooden parts of a window). It's almost impossible to get tape up straight on a smooth ceiling, and it won't stick at all to textured ceilings. As for windows, it takes longer to tape them than it does to clean the dried paint off later with a razor blade scraper.

WHERE TO MASK

If you're not painting it as part of the current project, mask along the top edge of your baseboard trim. The tape will protect the baseboard from drips and splatters falling from your roller. Mask over the fronts of electrical outlets.

If you *are* painting the baseboards, mask along the floor. Painter's tape only works well on hardwood floors, because they're so flat. If your floor is made of ceramic tile, laminate flooring, linoleum, or carpet, tape won't help very much. In those situations, you can use your 12-inch wallboard knife as a barrier between the paintbrush and the floor. Even then, you still need to be careful and paint slowly.

APPLYING PAINTER'S TAPE

When applying painter's tape, it's important to try getting it down in a straight line, and to make sure that it is stuck firmly to the surface.

1. APPLY FROM LEFT TO RIGHT if you're right-handed, holding the end of the tape in your left hand and the roll in your right (do the opposite if you're left-handed).

2. GUIDE THE EDGE OF THE TAPE up against the wall and gently press down on the tape as you move to the right. Then go back and press firmly with one finger along the entire length of the tape.

3. YOU CAN ALSO USE THE EDGE of a putty knife to press down on the masking tape to ensure that it adheres well to the surface.

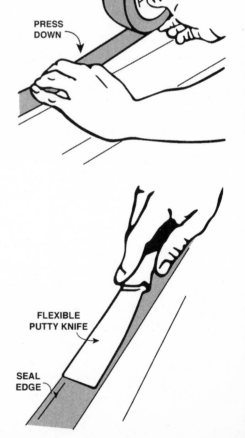

PRESS DOWN

FLEXIBLE PUTTY KNIFE

SEAL EDGE

IMPORTANT NOTE: Remember that painter's tape will not completely prevent paint from getting onto the surface underneath it. It's a deterrent, not a guarantee!

Let's review what you've done so far:

- ✔ Purchased paint and primer (if necessary)
- ✔ Removed everything possible from the room
- ✔ Put down drop cloths
- ✔ Taken everything off the walls, including nails, hooks, and old anchors
- ✔ Washed the walls (and the woodwork and doors, if you're painting them too)
- ✔ Prepared walls by filling holes and cracks with Spackle
- ✔ Sanded the walls and cleaned up the dust
- ✔ Caulked any gaping joints
- ✔ Applied masking tape where necessary

Having completed this checklist, you can now move on to the most gratifying and fun part of the paint job: painting the walls!

Painting the Ceiling and Walls

If you are planning on painting the entire room, there is a preferable order in which to paint the various surfaces in the room; it will minimize the likelihood of getting paint splatters on recently painted surfaces. Basically, the order goes from top to bottom:

1. Ceiling
2. Walls
3. Window and door trim
4. Baseboards
5. Doors

PAINTING THE CEILING

Ceilings are not painted as often as walls, mostly because they don't get as dirty, and because only a small percentage of people use colored ceiling paint as a decorative statement. This is a good thing:

Ceilings are difficult to paint, because you're working over your head. Any job that requires your body to be in an awkward or unusual position where you can't see what you're doing very well is, by definition, more difficult. There are a few ways to make painting a ceiling slightly less challenging, but I haven't yet found a way to make painting a ceiling fun!

1. USE AN EXTENSION POLE on your roller so you can reach the ceiling without being on a ladder, if it's at all possible.

2. GET A REALLY BRIGHT LIGHT in the room and move it around as needed so you can always see where you have already painted. There's nothing more frustrating than painting an area over and over again because you're not sure if you've already painted it or not.

3. WEAR A HAT AND SAFETY GLASSES to protect your hair, face, eyes, and glasses (if you wear them) from the fine spray of paint that the roller may generate.

4. USE A THICKER-NAP ROLLER than the surface might call for; it will allow you to get more paint on the ceiling more quickly.

5. SCHEDULE A GOOD MASSAGE for as soon as possible upon completion of the painting project. You'll need it.

The only good thing about painting ceilings is that there is very little preparation required. However, if the ceiling has suffered from water damage or has other holes or dings in it, it will require some of the same preparation described before for the walls.

The most common preparation I do for ceilings is to cover up water stains before painting. Regular primer is not sufficient to cover water stains; you need to use a sealing primer designed specifically for stains. KILZ and B-I-N primer are both good ones. It's okay to just apply the primer over the stained area: You don't have to prime the entire ceiling unless it's in really bad shape or very discolored.

Together, you and your paint roller or paintbrush make up

a paint application team. It's your goal to get the right amount of paint on the ceiling in the most efficient and effective manner. The first step in actually putting paint on a surface is called *cutting in*. When you cut in on the ceiling, you are applying paint with a brush (I use the 2½-inch sash brush) in a strip about 3 inches wide around the edge of the ceiling, up against the wall. Cutting in is necessary, because it's impossible to get a roller tight up against the wall without getting paint on the adjacent surface. If you're painting the ceiling, the adjacent surface is the wall; if you are painting walls, the adjacent surface will be the ceiling, another wall, or woodwork.

CUTTING IN

The cutting-in process requires a ladder or step stool:

1. POUR A SMALL AMOUNT OF PAINT (about 3 inches deep) into your handheld paint container. Dip your paintbrush into your paint container just far enough that you get paint on about 1 to 1½ inches of the tip of the paintbrush.

2. LIGHTLY TAP THE BRUSH against the sides of the container (do not scrape the brush against the container, or you will remove too much paint from the brush). Always start cutting in at a corner, and work out from the corner in both directions. Apply the paint to the edge of the ceiling in a line about 10 to 12 inches long, trying to avoid getting ceiling paint on the walls.

3. GO BACK AND FORTH OVER this area a couple of times with the brush, smoothing out the paint, until you have a line of paint that is about 3 inches wide and 10 to 12 inches long.

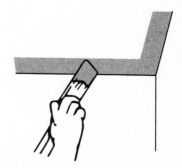

4. REPEAT STEPS 1 AND 2, extending your line out from the corner in both directions, until you have cut in an area that is about 3 feet long in each direction.

5. AFTER YOU HAVE CUT in this first section of the ceiling, you're ready to use the roller. Slide the roller pad over the metal bars of the roller until it fits snugly against the end.

6. SCREW THE ROLLER EXTENSION bar into the end of the roller and adjust its length so that you can easily reach the ceiling with the roller.

7. PUSH THE ROLLER INTO THE PAINT in the bucket or paint tray and roll it back and forth against the screen (if using a bucket) or the tray itself until the paint seems to be evenly distributed around the roller. You want to have a good amount of paint on the roller, but not so much that it's dripping off.

NOTE: One of the biggest mistakes that beginning painters make is not putting enough paint on the brush and roller. It may take you a few attempts to get this figured out, but you will get it eventually.

8. TAKE THE ROLLER (with the paint on it) and set it against the ceiling near the corner where you cut in. Move the roller across an area about 3 feet by 3 feet in the shape of a **W**. This gets the paint evenly distributed across the area.

9. USING LONG STROKES, move the roller across the area to spread out the paint. Only infringe into the cut-in areas by about an inch or so. Try to keep the roller from bumping into the walls. Once you

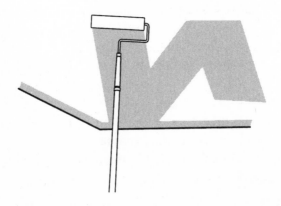

have spread the paint neatly and evenly over the area, making sure there are no visible lines left by the edge of the roller, you are ready to move on to the next part of the ceiling. Slide over from the just-painted area and cut in a new 3- to 4-foot-long section with your brush. Paint that section with your roller, repeating the techniques from steps 8 and 9. Repeat this process until you have completed your first row across the ceiling.

10. MOVE BACK TO THE LEFT SIDE of the room and start your next row. Moving in sections like this, across the ceiling and down the room, it will take you about two to three hours to paint a ceiling in a 10 by 12 room.

IT HAPPENED TO ME ONCE: The first few times I painted ceilings, I kept repainting areas over and over again because, when I looked at the ceiling while the paint was wet in some areas and dry in others, I thought I had missed several places. As ceiling paint dries, it plays special tricks on your eyes because of the way the light hits its no-gloss surface. Don't panic and keep repainting the same spots like I did. Instead, if you have followed the grid method of paint application that I just explained, wait several hours (until the paint is completely dry) before deciding if you missed any spots.

PAINTING THE WALLS

If you have just completed painting the ceiling, painting the walls is going to feel much easier.

The following set of instructions applies whether you are applying "primer" or "paint" to your walls. The techniques are the same. The words "primer" and "paint" are interchangeable at this point. If you start with a primer and follow it with two coats of paint, you will be a very good painter by the time you finish the third coat:

1. START BY POURING some paint into your bucket or roller tray. Also pour some paint into your handheld container.

IMPORTANT NOTE: If you're painting your walls with a custom-mixed paint color and you're going to use more than one gallon of paint, I suggest that you pour all of the paint into one larger container: Mixing the separate gallons together takes care of any slight difference in color that may result when the paint was mixed at the paint store. I use 5-gallon pickle buckets that I buy at the local deli (the pickle smell goes away very quickly!). If you're using an off-the-shelf color, this mixing is not necessary. That said, when I'm painting a larger room and know I will be using more than one gallon of paint—whether it's a custom color or off the shelf—I prefer working out of the 5-gallon bucket and using a paint screen to roll my roller against. It's easier to move a bucket than a roller tray around the room; also, I've never stepped in a bucket by accident, but I have stepped in more than one roller tray.

2. PLACE A NEW ROLLER PAD on the roller frame, get your 2½-inch sash brush, and you're ready to start.

3. ONCE AGAIN, YOU'LL START by cutting in. Take your 2½-inch sash brush, your handheld container of paint, and your step stool or ladder, and cut in a 3-foot-long area across the top of the wall, near the corner. Again, I work from left to right, because I'm right-handed. If you're left-handed, you'll probably want to work from right to left). Be careful,  go very slowly, and don't get paint on the ceiling. Your goal is a nice, straight line of paint just under the ceiling.

4. PROCEED CAREFULLY with the cutting in process and keep a wet rag handy, just in case you get a little paint on the ceiling. If you catch it while it's wet, paint comes off quite easily. After you've cut

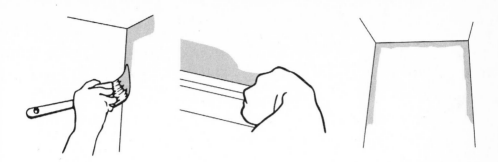

in a few feet across the top of the wall, cut in down the wall in the corner, all the way down to the baseboard, and then cut in about 3 feet across the bottom of the wall, above the baseboard. The cut-in area should be no more than 3 inches wide.

TIPS: Glasses are still a good idea, but I have to admit that I don't always wear them. Also, if this is your first time ever painting a wall, then I suggest picking the least visible wall as your starting point. Usually the wall behind the entrance door is a good place to start.

5. GET YOUR ROLLER, dip it in the paint, roll it against the screen or roller tray a few times, and put it on the wall in the upper left corner. Make the same **W** shape you made on the ceiling by moving up and down across a 3-foot by 3-foot area. Again, the **W** shape allows you to spread paint evenly over the entire section instead of just on the left edge, which would happen if you went straight up and down on the left side.

Slowly move the roller up and down across the area, smoothing out the paint and covering any unpainted spots. Pay careful attention as you move the roller into the cut-in areas at the top, side, and bottom of the wall. Only bring the roller about 1 inch into the wet, cut-in area. If you try to go farther in, or lose concentration and control of your roller, you will bump into the ceiling, wall, or baseboard, which you want to avoid.

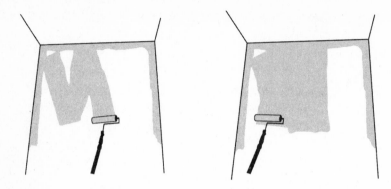

TIP: When you're cutting in, treat the painter's tape like it's allergic to paint: Try to get the least amount of paint possible on it. If you're not careful, paint will leak underneath the tape and onto the woodwork, and you may end up disappointed and discouraged when you remove the tape.

NOTE: Remember when I said painting doesn't require much of your brain but does require focus? Well, if you don't stay focused on where the roller or brush is at any given moment, you'll end up with lots of messes to clean up, and that takes the fun out of painting. Keep your focus on the location of the brush or roller, and let the rest of your mind wander.

6. AFTER YOU FINISH YOUR FIRST 3-by-3 section, repeat the process in the area beneath it. It will take three sections to complete most standard-size walls. If your walls are higher, you will need more sections. When you have completely covered the wall from top to bottom, take your roller (without adding any new paint to it) and roll it lightly over the entire area, from top to bottom. This will clean up any drips or lines that have been left by the roller during the initial painting process. Do this just once, and do it lightly.

7. MOVE ON TO THE NEXT SECTION OF WALL, cutting in at the top and

TIP: This is a great opportunity to work with a partner (hey, it worked for Tom Sawyer!). One of you can cut in, and the other can roll. If you need to stop or take a break, don't do it in the middle of a wall: Wait until you have completed a wall, and don't leave any wet cut-in areas—they'll have dried out by the time you return.

bottom and around any doorways or windows that you encounter. Remember, you only want to cut into as much area as you can get back to and roll over while the cut-in area is still wet.

8. WORK YOUR WAY AROUND THE ROOM, section by section, moving your drop cloths and light source as needed. Always make sure you have enough paint on the roller. You shouldn't need to be pressing on the roller really hard. If you do, there's not enough paint on the roller. When you've completed one trip around the room, give yourself a pat on the back. Now you just have to wait until the paint is dry, and then you can put on the second coat!

NOTE: Most paint manufacturers recommend that you wait at least four hours between coats of paint. I don't always adhere to that. Usually, by the time I finish one trip around the room and have something to eat, the first wall I painted is dry enough for a second coat. Drying time of paint is affected by temperature and humidity; the hotter and dryer the room, the faster the paint dries, and the higher the humidity, the slower it dries. If you are in doubt about whether or not to proceed with a second coat, wait until the first coat feels really dry to your touch.

TIP: If you're taking a break that's between an hour and overnight in length, wrap your roller and paintbrush in plastic wrap or a plastic bag and put them in the refrigerator to keep the paint wet. Take them out an hour or so before you plan to paint again so they can warm up. I've left rollers wrapped in the fridge for over a week before, and the paint was still wet when I needed them again.

The second coat of paint is an exact duplicate of the first coat, including the cutting-in process. One trick you can try on the second coat is to not go quite as close to the ceiling and woodwork as you did on the first coat when you cut in (I'm talking about $\frac{1}{8}$ of an inch or so).

Congratulations—you've finished painting the room! Now it's time for the finishing touches.

Removing the Painter's Tape

Stop! Do not touch the masking tape until you read this section! This step seems like it should be really obvious: You just grab an end and pull until all the tape is removed. Do not do this! If you do, you will have some nasty surprises. For example, paint that has dried with part of itself on the wall and the other part on the tape may come off in one piece and leave an ugly chunk of paint missing from your wall. You can fix this with a small brush and some paint if it does happen, but it is better to try and prevent it. This method works well for me:

1. USE YOUR UTILITY KNIFE (with a new blade) and gently cut along the edge of all the masking tape in the joint where the tape meets the wall. This will cut any paint that has dried and leave a nice, straight edge when the tape is removed.

2. AFTER YOU HAVE CUT all the way around, gently and slowly peel the tape back. Any paint that has leaked under the tape onto the woodwork will be covered when you paint the woodwork. If you're not painting the woodwork, this paint can be gently removed with a kitchen scrubber, a razor blade, or your fingernail.

Painting the Woodwork

Painting woodwork is the hardest part of the painting job, which is why so many people skip it and just paint the walls. If the woodwork is in good shape, you can skip repainting it, but if it is dinged up and really worn, then painting it is worth the effort. It's like when you get dressed up to go out: If you look great from the neck down but you don't bother brushing your hair, people are going to notice your hair more than your outfit!

Woodwork usually consists of baseboards, door and window trim, crown molding, chair rail, and even doors and windows themselves if they have wood detailing. Woodwork can be smooth, or it can have lots of fancy grooves and details.

The basic rule of thumb for the order of painting woodwork is "inside out, and top to bottom": You paint the inside of the door or window first, top to bottom, and paint the outside last (again, top to bottom).

For the different kinds of woodwork, you'll paint in this order:

1. Crown molding
2. Windows
3. Chair rail
4. Baseboard
5. Doors

PREPARING WOODWORK FOR PAINTING

If you're painting the whole room, it makes the most sense to prepare the woodwork at the same time you're preparing the walls; that way you're only dealing with water and sanding dust once. Here's a quick review of steps to prepare the woodwork for painting:

1. WASH THE WOODWORK with a mixture of TSP and hot water.

2. RINSE OFF THE TSP with clean, cool water.

3. USE A PAINT SCRAPER or your six-in-one painter's tool to scrape away any loose or flaking paint.

4. FILL LARGE HOLES, dents, and cracks with wood filler.

5. SAND OVER EVERYTHING lightly with a flexible sanding block (150-grit sandpaper).

6. REMOVE DUST with a vacuum or tack cloth.

7. PRIME ANY BARE WOOD that was revealed when you scraped off flaking paint.

IF YOUR WOODWORK HAS A STAIN AND POLYURETHANE FINISH

A current trend is to paint woodwork that was previously finished with stain and polyurethane. This used to be a difficult job that involved a great deal of sanding to remove the glossy finish of the polyurethane so the new paint would stick. I did it in my family room in 1993 and did not enjoy the job. Now, however, a new product has come along that completely transforms this job into a simple painting project.

BONDING PRIMER is a special primer that has been designed to stick to old polyurethane or varnish without requiring any sanding. You just need to clean the woodwork with TSP, fill any holes with wood filler and sand those down, and then you can apply the bonding primer according to the directions below for painting woodwork.

NOTE: If you are overwhelmed after reading about the level of preparation work involved in painting a room "correctly," and you are ready to throw this book down and just go to the movies instead, relax. You're not a professional painter, and you don't need to become one. Many women will not attempt to do a job at all if they are afraid that they can't do it perfectly; I don't want you to feel that way. Your paint job will look great if you end up somewhere in between "perfect" and "good."

I want you to know the *right* way to do the job, but remember that you have free reign to do the job *your* way, within the limits of your time, budget, physical ability, need for perfection, and willingness to laugh at yourself. It's up to you to figure out what "good enough" means to you!

SHOULD I PUT DOWN ANY MASKING TAPE?

I *do not* recommend that you put masking tape on the walls you recently completed painting in order to protect them from your woodwork paint. Again, my suggestion is that you proceed slowly and carefully; that way, the paint will only go where you want it to. Also, even though "extra-gentle" masking tape can supposedly be used in this type of situation, it might still damage your recently painted wall. If you do get some woodwork paint on a wall, you can just touch up that spot with wall paint later.

LET'S PAINT THE WOODWORK, ALREADY!

Tools you will need:

- ✔ 2½-inch sash brush
- ✔ Smaller sash brush (if you're painting window mullions)
- ✔ Handheld paint container
- ✔ Wet rag
- ✔ Step stool

1. FILL YOUR HANDHELD PAINT container about halfway up with your woodwork paint, and get your brush and rag (and step stool, if needed). You should still be working over a drop cloth. Of the painting you have done so far, painting woodwork is most similar to the cutting-in process. No roller is involved here; you just work with a paintbrush.

2. DIP THE BRUSH INTO YOUR PAINT container, tap it against the side of the container, and then touch the brush to the woodwork. I can usually paint an area 2 to 3 inches wide and 10 to 15 inches long with each load of paint on my brush. If you can't cover that much area with one load of paint, try working with a little more paint on the brush—it will make the job easier.

3. YOU NEED TO MAKE SURE THAT you work the paint into the corners and crevices. Once you've smoothed the paint over the intended area, go back over it with one long, smooth stroke, and then move onto the next area. The rule of thumb for woodwork brushstrokes is to work from the dry area into the wet area. Repeat the process with the next area, moving your paintbrush back into the wet paint you just applied about an inch or so.

4. WORK YOUR WAY AROUND THE ROOM, painting the woodwork from inside to outside and top to bottom. When you get to a window, start with the wood that's in contact with the glass. Feel free to get some paint on the glass (again, it's easier and takes less time to scrape dried paint off glass with a razor blade scraper than it takes to mask the entire area. Painting woodwork is not a job that can be rushed, and your patience will be rewarded. Take the time to work slowly and carefully. Use the time to learn how to focus part of your mind on the painting and let the other part wander. Meditate while you paint!

TIP: The goal when applying paint to woodwork is to end up with a smooth, even distribution of paint, with no visible drips or dribbles. Drips and dribbles often aren't immediately visible. After I have completed a length of woodwork and started on the next area, I go back and check the first area, looking closely for drips, dribbles, and sags. It's kind of like checking yourself in the mirror one last time before you leave the house to make sure you don't have lettuce between your teeth, or that your skirt isn't tucked into the back of your underwear. If you find an imperfection, use your brush (without adding more paint to it) to smooth it out before it dries. This is one of the reasons to use good paint instead of cheap paint: With good paint, you have more time to fix your mistakes; cheap paint is less forgiving.

Painting the Doors

I usually paint the doors in a room after I have completed the other woodwork; for some reason, they seem like a separate project to me. Before you paint, remove the doorknob and latch (see Chapter 5), and put masking tape over the hinges to protect them from the paint. Some people prefer to remove doors from their hinges and paint them lying flat. This method is easier in some ways but requires taking all the doors off, lifting them and setting them on a flat surface. I have tried both methods, and I believe that it's easier to paint them where they hang.

If your door is smooth, with no raised panels or glass inserts, you can paint it as if it were a small wall. Apply the paint with a brush or small roller in sections 4 to 6 inches wide, from the top down. Complete one "top to bottom" section and then move over and

repeat until you've painted the entire door surface. If you're painting
a raised-panel door, you need to use a brush for the whole thing.

For doors with raised panels:

1. PAINT EACH PANEL from the inside to the outside, top to bottom.

2. PAINT THE HORIZONTAL AREAS above and below the raised
panels, top to bottom.

3. PAINT THE VERTICAL AREAS to the left and right of the panels, top
to bottom.

4. PAINT THE TOP, EDGES, AND BOTTOM (if you can get to it) of the
door, being careful not to get paint on its other side.

You should be especially vigilant when looking for drips and
dribbles on raised-panel doors, because there are so many corners
where paint can pool. It usually takes me about 15 minutes to paint
one side of a door with one coat of paint. If you're painting a door
for the first time, plan on it taking you 25 to 30 minutes per side.

When you finish painting the door, go back and look it over
one last time for drips and dribbles, cleaning them up as you go.

Touching Up and Cleaning Up

The final two steps in the painting process are touching up and
cleaning up. Touching up allows you to hide or minimize any
mistakes you may have made, and cleaning up leaves the room and
your equipment looking like new.

One of the toughest lessons I have learned from doing work around the house is how to answer to the question, "Is it good enough?" I don't mean that in the throwaway sense of "Whatever, it's good enough." I mean looking at the job and deciding if the quality level you achieved, given the time and energy you expended, is good enough for you. Perfection is impossible, and trying for it will make taking on jobs around the house overwhelming. This is supposed to be fun and satisfying, not disheartening. When you step back and look at the room you've painted, it's important to see what you've accomplished, not the mistakes you've made.

I'm talking about this now because the final touch-up phase can bring out the latent perfectionist in anyone. Try to remember that you are the only one who will see most of the little mistakes that you made while painting a room. Once the room is filled up with furniture and people, the little details disappear.

For touching up, I use a small brush, either a 1-inch sash brush or one of the little paintbrushes from my children's craft projects. Using small containers of ceiling paint, wall paint, and woodwork paint, I walk around the room, looking for obvious places where I got wall paint on the ceiling or woodwork paint on the wall. Then I take a small amount of the appropriate paint and paint over the mistake. It's important to know when to stop. Just deal with anything that is really big and visible or that you know will drive you crazy every time you're in the room. Let it dry, and then let it go!

REMOVING PAINT FROM WINDOWS

One of the final steps in finishing a paint job is to remove any paint that got onto glass in your windows or doors. This is a simple, three-step process:

1. USE YOUR UTILITY KNIFE OR the edge of a razor blade to score along the seam where the glass meets the wood. Doing this will allow you to remove just the paint on the glass and prevent you from accidentally removing some of the paint on the wood.

2. SET A RAZOR-BLADE SCRAPER flush on the glass and scrape away the dried paint. It comes off in really cool curls. Check for drips of paint in the center of the glass as well.

3. USE A VACUUM CLEANER to pick up the paint curls, as they tend to stick where they land.

WASHING PAINTBRUSHES

I will admit up front that a pet peeve of mine is dirty paintbrushes. When I go to a woman's home to do a painting project with her, she'll usually offer me paintbrushes she has used on previous projects to work with. I pick them up, and they're stiff with old paint. You can't paint well with brushes that are stiff and dirty.

If you spend $15 to $20 on a good paintbrush and wash it correctly after each use, it will last for years. This is how I suggest you wash your brushes after each use (or at the end of the job, if you've been refrigerating them overnight in plastic between coats):

1. SOAK THE BRUSH IN WARM water and dish soap for an hour or so (or as long as overnight).

2. USING A WIRE BRUSH OR COMB, work down from the metal strip toward the tips of the bristles, loosening the paint that has embedded itself into the paintbrush.

3. RUN THE BRUSH UNDER WARM water and squish it against the bottom of the sink, first on one side, then on the other. Keep repeating these steps until the water runs clear and there's no more paint in the brush.

4. HOLD THE BRUSH HANDLE BETWEEN the palms of your hands and move your hands back and forth, quickly, in opposite directions. This will make the brush spin, and remove excess water.

5. HANG THE BRUSH TO DRY, or wrap the bristle area gently in a paper towel and lay it down flat.

6. WHEN THE BRUSH IS DRY, return it to the cardboard cover it came in. This helps the brush to maintain its shape.

WASHING PAINT ROLLERS

I used to spend 15 to 20 minutes washing out a paint roller at the end of the day. I hated this part of clean up, but felt that it was really wasteful to throw out perfectly good rollers just because I didn't feel like cleaning them. Then I discovered the six-in-one painter's tool, and my life changed forever: Its rounded edge is designed to fit perfectly over the contour of a paint roller and squeeze out the paint.

1. SCRAPE THE EDGE OF THE TOOL along the contour of the roller and squish out the paint. Do not put the scraped paint back into the paint can—it's full of yucky stuff you don't want in there. Scrape the paint into a trash can, working your way around the roller several times.

2. WHEN THE ROLLER SEEMS RELATIVELY DRY, move to the sink and run warm water over it. Soap it up with dish detergent and—keeping it under the stream of warm water—continue scraping it with the six-in-one painter's tool until the water runs clear.

3. STAND IT ON END on a paper towel until it's dry.

NOTE: I have to admit that I don't always clean my rollers these days. Sometimes I'm just too tired to bother, and when I weigh the cost of my time and energy against the cost of a new roller, I toss the roller out.

FINAL THOUGHTS ON PAINTING

As you can see, painting a room well is much more involved than you would expect if you have watched any of the quick-design shows on television. If you have followed the steps in this chapter and done the best job you can, your paint job will last for many years. If you have small amounts of paint left over in large paint cans, transfer it to a small glass jar or plastic container—it will store better and last longer. Mark it with the name and manufacturer of the paint and today's date. You might need this information at a later time. Now put the furniture back, hang your pictures on the walls, and enjoy your room!

7. IT'S NOT ALL BUBBLE BATHS

The bathroom is what I like to call a project-rich environment. Though it's usually the smallest room in the house, it provides a seemingly endless list of repair opportunities and home improvement project possibilities. Bathroom projects can be divided into at least two categories: water-related and non-water-related (which you'll find in Chapter 8).

WATER-RELATED PROJECTS:

✔ Turning off the main water supply line
✔ Fixing a leaky faucet
✔ Basic toilet repair
✔ The sink pop-up thingy
✔ Installing a new showerhead
✔ Sink aerators
✔ Replacing caulk
✔ Repairing grout

NON-WATER-RELATED PROJECTS:

✔ Replacing a medicine cabinet
✔ Installing safety grab bars
✔ Installing toilet paper and towel bars that stay on the wall
✔ Updating vanity or cabinet hardware
✔ Painting an old, ugly vanity

The projects on the non-water-related list are often found on a woman's "Wouldn't it be nice" list, while the water-related projects are always on the "I know I have to" home maintenance list.

IT HAPPENED TO ME ONCE: I continue to be amazed by how some clients I have visited over the years can remain in complete denial about the extent of damage their seemingly small, innocuous water problems are causing. I'll give you two examples.

STORY #1: Several years ago, I was hired by a new client to repair some drywall adjacent to a tub surround that had been damaged by water. While I was fixing the drywall, I noticed that there was water around the base of the toilet. More water appeared each time the toilet was flushed. I finished the first round of wall repair and informed my client about the problem that I noticed with her toilet. She said that there had been water on the floor for a long time, but she thought she was just splashing water from the vanity onto the floor. I strongly suggested she call a plumber and departed. I returned a few weeks later to finish the wall repair, and I checked to see if the toilet had been repaired. It hadn't. She was completely ignoring the water issue. If she had called a plumber when she first noticed the problem, it would have been a simple matter of replacing the wax ring under the toilet. By the time she got around to getting it fixed, however, it was going to require repairs to the subfloor, as well as new linoleum.

STORY #2: About a year ago, I was hired to do regular handywoman work at a retirement home for nuns. I stop by about one day every couple of months and take care of whatever has shown up on their to-do list. The sister in charge had told me that one of the bathtub surrounds needed new caulk. When I arrived, I discovered that a long piece of gray duct tape had been placed over the joint where the tiled tub surround met the tub. When I started to remove the duct tape, the wall tiles came off with it. I removed about twenty wall tiles and discovered that part of the wall behind the tile was completely destroyed by long-term exposure to water and needed to be rebuilt.

I could fill this book with similar stories, but instead I'll simply restate my point: In both of these situations and with 95 percent of all others, if the repair had been done at the first suspicion of a problem, it would have been a minor one. Unless you suffer a catastrophic flood, it takes a long time for most water damage to occur. If something gets wet just once, it will dry out and will probably be fine; if it gets wet and remains wet for months or years, however, the extent of the damage is always major and will usually involve mold, or even insects. I have found termites or carpenter ants living happily in someone's rotted wood on more than one occasion when I was dealing with water damage. Don't let that happen to you.

After reading this book, I hope that you will have the knowledge and information you need to nip some water-related problems in the bud on your own. If you don't feel comfortable taking on any kind of water-related issue, make sure you call a plumber at the first suspicion of a problem. Whatever you pay the plumber will be much less than you would pay to fix the damage caused by the problem years down the road if it goes unchecked.

Where Water Comes from and Why That's Important to Know

Whenever I speak to a group of women, I always ask if they know where the main water shut-off valve is located in their home. Usually, fewer than half the women raise their hands. So I give them a homework assignment: Go home and locate your main water supply shut-off valve.

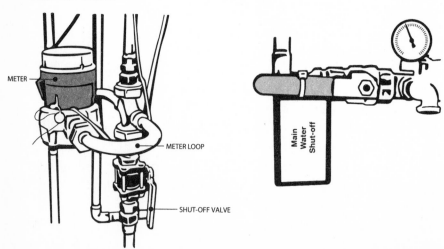

METER

METER LOOP

SHUT-OFF VALVE

Main Water Shut-off

Here's why: If you ever walk through your doors and discover that the hose burst on your washing machine, or that your toilet is overflowing, the fastest way to stop it is to shut off the water supply to the entire house. The location of the shut-off valve will vary, depending on what region of the country you live in, and whether you have a well or your water is supplied by your city or town.

IMPORTANT NOTE: The shut-off valve is usually located inside the house, on the side of the house closest to the street (if you have town water), or close to the well (if you have a private water supply). It will often be in your "mechanical" room, which can contain your hot water heater, furnace, water treatment system, etc. Take the time to find it so you'll know where it is if you ever need it.

There are other shut-off valves located throughout your home, usually (but not always) wherever there are faucets or toilets. Modern plumbing code requires shut-off valves for each faucet, but if you have some ancient plumbing, you may be missing a valve or two. If you look under your kitchen sink and bathroom vanity, you should see a shut-off valve for both the hot and cold supply lines, which provide water to the faucet.

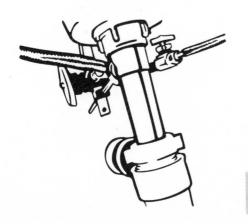
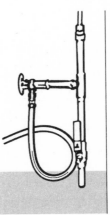
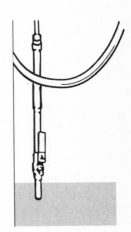

Each toilet has its own shut-off valve. If your shower has a shut-off valve, it may be hidden in the wall behind the shower. Sometimes there's access to the shower's plumbing through an adjacent closet, but not always.

Your washing machine also has its own shut-off valve, on the wall where the hoses are attached. Now don't you feel more secure knowing that there all these places in your house where you could turn off the water if you needed to?

Can I Fix a Leaky Faucet Myself?

The answer is "Yes . . . possibly." There are too many kinds of faucets for me to be able to explain them all in detail in a book of this size. But there are two very common types of kitchen and bathroom faucets (ball-type and cartridge) that are reasonably simple in design and are worth the effort of trying to repair before calling for professional help. Unfortunately, it's impossible to know what type of faucet you have without taking it apart, unless you still have the paperwork from when you purchased it.

Here's how I think about it: Best case, you invest a couple of hours of your time and fix an annoying, water-wasting leak; worst case, you can't fix the leak, and after a couple of hours you call a plumber. At least you will have had the satisfaction of trying, and you can ask the plumber what you should have done differently, if anything.

I'll tell you the truth about plumbing (it's something your mother would have told you, if she had only known): Plumbing—especially old plumbing—does not like to be touched! In several instances, I did everything correctly on a plumbing repair but still ended up with a leak. It goes like this: In order to try repairing a leaky faucet, you have to close the shut-off valves in the cabinet under the sink. You take apart the faucet, replace the suspicious parts, and put the faucet back together. You open the shut-off valve and—hoorah!—the faucet no longer leaks. Then you look under the cabinet and notice that the cold water shut-off valve is leaking. You did absolutely nothing wrong. The shut-off valve is leaking purely because you touched it. This happens to plumbers all the time. The only difference is that they're prepared to handle it by replacing the shut-off valve if they have to.

I don't want to scare you away from trying to accomplish some minor plumbing repairs. I'm just trying to save you from some of the anguish I have suffered over the years. All my lowest self-esteem days have come on days that I took on plumbing projects without understanding how fickle pipes and valves can be. I want you to be prepared so that if your plumbing throws you a curveball, you don't blame yourself. Instead you'll say: "Oh, Marie said this might happen! It's not my fault. I'll just call the plumber."

One last thought before we get started trying to fix a leaky faucet: *Never start plumbing projects late on a Sunday afternoon.* Always start them early, and on a day when stores are open and plumbers are available if needed.

FIXING A LEAKY FAUCET

Your faucet may be dripping from the spout, or it may be leaking at the base of the handle. Regardless of where the water is showing up, the workings of the faucet are all inside the handle area, and that's where the work needs to be done.

REPAIRING A CARTRIDGE FAUCET

Tools you will need:
- ✔ Utility knife
- ✔ Phillips head screwdriver
- ✔ Water pump pliers
- ✔ Needle-nose pliers

Materials you will need:
- ✔ Paper towels
- ✔ Heat-proof grease
- ✔ New cartridge (with washers and springs)

You won't know what kind of cartridge you need until you remove the old one. You should plan on taking a trip to the hardware store once you have disassembled the old faucet.

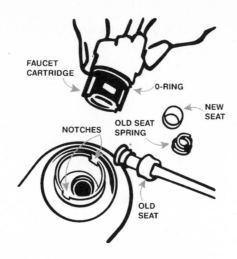

STEP ONE: TAKE THE FAUCET APART

1. CLOSE BOTH SHUT-OFF VALVES (hot and cold) underneath the sink by turning them all the way to the right (clockwise). If you're not able to close one or both valves, you can close the main water valve to the house.

2. CLOSE THE DRAIN, and then put a towel over the bottom of the sink to catch any parts that fall (because they *will* fall!).

3. LAY A TOWEL OUT ON the counter to place the parts of the old faucet on as you remove them.

4. USE THE BLADE OF A UTILITY KNIFE to pry off the index cap on top of the faucet. The index cap is the small, round piece of metal or plastic that may say "hot" or "cold." Lay the index cap on the towel.

5. UNSCREW THE HANDLE screw that was hidden by the cap. Place it on the towel, next to the index cap.

6. REMOVE THE FAUCET handle by lifting it straight up. Place the handle on the towel, next to the handle screw.

 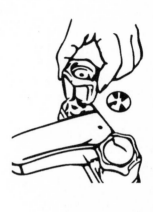

7. REMOVE THE THREADED retaining ring with a pair of water pump pliers. There is usually an area near the top where the pliers fit naturally. Unscrew the ring by moving the pliers counter-clockwise. Place the retaining ring on the towel, next to the faucet handle.

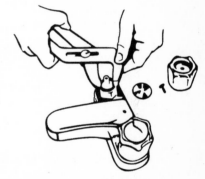

8. USE YOUR HANDS OR A PAIR of pliers to remove the cartridge by lifting it up and out. Set it on the towel, next to the retaining ring.

9. LOOK DOWN INTO THE OPENING you have created in the faucet; you'll see a small, black valve seat. Remove it with a pair of needle-nose pliers. Set the valve seat on the towel, next to the cartridge.

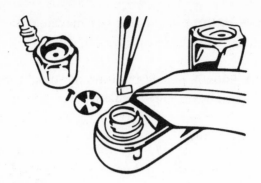

10. REMOVE THE SMALL SPRING that was covered by the valve seat and place it on the towel, next to the valve seat. If you are not sure which handle is leaking, repeat steps 1–10 on the other faucet handle.

NOTE: By laying all the pieces on a towel as you remove them, you have them in the correct order for replacement. When it's time to put the faucet back together, you'll start at the end of your line of parts and work your way back to the beginning of the line. That way, there's no way you can forget a part or put it in at the wrong time.

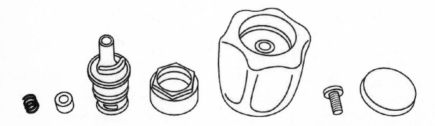

Now it's time for a trip to the hardware store. Place your cartridge, little black valve seats, and springs in a container and take them with you. When you get to the store, ask for a replacement cartridge that matches yours and a new set of valve seats and springs. This is also a great time to pick up some heat-proof grease if you haven't gotten it yet. Once you have everything, it's time to start putting it all back together.

STEP TWO: PUT THE FAUCET BACK TOGETHER

1. PUT A SMALL AMOUNT OF heat-proof grease on your pinky finger or on a cotton swab and rub it inside of the little hole (or holes) from which you removed the valve seats and springs.

2. PLACE THE NEW SPRING INTO its hole, making sure that the biggest end of the spring is in the bottom of the hole.

3. SET THE NEW VALVE SEAT over the spring. You may need to use the needle-nose pliers to do this.

4. SPREAD SOME HEAT-PROOF grease around the outside of the new cartridge and set it in the opening. In order to make sure the cartridge is set all the way into the opening, you'll have to fit the little tab on the cartridge into a corresponding slot on the metal surrounding the cartridge.

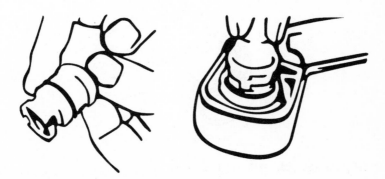

5. PLACE THE RETAINING RING over the cartridge and screw it back into place with the water pump pliers.

6. SET THE FAUCET HANDLE back into place.

7. REPLACE THE SCREW in the top of the faucet handle.

8. POP THE INDEX CAP back into its place.

9. THE TOWEL ON THE COUNTER should now be empty: You have replaced the cartridge and washer with new ones, and everything else went back where it belonged.

10. OPEN THE SHUT-OFF VALVES by turning them counter-clockwise (or, if you turned off the main water valve for this, go turn it back on).

11. OPEN YOUR FAUCET; the leak should be gone. Congratulations!

REPAIRING A BALL-TYPE FAUCET

Tools you will need:
- ✔ Utility knife
- ✔ Phillips head screwdriver
- ✔ Water pump pliers
- ✔ Needle-nose pliers
- ✔ Allen wrenches

Materials you will need:
- ✔ Paper towels
- ✔ Heat proof grease
- ✔ Masking tape
- ✔ Faucet ball (with new valve seats and springs)

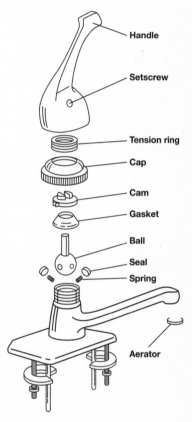

Handle

Setscrew

Tension ring

Cap

Cam

Gasket

Ball

Seal

Spring

Aerator

This kind of faucet is called a ball-type faucet because the part that controls the flow of water is shaped like a ball. The process to replace the ball and fix the leak is almost identical to the process outlined for a cartridge type faucet, but some of the parts are slightly different.

STEP ONE: TAKE THE FAUCET APART

1. CLOSE BOTH SHUT-OFF VALVES (hot and cold) underneath the sink by turning them all the way to the right (clockwise). If you're not able to close one or both valves, you can close the main water valve to the house.

2. CLOSE THE DRAIN and put a towel over the bottom of the sink to catch any parts that might fall.

3. LAY A TOWEL OUT on the counter to place the parts of the old faucet on as you remove them.

4. LIFT UP THE FAUCET HANDLE and look on the underside of its base for an opening. Sometimes the opening is covered by a small plastic disc that has the faucet name on it, or a red/blue symbol denoting hot/cold. Pry this piece off with a utility blade and set it on your towel.

5. YOU'LL FIND A SCREW INSIDE the opening. It may be a regular Phillips head screw, but more likely it's a set screw, for which you will need the appropriate-size Allen wrench. It may take a couple attempts to match the wrench with the screw; when you do, loosen the screw by turning it to the left (counter-clockwise). If it is a set screw, you don't have to remove it completely; just loosen it until you can lift the handle off. Set the handle and screw on the towel, next to the little plastic thing you removed first.

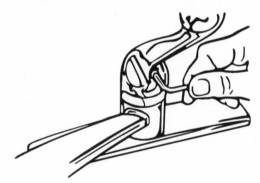

6. USE A LARGE PAIR OF WATER PUMP pliers to remove the faucet cap by unscrewing it. You may want to place a little masking tape on the teeth of the pliers to protect the finish on your faucet cap.

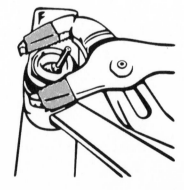

7. SET THE FAUCET CAP on the towel, next to the handle.

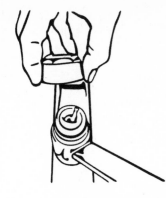

8. LOOSEN THE FAUCET CAM with the same pliers and remove it. Set it on the towel, next to the faucet cap.

9. REMOVE THE CAM washer and set it next to the faucet cam.

10. REMOVE THE BALL and set it next to the cam washer.

11. LOOK UNDER WHERE THE BALL was and remove the two black valve seats and the springs underneath them. Set the valve seats and springs on the towel, next to the ball.

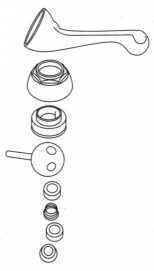

Now you're ready for your trip to the hardware store. Take your ball and valve seats with you and ask the helpful hardware person for a replacement, along with a tube of heat-proof grease.

STEP TWO: PUT THE FAUCET BACK TOGETHER

In order to put the faucet back together correctly, you're going to start at the end of the line of parts lying on the towel and work backward, putting them back in place one at a time.

1. PUT A SMALL AMOUNT OF heat-proof grease on your pinky finger or on a cotton swab and rub it inside of the little holes from which you removed the valve seats and springs.

2. PLACE THE NEW SPRINGS INTO their holes, making sure that the biggest end of each spring is in the bottom of the hole.

3. SET THE NEW VALVE SEATS over the springs. You may need to use the needle-nose pliers to do this.

4. SPREAD SOME HEAT-PROOF GREASE around the outside of the new ball, and set it in the opening. The ball may have a little metal tab on it that corresponds to a small opening into which it must fit. Play around with it until the ball feels like it settles into place.

5. PLACE THE NEW CAM washer over the ball.

6. PLACE THE CAM OVER the cam washer. There should be a little metal tab on one side of the cam that fits into a corresponding notch on the faucet body. Press the cam into place, with the tab in the notch.

7. SET THE CAP BACK IN PLACE, and tighten it with a pair of water pump pliers.

8. SET THE HANDLE BACK in place and tighten the screw, holding it in place.

9. REPLACE THE LITTLE plastic tab over the screw (if there was one).

10. OPEN THE SHUT-OFF valves by turning them counter-clockwise (or, if you turned off the main water valve for this, go turn it back on).

11. OPEN THE FAUCET and see if your leak is gone. If it is, pat yourself on the back. Congratulations!

GENERAL THOUGHTS ON FAUCETS AND FAUCET REPAIRS

Your faucets may not look like either type I have described here, or they may be the same kind but not have all the parts listed, or they may have more parts than I mentioned. You're not going to know exactly what you have until you open it up. There are many resources available to you in addition to this book: There are entire books on plumbing that cover a wider range of faucets and faucet issues; if you know what kind of faucet you have, the company might have a website with repair information available; and, if all else fails, you can always do an Internet search. Just type in "How to fix a leaky faucet?" and be prepared to wade through the responses you get.

Because plumbing presents unique challenges, it is that much more rewarding when you solve a problem. If you're someone with a lot of patience who likes to work through issues and who can handle possible setbacks, you may really enjoy working on the minor plumbing issues in your home. If you're someone with less patience and/or someone who doesn't like uncertainty, risk, and solving problems, then plumbing may not be something you choose to take on. That is completely okay.

Even though I can do plumbing, at this point in my life I often call a plumber to do the nastier jobs that I just don't want to mess with. It's important to know your strengths and weaknesses, and choose your projects accordingly.

Getting to Know (and Fix) Your Toilet

For something that we have spent countless hours of our lives on top of, it's remarkable how little most of us know about how a toilet works and how to fix its minor problems. Like many things in our lives, we really don't notice our toilet until it stops working. Most residential toilets are gravity-feed toilets, which means that it's the force of the water dropping from the tank into the bowl that flushes away the waste. When the toilet handle is pressed down, it lifts up the trip lever, which lifts up the flapper ball. The flapper ball covers a large opening from the tank into the bowl; when it lifts, it allows water to flow from the tank into the bowl.

When your toilet is working properly, this entire process is invisible to you. However, three minor (but annoying) problems often arise: the handle can break or get loose, the water level can rise too high, and the flapper ball can wear out. Each of these problems is relatively easy to fix, and only one requires shutting off the water. But before we get into all that, let's start by getting to know your toilet.

All the interesting things that can go wrong with your toilet (and that don't involve a foreign object getting flushed) take place in or on the toilet tank.

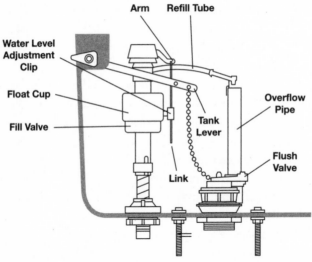

Water enters most toilet tanks through a small pipe located on the lower left-hand side of the toilet tank. The bottom of this pipe is attached to the shut-off valve, which is connected to the cold water pipe (which comes out of the wall or up through the floor near the toilet). It's important to know where this shut-off valve is, in case of an emergency (like an overflowing toilet), and for some repairs.

The top of the water pipe or hose connects to the bottom of toilet tank and lets water enter the tank through the ballcock. (Yes, that is what it's called. I could never make up a name that funny.) Older toilets and some current ones have a float ball attached to the ballcock. In many modern toilets, the two are combined; these have a float cup ballcock (try saying that three times, fast) to control the water level in the toilet tank.

Now that we know what the parts in the toilet tank are and what they do, let's fix those three simple problems I mentioned before, starting with the toilet handle:

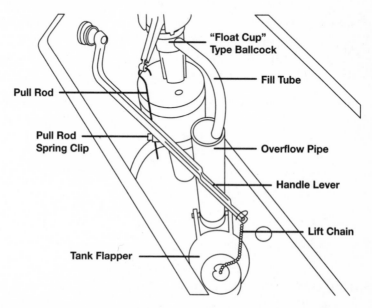

"Float Cup" Type Ballcock

Fill Tube

Pull Rod

Pull Rod Spring Clip

Overflow Pipe

Handle Lever

Lift Chain

Tank Flapper

TIGHTENING OR REPLACING THE TOILET HANDLE

Tools you will need:
✔ Water pump pliers

Materials you may need:
✔ A new handle (with trip lever attached)

IMPORTANT NOTE: Before you go to buy your new handle, take note of where exactly it is located on the toilet. It may be on the right or left side, or it may be on the front of the toilet. If you don't know where it is, you can't buy the correct replacement, which is very frustrating.

1. REMOVE THE LID from the toilet tank and set it aside.

2. START BY TIGHTENING the connecting nut that holds the toilet handle in place on the inside of the toilet tank.

IMPORTANT NOTE: The connecting nut is reverse threaded! That means that it twists in the opposite direction from other nuts: You turn it clockwise to loosen it, and counter-clockwise to tighten it. My mother taught me this one!

3. IF TIGHTENING THE CONNECTING nut solves your handle problem, you're done; if it doesn't, then you need to buy a new handle. The best thing to do is remove the old one and take it with you to the hardware store. To remove the handle, start by completely loosening the connecting nut.

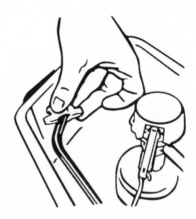

4. UNHOOK THE LIFT CHAIN by removing the hook from its hole in the trip lever; but before you do so, make a note of which hole it was in. You'll want to know that when you put it back later.

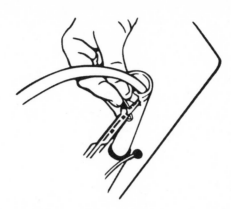

5. NOW SLIDE THE HANDLE and trip lever out of the hole in the toilet tank, and go buy a replacement.

6. PUT THE NEW HANDLE and trip lever through the hole in the tank. Slide the nut onto the trip lever, and move it all the way to the end. Start tightening the connecting nut by turning it counter-clockwise with your fingers. Use your pliers to finish tightening the nut.

7. REATTACH THE LIFT CHAIN to the trip lever by placing the hook back in the hole where it was originally located.

8. PLACE THE LID BACK ON the tank, and you're done. Congratulations! Aren't you glad you didn't hire a plumber to do that?

THE MYSTERY OF THE PHANTOM FLUSH

Have you ever been brushing your teeth and heard the toilet making sounds all by itself? It's usually one of two sounds: Either it sounds like water is running (and, if you can catch it happening, you'll see water filling the bowl), or it sounds like water is filling the tank and shutting off. In order to figure out which phantom is visiting your toilet, you need to do a little detective work.

1. LIFT THE LID OFF THE TOILET tank and look inside. The water level in the tank should be about 1 inch below the top of the fill pipe. If it isn't, and the water is even with the very top of the fill pipe, then it's overflowing, and that's why your toilet is running. The water level needs to be adjusted.

2. IF THE WATER LEVEL LOOKS to be okay, the problem is with the flapper ball—reach into the tank and press down on it. If the water stops leaking into the tank, it means that your flapper ball is worn out and needs to be replaced.

ADJUSTING THE TOILET'S WATER LEVEL

Tools you will need:
✔   Your hand

Materials you will need:
✔   None

If your toilet has a float ball attached to the ballcock by an arm, you adjust the water level by bending the arm:

1. GRAB HOLD OF THE ARM with both hands and bend it slightly downward.

2. FLUSH THE TOILET AND SEE if the new water level is lower than the original one. If it isn't, keep bending the arm down and test-flushing the toilet until the water level is about 1 inch below the top of the fill pipe.

3. PUT THE LID BACK on the toilet tank.

If your toilet has a float cup ballcock, the adjustment is slightly different, but the results will be the same:

1. LOCATE THE SPRING CLIP on the pull rod and pinch it together with your fingers.

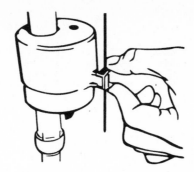

2. SLIDE IT DOWN the pull rod a little bit.

3. FLUSH THE TOILET AND SEE if the new water level is lower than the original one. If not, keep moving the spring clip down until the water level is about 1 inch below the top of the fill pipe.

4. PUT THE LID BACK on the toilet tank.

REPLACING THE FLAPPER BALL

The previous fixes could be done with the water in the toilet tank, but this one can't, so you have to start by emptying the tank:

1. CLOSE THE WATER SHUT-OFF valve (located on the floor or wall near the toilet) by turning it all the way to the right. If it hasn't been closed in a long time, you may need some pliers to help you with this step.

2. REMOVE THE LID from the tank.

3. HOLD THE TOILET HANDLE down until as much water as possible drains out of the tank and into the bowl.

4. REACH INTO THE TANK and unhook the lift chain from the trip lever, taking note of which hole it was connected to.

NOTE: If your memory is anything like mine, write this down, because you won't remember later!

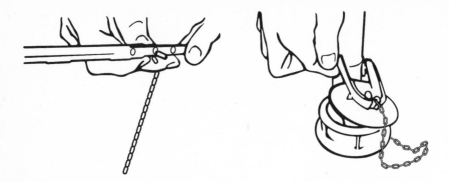

5. UNHOOK THE FLAPPER BALL from the ears on the fill pipe by unsnapping it, or by prying it off.

6. TAKE THE FLAPPER BALL with you to the hardware store and ask for a replacement.

SHOPPING NOTE: There are some universal replacement flapper balls that work on many toilets, but they don't work on all of them. The folks at the hardware store will be able to tell you which replacement flapper ball you need.

7. THE FLAPPER BALL YOU BUY may have some extra parts that you don't need. When you get it home, remove or add whatever is necessary to make it look like your old one.

8. ATTACH THE NEW FLAPPER BALL to your fill pipe in the same way the old one was attached.

9. BEFORE ATTACHING THE NEW CHAIN to the trip lever, you need to make sure it's the same length as the old one. If it's too short, the flapper ball can't close completely, and if it's too long, it can get caught under the flapper ball and keep it from closing tightly. Cut the chain to length with a pair of scissors.

IT HAPPENED TO ME: I was once in the bathroom at my doctor's office and noticed that the toilet was running, so I did what any self-respecting handywoman would do: I took the lid off the toilet tank and looked inside. The lift chain was too long and was getting stuck under the flapper ball. So I fixed it.

10. ONCE THE CHAIN is the right length, you can reattach it to the correct hole in the trip lever.

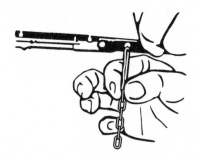

11. PLACE THE LID BACK on the toilet tank.

12. OPEN THE SHUT-OFF VALVE by turning it all the way to the left, and then back to the right about half a turn.

13. CONGRATULATIONS—you did it!

The Sink Pop-Up Thingy (Drain Stopper)

The technical term for the sink pop-up thingy is the pop-up sink drain stopper. I don't know why all these bathroom terms are tongue twisters, but they are. Feel free to rename them (as I clearly have) for your own purposes! Whatever you call it, that thing at the bottom of your bathroom sink hides a multitude of sins. It is important for you to know how to adjust it when it's not working correctly, and how to remove it for cleaning when it's causing drain problems.

IT HAPPENED TO ME ONCE: When my bathroom drain was draining very slowly, I assumed that the problem was in the trap underneath the sink. I removed the nut at the bottom of the trap, drained out the water, and stuck my finger and a coat hanger up inside, but found no clog. So then I assumed that the problem must be further down the drain system. I poured a rather caustic drain cleaner into my sinks and waited for it to eat away the clog. It didn't.

As a last resort, I removed my pop-up sink drain stopper . . . and I was disgusted by what I saw. It was completely covered in a ball of hair, soap scum, and black slime caused by hair products and all the other things we thoughtlessly send down the drain. I cleaned it off, put it back into the sink, and ran the water, and the "clog" was gone.

A little regular maintenance and an occasional cleaning can prevent the kind of mess I ran into.

CLEANING YOUR POP-UP SINK DRAIN STOPPER

Tools you may need:
- ✔ Water pump pliers
- ✔ Flashlight
- ✔ Old toothbrush

Materials you may need:
- ✔ Cleaning supplies
- ✔ A strong stomach!

1. MAKE SURE THE DRAIN STOPPER is in the full, open position. Try turning it counter-clockwise, hard, and then lifting it out. Some will come out like this, but many won't. If yours does, proceed to step 6. If it doesn't, go on to step 2.

2. USE YOUR FLASHLIGHT TO illuminate the area underneath your sink; this area's usually in a vanity, but sometimes it's in plain view.

3. DIRECTLY BEHIND THE DRAIN tailpiece—it's not visible from the

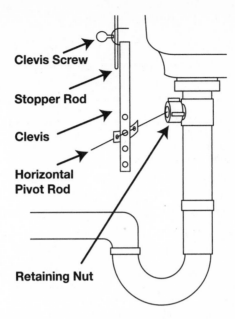

Clevis Screw

Stopper Rod

Clevis

**Horizontal
Pivot Rod**

Retaining Nut

front of the plumbing—is the drain stopper rod, which is connected to the clevis, which is connected to the drain pivot rod. The end of the drain pivot rod that you can't see is what's holding the pop-up drain stopper in the drain.

4. UNSCREW THE RETAINING NUT (the nut that's holding the pivot rod in place) with your fingers or the pliers.

5. SLOWLY PULL THE PIVOT ROD OUT of the tailpiece, being careful to catch any little pieces that might fall (I once lost a washer that I didn't know was there during this step).

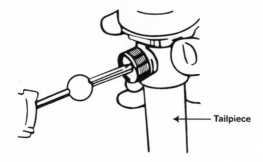

Tailpiece

6. NOW THE POP-UP SINK DRAINER should easily lift out of the sink for cleaning. While it's out of the drain, take the opportunity to clean the drain. Shine your flashlight down into the drain—you may be surprised at what you see. Use an old toothbrush to scrub the walls of the tailpiece.

7. ONCE THE SINK STOPPER IS clean, set it back into the drain.

8. PUT THE PIVOT ROD BACK IN place and gently hand-tighten the retaining nut.

9. TEST TO SEE IF THE SINK STOPPER is being held in place by the pivot rod by lifting the stopper lever up and down.

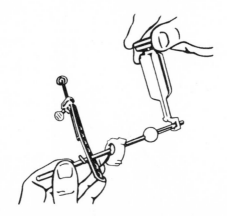

(These are the parts out of the sink, so you can see what is happening inside the tailpiece.)

10. IF IT ISN'T, YOU'LL HAVE TO remove the pivot rod and change the orientation of the sink stopper until it's in the correct position for the pivot rod to "catch" it.

11. ONCE EVERYTHING IS WORKING correctly, finish tightening the retaining nut by hand. If you need to use pliers to do this, use them gently. If you overtighten the retaining nut, the sink stopper will not move up and down easily.

 **TIP:** Pour really hot water down your drains once a month. This will help prevent the yucky build-up in the drains and on the sink stopper. Remove the sink stopper once a year for cleaning, whether you think it needs it or not. (My mother taught me this one too.)

FIXING YOUR SINK POP-UP DRAIN STOPPER

If your sink pop-up drain stopper doesn't move up and down anymore, it's probably because the pivot rod has slipped out of its hole in the clevis. What the heck is a clevis? It's the thing that connects the drain stopper rod to the drain pivot rod. There's a little bent piece of metal called a spring clip that holds the end of the pivot rod onto the clevis. Sometimes the spring clip falls off, preventing the sink stopper from moving up and down, but you can replace it easily:

1. SLIDE ONE END OF the spring clip onto the pivot rod.

2. PUT THE END OF THE PIVOT rod into a hole on the clevis.

3. SLIDE THE OTHER END OF the spring clip onto the end of the pivot rod protruding through the clevis. There should be tension in the spring clip.

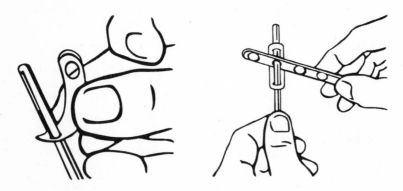

4. IF THERE'S NO TENSION IN the spring clip, you need to open it up a little by pulling the ends away from each other; then you can reattach it to the pivot rod.

5. MOVE THE PIVOT ROD UP and down. The drain stopper should now move with it. If the drain stopper does not open or close all the way, you need to move the end of the pivot rod to a new hole in the clevis.

6. I WISH I COULD TELL YOU EXACTLY which hole you need to use, but I can't. Experiment by moving the pivot rod into a new hole, reattaching the spring, and testing it. Continue trying different holes until the drain stopper opens and closes to your satisfaction.

Showerheads

Removing an old showerhead and replacing it with a new one is a favorite project of mine, because it doesn't involve shut-off valves. Remember what I said at the beginning of this chapter about plumbing not liking to be touched? Well, you don't have to touch any "real" plumbing in order to replace your showerhead. You just have to make sure the shower handle is in the "off" position, and then you're

ready to start. However, to be safe, stand to the side when you finish
unscrewing the showerhead; there's usually some water still in the
pipes, and you may get an unexpected shower if you're standing
directly in front of the head.

REPLACING A SHOWERHEAD

Tools you will need:
✔ Waterpump pliers

Materials you will need:
✔ Masking tape
✔ Teflon plumbing tape
✔ New showerhead

1. WRAP SOME MASKING TAPE around the
teeth on your pliers to prevent scratching
the surface on the showerhead.

2. UNSCREW THE SWIVEL BALL nut by turning the pliers counter-
clockwise.

3. CLEAN OFF THE THREADS AT THE end of the shower arm, removing
any old tape or debris.

4. WRAP A PIECE OF TEFLON TAPE (about 4 inches long) around
the threads, clockwise, pulling it tight so that it stretches and grabs.
Smooth down the end. This tape helps seal the joint between the
threads and the swivel ball nut, preventing leaks.

5. SCREW THE SWIVEL BALL NUT of the new showerhead on to the threads by hand, and then finish tightening it with your pliers.

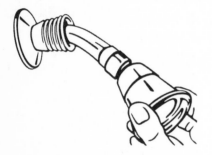

6. TURN THE WATER ON TO SEE if you have any leaks; if you do, continue to tighten the nut until the leaking stops.

7. ENJOY YOUR NEW showerhead.

TIP: If you like your old showerhead but it doesn't seem to work as well as it used to, try cleaning it before replacing it. First, fill a quart- or gallon-size bag with equal parts vinegar and water. Place the bag over the showerhead so that it is fully submerged. Tie the bag in place and leave it there overnight (or longer). The vinegar can dissolve any mineral build-up in the showerhead that's clogging the holes.

Cleaning and Replacing Sink Faucet Aerators

Tools you will need:

✔ Water pump pliers

Materials you will need:

✔ Masking tape
✔ Toothbrush

Each of your kitchen and bathroom faucets has an aerator on its tip that reduces water flow and evens out the water pressure. Over time, aerators can get clogged with minerals and tiny rocks. This almost always happens when the main water supply has been shut off for plumbing repairs. When the water is turned back on, debris in the pipes flows to your faucets and gets caught in your aerators. If you have noticed that your water pressure seems reduced, or that the water is coming out of your faucet unevenly, it's time to remove your aerators and clean or replace them.

CLEANING YOUR SINK FAUCET AERATOR

1. CLOSE OR PLUG THE DRAIN in your sink, lay a towel down in the sink to catch any parts that may fall, and lay another towel down to the side to place the parts you remove on.

2. WRAP SOME MASKING TAPE around the teeth on your pliers to avoid scratching your aerator.

3. UNSCREW THE AERATOR with the pliers by turning it counter-clockwise. Once you get it loosened, you'll be able to unscrew it with your fingers.

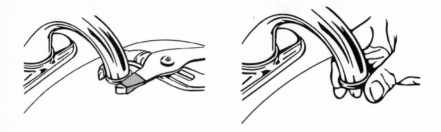

4. CAREFULLY DISASSEMBLE IT by laying the parts down on the towel you put to the side, in the order they were removed.

5. CLEAN EVERYTHING, especially the screen, with the toothbrush.

6. REASSEMBLE THE AERATOR and reattach it to the faucet by turning it clockwise. Tighten it with the pliers.

7. TURN THE WATER BACK ON and see if cleaning the aerator solved your problems.

8. IF IT DIDN'T, YOU'LL need to replace the old aerator with a new one.

REPLACING YOUR SINK FAUCET AERATOR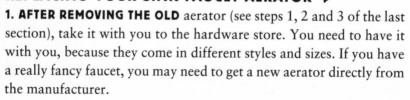

1. AFTER REMOVING THE OLD aerator (see steps 1, 2 and 3 of the last section), take it with you to the hardware store. You need to have it with you, because they come in different styles and sizes. If you have a really fancy faucet, you may need to get a new aerator directly from the manufacturer.

Variations of Aerators

2. WHEN YOU GET HOME, screw the new aerator (clockwise) onto your faucet and test for leaks. Tighten it as much as necessary.

TIP: Clean your aerators once a year and you'll probably be able to avoid ever having to replace them! Always clean your aerators out after any plumbing repair that required the water to be shut off.

Removing and Laying Caulk

One of the simplest but most effective deterrents against future water problems in your bathroom is a bead of caulk. Caulked joints are most commonly found in your shower stall and tub surround. You may also find caulk on the joint where countertops meet the wall, and around the shower handle escutcheon (for a lot more information about caulk, read Chapter 2.)

People usually don't notice the caulked joints in their homes until the joints start to look really gross, or until they notice a leak somewhere and trace it back to a defective caulk joint. There is no reason to disturb your caulked joints as long as they are mold- and mildew-free and still doing their job well. But eventually, many caulked joints will need to be removed and replaced with new caulk.

REMOVING OLD CAULK

Tools you will need:
- ✔ Six-in-one painters tool
- ✔ Razor blade scraper

Materials you may need:
- ✔ Cleaning supplies ·
- ✔ Clean cloth/scrubber
- ✔ Caulk-Be-Gone product (for removing latex caulk; see the Shopping Tip below for details)

As soon as you start trying to remove your old caulk, you'll find out if it's silicon or latex. Old silicon caulk remains pliable and somewhat soft, while old latex caulk is very hard, brittle, and difficult to remove.

1. USE THE POINTY END OF THE painter's tool to get under an end of the caulk and lift it up a little. If you can grab onto the end with your fingers and start pulling the caulk up, then you have silicon caulk. If the caulk is very hard and almost impossible to dig out, you have latex caulk.

SHOPPING TIP: If you have latex caulk, there's a product you can buy that really helps with the removal process. It's called Caulk-Be-Gone, and it's made by DAP. You can usually find it in the caulk aisle at major home centers; I've never had luck finding it at my hardware store. Buy a tube, cut the tip off with scissors or a utility knife, and spread a bead of it onto your old latex caulk. It looks like green toothpaste. Be liberal with it, and let it sit for at least two hours. Then proceed to step 2.

2. DIG THE CAULK OUT OF the joint, using the painter's tool or whatever other tool you find that works.

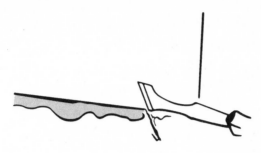

3. USE THE RAZOR BLADE scraper to scrape up any pieces or residue left behind.

4. THOROUGHLY CLEAN THE AREA with soap and a scrubber of some sort. Wipe the area dry, making sure all the old caulk is gone, no soap residue remains, and the area is squeaky clean. The new bead of caulk will not adhere well unless the area is really clean.

LAYING A NEW BEAD OF CAULK

Tools you will need:
- ✔ Caulking gun
- ✔ Utility knife

Materials you will need:
- ✔ Tube of caulk
- ✔ Paper towels or rags

Laying down caulk is a somewhat difficult job that looks easy when you see someone else that has lots of experience doing it. I am living proof that—with enough practice—anyone can become quite proficient with a caulking gun.

1. START BY CUTTING THE TIP off your tube of caulk with a new blade in your utility knife. Make the cut at an angle, starting about $\frac{1}{8}$ of an inch from the tip and cutting back, toward the tip. Do not cut straight across the tip.

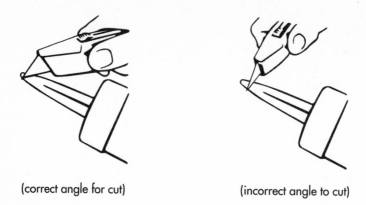

(correct angle for cut)   (incorrect angle to cut)

2. PUNCTURE THE SEAL AT THE BASE of the nipple, using a long nail or the pointy part of your caulking gun.

3. PLACE THE TUBE OF CAULK INTO the gun and squeeze the trigger gently, just until a small amount of caulk comes out the tip.

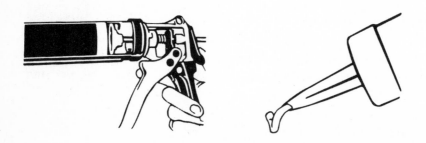

4. DISENGAGE THE TRIGGER, and then wipe the tip clean with paper towel or rags. I use paper towels; caulk doesn't wash out of fabric.

IMPORTANT NOTE: I strongly recommend that you take some time to practice using the caulking gun before you try laying your actual beads of caulk for this project. Even if you have to buy an additional tube of caulk just for practicing, it will be worth it.

IT HAPPENED TO ME ONCE: I was once hired by a woman to help her with a list of projects, including teaching her how to caulk her kitchen countertop where it met the backsplash. I demonstrated how it was done, explaining my technique as I went along, and then I handed her the caulking gun and she stepped up to the countertop. She proceeded to lay down a perfect bead of caulk. My jaw dropped—no one does that well the first time! She looked at the expression on my face and said, "I frost cakes."

5. SET THE TIP OF THE TUBE OF CAULK in a corner, or at the end of the area you are caulking, and gently squeeze the trigger. Start pulling the caulking gun toward you and move slowly along the joint.

Your goal is to make a thin, even bead of caulk, with no gaps or lumps. The rule of thumb with caulk is "less is more." You can always go back and add some if necessary. It is much harder to remove excess!

6. WHEN YOU GET TO AN END point, disengage the trigger and set the tube down on a rag or paper towel (the tube will often leak caulk even after you have disengaged the trigger).

7. NOW IT'S TIME TO SMOOTH out the bead of caulk. You want a smooth, concave bead, with no gaps. There are numerous tools and gadgets on the market for smoothing out caulk, and I have tried several—none have measured up to my tried and true trusty tool, my index finger. I wet the tip of my finger (yes, I stick it in my mouth) and gently pull it along the bead of caulk, occasionally lifting it to wipe any excess caulk onto a rag.

8. IF, AFTER SMOOTHING OUT the caulk, you notice a gap, apply a small amount to that area and smooth it out.

9. REPEAT THESE STEPS UNTIL you have covered all the areas needing caulk.

10. CONGRATULATIONS! You have just completed a rather difficult job. Rest assured that next time it will be easier, and you will get better with practice.

IMPORTANT NOTE: Tubs and showers should not be used for 24 hours after applying new caulk.

Grout

If you have tile on the walls of your tub or shower, it's important that the grout between those tiles is in good condition. While grout does have an aesthetic purpose, its real reason for existing is to seal the space between the tiles, preventing water from getting behind them. I have lost count of the times I have been called to replace tile and the wall behind it because water had gotten behind the tile and done major damage. Prevention through ongoing maintenance is much easier than major repairs will be.

Next time you're cleaning the tile in your bath or shower, look closely at the grout lines. Pay special attention to the bottom 4 feet of tile and grout. You're looking for any areas where the grout appears to have fallen out or is loose. Grout should be rock hard, and you shouldn't be able to move it. If you find any areas that look suspicious, mark them with a pencil or a piece of tape.

REPAIRING GROUT

Tools you will need:
- ✔ Grout removal tool (or utility knife with new blades)
- ✔ Putty knife
- ✔ Rubber spatula
- ✔ Vacuum cleaner

Materials you will need:
- ✔ Grout
- ✔ Container for mixing
- ✔ Whisk or fork
- ✔ Grout removal sponge (or new kitchen sponge)

TIP: You can purchase a grout removal tool if you like. I own two, but I usually use my utility knife, and it does a better job for me. The secret is to change the blade often; it gets dull very quickly doing this kind of dirty work!

1. USE YOUR UTILITY KNIFE (or grout removal tool) to scrape away all the loose grout that you can find. Be very careful. I keep both hands on the knife to reduce the chances of hurting myself. Anytime you're exerting force on a knife containing a sharp blade, you want to be constantly aware of where your fingers are in relation to the blade.

2. CONTINUE SCRAPING UNTIL you have removed all the loose or damaged grout.

3. USE THE VACUUM CLEANER over each grout line to clean the area and remove anything left behind by your knife.

4. WIPE THE SURFACE clean with a damp sponge.

SHOPPING TIP: If your grout is white or off-white, you may be able to purchase small tubs of premixed grout. Purchase a grout color that most closely matches your grout, but don't worry if it is not perfect. It's very difficult to match existing grout colors. Also, most shower and bath tiles use unsanded grout because the grout lines are less than $\frac{1}{8}$ of an inch wide. If your grout lines are wider than that, you will need sanded grout.

5. IF YOU WERE ABLE TO PURCHASE premixed grout, move on to step 6. If not, you'll need to mix some grout. The instructions on the package tell you how much water to use if you're mixing the entire package of grout. It's highly unlikely that you will need that much grout, however. I suggest mixing small amounts at a time; you can always mix another batch if you run out. Start by putting a ½-cup of cool water in a clean plastic container. Slowly add small amounts of grout and stir it with a whisk, a fork, or your spatula. Continue adding grout and stirring until the mixture is the texture of a thick pudding. It should not be wet and runny; nor should it be so stiff that you can hardly move it. Let it set for a few minutes.

6. TAKE A SMALL AMOUNT OF grout on your spatula or putty knife and press it into the grout lines that you cleaned out. Press hard to ensure that the grout really fills them up. Don't worry about it if you get some new grout onto the existing grout; you'll wipe it off later.

7. LET THE GROUT SIT for about 10 minutes.

8. USING A DAMP (NOT WET) sponge, gently rub over the areas where you put the new grout. Use the sponge to shape the grout so it's concave, not convex. Wipe off any excess grout that's lying on top of the tile; you want the grout to be *between* the pieces of tile, not on top of them! Be careful not to wipe the grout out of the lines. You're trying to match the new grout lines to the existing grout lines.

9. STOP WIPING ONCE ALL THE GROUT lines look good and no large amounts of excess grout remain on the tile surfaces. *Do not* try to get the tile perfectly clean at this point. It will have a haze on it (created by grout residue) that you will remove later, when the grout is drier.

10. LET THE GROUT SIT for at least a couple of hours.

11. WIPE THE ENTIRE SURFACE of the tile with a soft, dry, clean cloth. This should remove any remaining grout haze.

12. DO NOT USE THE TUB or shower for at least 24 hours.

13. CONGRATULATIONS! You have completed a less-than-fun job that's extremely important to maintaining the integrity of your house.

FINAL THOUGHTS ON WATER-RELATED BATHROOM PROJECTS

If you just completed a project in this chapter, you should be very proud of yourself. After electrical projects, we women seem to have the most trepidation about taking on plumbing projects . . . which is why it's so satisfying to sit on your toilet that no longer leaks, take a shower under your new showerhead, and wash your hands under your clean aerator or new faucet. Not only will your bathroom look and feel better now, but you can also rest assured that you are avoiding expensive water-related repairs down the road.

8. BUT WAIT, THERE'S MORE: NON-WATER-RELATED BATHROOM PROJECTS

When I said the bathroom was a project-rich environment, I meant it! Now that you have taken on and successfully completed the water-related projects, it's time to move on to the many non-water-related projects in the bathroom. Bathrooms get a lot of wear and tear, because every member of the family uses them each day. The kitchen is really the only other room that takes the same amount of abuse as the bathroom.

If you don't have money in the budget for a major remodel, don't worry: There are several simple things you can do to update the look and feel of your bathroom. In this chapter you will learn how to:

✔ Replace your towel bars and toilet paper holder
✔ Remove and replace your medicine cabinet
✔ Install safety grab bars
✔ Update your old vanity with paint and hardware

If, in addition to the above projects, you put fresh paint on the walls and buy some new towels, bathmats, and a new shower curtain, you'll feel like you have a brand new bathroom (but it will cost you a fraction what a major remodel would).

Towel Bars and Toilet Paper Holders

I have been asked to replace towel bars and toilet paper holders more frequently than I've been asked to do any other bathroom project. Usually this is because the towel bars and toilet paper holders were installed with wall anchors that were insufficient for the job. Towel bars installed with small plastic anchors were never intended to hold a person's body weight, but people treat them as if they were.

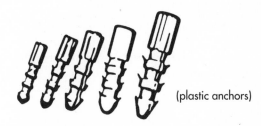

(plastic anchors)

Over time, the stress of people leaning on and pulling towels over towel bars will weaken the hold of most wall anchors. Since towel bars are almost never located over studs, you usually need to use wall anchors, and it's extremely important that they be of a certain quality.

Until I started installing towel bars for my clients, I had never realized the wide range in quality that exists in the world of towel bars. Once I installed my first towel bar and toilet paper holder made by Baldwin, I was sold on the value of paying for quality. The folks at Baldwin understand that bathroom hardware needs to be installed with toggle bolts, so they include toggle bolts with all their products. Manufacturers of lower-quality hardware products include simple plastic anchors with their products, almost guaranteeing that they will fall off the wall at some point in the future.

If Baldwin products don't fit your budget—or you just don't happen to like their style—don't panic. You can buy your own toggle bolts. As long as you install your hardware (new or old) with the right materials, your towel bar will remain on the wall until you decide to take it down.

REPLACING TOWEL BARS AND TOILET PAPER HOLDERS

Tools you will need:
- ✔ Power drill
- ✔ Drill bits
- ✔ Hammer
- ✔ Utility knife
- ✔ Phillips head screwdriver (or screwdriver bit for your drill)
- ✔ Pencil
- ✔ Eraser
- ✔ Steel measuring tape
- ✔ Level
- ✔ Scissors
- ✔ Allen wrench (also known as a hex wrench), or a really small flathead screwdriver

Materials you will need:
- ✔ ⅜- or ½-inch toggle bolts
- ✔ Masking tape

If you're reinstalling or replacing your existing towel bar because it's unstable or starting to fall out of the wall, you need to start by completely removing it from the wall. If you're installing a new towel bar, skip to the instructions at the bottom of page 207.

REMOVING THE OLD TOWEL BAR

1. LOCATE THE SET SCREWS on each of the towel rod's end brackets. If your bracket is made of wood, the screws will be on its face, but they may be hidden by small wood dowel pieces. Pop the dowels out with the blade on your utility knife and remove the screws holding the brackets to the wall. If your brackets are metal, the screws will be located on the underside of the end brackets.

NOTE: Take a walk through your bathroom and see if you can find any screws visible in any of the bathroom hardware, including the faucet, towel bars, toilet paper holder, and robe hooks. I've often wondered if there's some sort of law stating that all screws in bathroom hardware must be hidden, and that once you find them, they must be incredibly difficult to unscrew! Screws in metal bathroom fixtures are either small flathead screws, or (more often) set screws that require an Allen (hex) wrench. New bathroom fixtures come with the correct-size Allen wrench for installation, but if you are removing an old fixture and the original wrench is nowhere to be found, you will have to pick up a small set of Allen wrenches at the hardware store. You will need patience to locate and loosen the screws on most brackets.

2. USE A VERY TINY SCREWDRIVER (I had to buy one just for this purpose) or Allen wrench to loosen the set screw. You don't want to unscrew the set screw completely; just keep loosening it until you can pull the end bracket off the mounting hardware. Repeat on the other end bracket.

3. REMOVE BOTH PIECES of mounting hardware by unscrewing the screws holding them to the wall with either a handheld screwdriver or your power drill (set up as a screwdriver).

4. REMOVING THE EXISTING WALL anchors may be easy or hard. If they are already really loose, they should just pull out of the wall. Often, several will be loose but one or two will still be solid. I suggest that you remove them all and replace them with toggle bolts. Some anchors can be cut out with the blade of your utility knife: Do it carefully, and always keep your fingers out of the way. Others can be pushed into the wall: Set the tip of a Phillips head screwdriver against the anchor, and tap the end of it with a hammer until the old anchor disappears into the wall. Follow the directions later in this chapter for rehanging a toilet paper holder with toggle bolts, starting with step 2 because a toilet paper holder is just like a very small towel bar.

INSTALLING THE NEW TOWEL BAR

In order to install your new towel bar, you need to measure for where to install the mounting hardware. Most towel bars are mounted about 48 inches off the floor; that said, you should choose a height that's comfortable for you—just make sure the towels won't hit the floor while hanging on the rod. Place the rod in the end pieces and hold the whole thing up on the wall. Move it around until you have it where you want it.

1. USE A PENCIL TO MAKE A ROUGH mark on the wall indicating approximate location.

2. USE A LEVEL TO MAKE A LINE indicating where the towel bar will go.

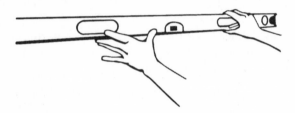

3. FOLLOW THE DIRECTIONS THAT COME with your towel bar if they include plastic toggle anchors or toggle bolts. If your towel bar comes with plastic anchors or self-drilling drywall anchors, replace them with ⅜-inch toggle bolts and follow the directions in the next section for hanging a toilet paper holder with toggle bolts.

4. USE YOUR STEEL MEASURING TAPE to mark exactly where each piece of mounting hardware should go on the line you made with your level.

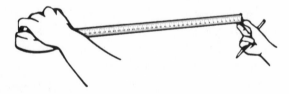

5. YOUR TOWEL BAR MAY COME WITH a template, which could either be inside the box with the bar, or on exterior of the box itself. If you have one, tape the template to the wall and use it to make exact measurements.

6. SET THE MOUNTING HARDWARE on the wall and use a pencil to mark where you'll drill the holes.

7. USE A ⅜-INCH drill bit to drill each hole.

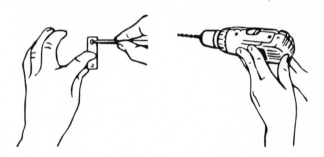

8. FOLD UP THE PLASTIC TOGGLE anchors and push them into each hole.

9. INSERT THE LITTLE RED PIN that came with the anchors into the hole until you feel the anchor "pop" behind the wall.

10. USE YOUR DRILL OR HANDHELD screwdriver to mount the hardware onto the anchors.

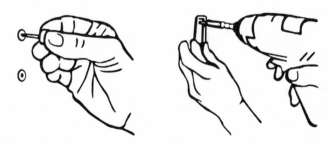

11. SET ONE TOWEL BAR BRACKET onto the mounting hardware and jiggle it until it's flush with the wall.

12. TIGHTEN THE SET SCREW with the Allen wrench that should have come with the towel bar.

13. SET THE TOWEL BAR IN PLACE and repeat steps 10 and 11 with the other end bracket.

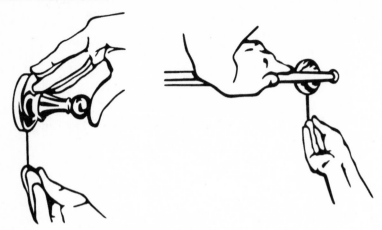

14. CONGRATULATIONS—you're done!

REHANGING A TOILET PAPER HOLDER

1. REMOVE THE EXISTING toilet paper holder hardware.

2. USE A SPADE BIT OR A DRILL bit that is slightly bigger than the widest part of the toggle to enlarge the existing holes in the wall.

3. PLACE THE TOGGLE BOLTS through the mounting hardware and screw the toggles onto the bolts so that the wings close onto the longest part of the bolt.

4. SQUEEZE THE WINGS TOGETHER and carefully insert the toggle bolt into the holes in the wall.

5. YOU MAY HEAR A CLICKING SOUND as the wings pop open. Tug on the mounting hardware to make sure the wings are fully open and engaged against the back of the wall.

6. TUG SLIGHTLY ON THE MOUNTING hardware and use your power drill (with the correct bit in it!) to start tightening the toggle bolt. If you have more than one toggle bolt in each piece of hardware, alternate between them, tightening each one a little bit at a time in order to keep the spring-loaded wings of the toggles tight against the back of the wall.

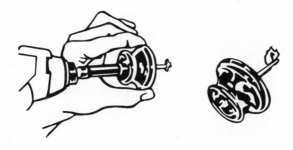

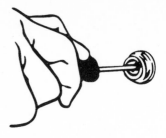

7. SWITCH TO A HANDHELD SCREWDRIVER for the last few turns; it will give you a better feel for "just-enough" tightness. It *is* possible to overtighten toggle bolts and break the toggle. Snug against the wall is all you need, nothing more.

8. REPEAT THE PROCESS with the other piece of mounting hardware.

9. LAY A LEVEL ACROSS BOTH pieces of hardware. If the bubble isn't right in the middle of the black lines, you need to adjust one of the mounting hardware pieces.

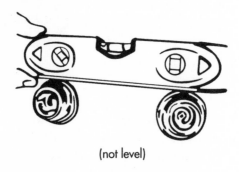

(not level)

10. TO ADJUST THE MOUNTING hardware, slightly loosen the toggle bolt (or bolts) on one piece of hardware, then move the hardware up or down until you reach level. Retighten the toggle bolt(s).

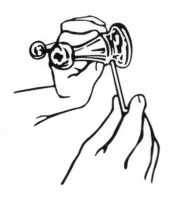

11. PLACE ONE END BRACKET on the mounting hardware. You may have to jiggle it a little bit until it rests solidly against the wall. Tighten the set screw with the Allen wrench provided, or with a small screwdriver.

12. INSTALL THE OTHER END BRACKET. Make sure your set screws are nice and tight.

13. CONGRATULATIONS! A toilet paper holder (mounted correctly) is a thing of beauty. Stand back and admire your work.

Medicine Cabinets

Removing your medicine cabinet and replacing it with a new one is really quite straightforward, as long as your new medicine cabinet is the same size as your old one. Older medicine cabinets are inset in the wall, so the new medicine cabinet has to fit into the same size hole.

REPLACING YOUR MEDICINE CABINET

Tools you will need:
- ✔ A Phillips head or flathead screwdriver
- ✔ Steel measuring tape
- ✔ Power drill with screwdriver bits

Materials you will need:
- ✔ A new medicine cabinet
- ✔ 4 1½-inch screws

1. COMPLETELY EMPTY THE contents of your medicine cabinet. This is a great opportunity to throw away expired medication, five-year-old makeup, and dried-out bandages.

2. REMOVE THE SHELVES to give yourself better access to the screws.

3. HOLDING THE MEDICINE CABINET in place, unscrew three of the four screws.

4. WHEN YOU START UNSCREWING the final screw, make sure you or someone else is holding the cabinet, as it may start to fall out of the wall once that last screw is loose.

5. REMOVE THE MEDICINE cabinet from the wall.

6. USE YOUR STEEL TAPE to measure the dimensions of your hole.

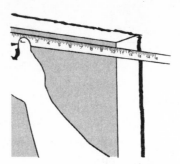

SHOPPING TIP: Take these dimensions with you when you go shopping for your new medicine cabinet. The holes are usually one of a few standard sizes. Make sure the new medicine cabinet you buy is the right size for your wall; it's very frustrating to get home and have a cabinet that is too big or too small, and neither problem is easy to fix.

7. PLACE YOUR NEW MEDICINE cabinet into the opening and screw it into place, following the directions included with the cabinet.

8. LOAD IT UP, and you're all done!

Safety Grab Bars

Some of my favorite clients are women in their sixties, seventies, and eighties who are committed to remaining in their own homes as long as possible. I like to do what I can to support them in that desire, and one way I do that is by making their bathrooms easier and safer to use with the installation of safety grab bars.

I have been asked to install grab bars near toilets and inside and outside tubs and showers. The location really depends on what each person needs. Grab bars basically give you something solid to hold on to while you're doing something that makes you vulnerable to falling, like stepping into a tub. There is no right or wrong place to install grab bars—they just need to be installed correctly.

Grab bars can be found at most hardware stores and home centers, and they come in a variety of lengths and materials. The two most common choices are white and stainless steel.

INSTALLING A SAFETY GRAB BAR

Tools you will need:
- ✔ Power drill with ½-inch and ⅛-inch drill bits
- ✔ Spade bit or tile bit (if installing in tile)
- ✔ 2- or 4-foot level
- ✔ Stud finder
- ✔ Pencil
- ✔ Screwdriver bit
- ✔ Screwdriver

Materials you will need:
- ✔ Safety grab bar and the installation materials that come with it
- ✔ Possibly: silicon caulk and caulking gun
- ✔ ⅜-inch toggle bolts
- ✔ Masking tape

A safety grab bar is really just an oversize towel bar with a different purpose; as such, its installation is almost identical to that of a towel bar or toilet paper holder (with a few minor exceptions). Just like a towel bar, a grab bar's gotta go where it's gotta go, regardless of where the wall studs are.

If you can locate studs to hang one or both ends of the grab bar on, however, it will make the installation a little bit easier. If you're installing the grab bar on a tiled wall, you won't be able to use a stud finder to locate the studs.

To install a grab bar:

1. HOLD THE GRAB BAR on the wall and determine where you want it to go. A grab bar

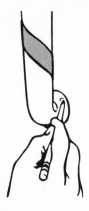

can be positioned horizontally, vertically, or in any angle in between that meets your need.

2. ONCE YOU'VE DECIDED WHERE you want the grab bar, you need to mark the location of the three holes on each end on the wall. You might want someone to hold the grab bar in place while you make the marks; it tends to slip if you are holding it with only one hand.

TIP: The large, circular disks that will eventually cover the screws once the grab bar is attached to the wall tend to slide around during installation and get in the way. Use a piece of masking tape to hold them in the center of the grab bar, out of your way, until you're ready for them.

3. IF YOU'RE NOT DEALING with tile, use a stud finder to see if your marks have landed on a stud.

4. SINCE A STUD IS ONLY 1½ inches wide, it's impossible for all three marks to land on one. Predrill each mark with a ⅛-inch drill bit to verify which holes are on studs and which are not.

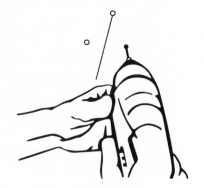

5. FOR THE MARKS NOT ON STUDS, you will need to drill a large hole for the toggle bolts that came with the grab bar.

6. THEY NEED TO BE VERY BIG TOGGLE BOLTS, because they have to be able to support an adult's body weight. Use your ½-inch drill bit or spade bit to drill holes for your toggle bolts.

IMPORTANT NOTE: If you're drilling through ceramic tile, porcelain tile, or marble, you'll need to purchase two special tile/glass bits. They will cost about $8, and their tips will look like a small, flat shovel. I know: It's scary to drill into tile. The first time, I was terrified that the tile would crack. Since then I have drilled into tile many, many times, and it has never cracked. I've encountered tile so difficult to penetrate that I've even had to have an extra person lean on the drill with me to get through it. So don't be afraid, and don't hesitate to ask for help either. You may also want to keep a spray bottle full of water on hand to squirt on the hole (for cooling purposes) between drilling attempts, because the bit gets very hot.

Start drilling with a small ⅜- or ¼-inch tile bit. When drilling through tile, only use the tile bit until you are through the tile and the backer board (which may be cement board or special wallboard). Once you think you've made it through both those layers (about ¾ of an inch in), switch to a regular ⅛-inch drill bit to finish drilling. This will allow you to find out if there's a stud at that location. If you hit a stud, stop drilling: You can use a screw instead of a toggle bolt. (If you had kept drilling with the larger drill bit, the resulting hole would be too big for a screw to hold.) If you didn't hit a stud, you need to redrill the hole with a ½-inch tile bit to make room for your large toggle bolt.

7. PLACE YOUR TOGGLE BOLTS through the holes in the grab bar at the appropriate locations. Don't do anything with the holes on top of studs: You won't deal with those until the end.

8. SQUEEZE IN THE TOGGLE WINGS, and stick the toggle bolts through the holes in the wall.

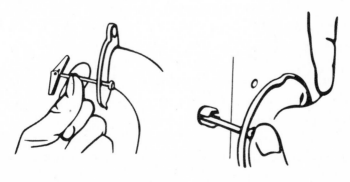

TIP: If you have trouble getting the toggle to fit into the hole (this often happens to me), you will need to make the hole a little bit bigger. Place the drill bit in the hole and try to move it around against the edges of the hole while it's spinning. This should make the hole big enough for the toggle.

9. MAKE SURE THAT THE TOGGLE has fully opened behind the wall.

(You can't see it, but this is what it looks like behind the wall.)

TIP: If I don't hear the toggle click, I often shine a flashlight into the hole so I can see if either of the toggle wings is stuck in the hole. Do this with all your toggle bolts, gently pulling on the grab bar to make sure the wings are all resting against the back of the wall.

10. NOW COMES THE HARDEST PART; you'll definitely want a helper for this step. Put the screwdriver bit in your power drill and start tightening the toggle bolts. You can only tighten each toggle bolt a little bit at a time, and you have to alternate from one end of the grab bar to the other. The whole time you're doing that, you need to be holding the grab bar away from the wall. Have your helper keep tension on the grab bar, pulling it away from the wall, as you tighten the toggle bolts. Keep working on each toggle bolt until the grab bar feels snug (but not too tight!) against the wall.

 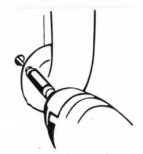

(toggle bolt at the top of grab bar)   (toggle bolt at the bottom of grab bar)

11. IF YOU'RE INSTALLING THE grab bar horizontally or vertically, now would be the time to get out your level and check to see if it's plumb (level). If you need to adjust the grab bar, loosen the toggle bolts on one end just enough so that you can move it. Then retighten the toggle bolts. I like to use a handheld screwdriver for the final adjustments so I can really feel what's happening.

12. NOW THAT YOU HAVE TAKEN CARE of the holes that aren't over a stud, you need to deal with the ones that are. For these holes, you can use the long, stainless steel screws that should have come with your grab bar. Predrill each location first with a $\frac{1}{8}$-inch drill bit.

13. FIT YOUR DRILL WITH THE screwdriver bit, and screw in the screws. Make sure that you press hard on the back of the drill so that the drill's tip is firmly embedded in the head of the screw. These screws are usually 2 inches long, and your predrilled hole is not that deep. It's easy to strip the head of the screw if you don't make sure the screwdriver tip is seated deeply in the head of the screw, put all your weight behind the battery-powered screwdriver, and go slowly.

14. DO A FINAL CHECK ON ALL THE SCREWS and toggle bolts with a handheld screwdriver.

15. SNAP THE END COVERS INTO PLACE. This sounds easy, but sometimes it's really difficult. If you're having trouble, try turning it, then press on it hard until it snaps on.

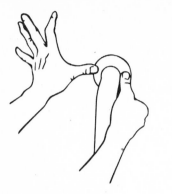 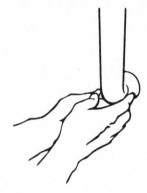

16. IF YOU INSTALLED YOUR GRAB BAR in tile, put some silicon caulk in your caulking gun and run a small bead of caulk around both end covers where they meet the tile. It's important to seal this joint so that water can't get behind the end covers and into the holes you made in the tile.

17. CONGRATULATIONS, YOU'RE DONE! Whether you installed these safety bars in your own home or in the home of an older person whom you love, you can feel confident that whoever is using them will be safer and feel more secure.

Bathroom Vanities

If you have an older-model bathroom vanity that is ugly but still in good shape, relax: There's a simple and inexpensive way to update it without having to replace it entirely. You can just paint it and change out your hardware. Some really wonderful paint products have been developed in recent years that make it easy to paint over both wood and Formica cabinets.

PRODUCT TIP: Bonding Primer is designed to stick to polyurethane/varnish. That means you can turn stained woodwork into painted woodwork without having to sand away all the old polyurethane/varnish first.

SHOPPING TIP: If you have a vanity made out of something other than wood, I suggest that you remove a drawer and take it with you to a good paint store: They'll tell you exactly what you need in order to paint it. Bring your drawer and door pulls with you when you go shopping for new ones too. If you're replacing all the knobs, it is quite easy to just get new ones. However, if you're replacing handles, you need to be more careful: There are two openings on the back of each handle that screws go into to hold the handle onto the drawer, and the holes on the new handle need to be the same distance apart as the holes on the old handle.

SPRUCING UP YOUR OLD VANITY

Tools you will need:

✔ Screwdriver
✔ Painting supplies (see "Painting the Woodwork" in Chapter 6)

Materials you will need:

✔ New drawer and door pulls
✔ TSP (Trisodium phosphate, a really strong detergent)
✔ One quart each of primer and paint (see Product Tip above.)

1. REMOVE ANY DRAWERS and doors on your vanity. The drawers should just pull out. Unscrew the door hinges from the cabinet face and then from the doors themselves. Place them in a bag or bowl for safekeeping.

2. CLEAN THE CABINET THOROUGHLY with TSP and hot water. Pay special attention to the areas around the door handles, and the wall nearest the toilet. Rinse the TSP off with clean water. Dry everything with a clean rag.

3. SAND THE ENTIRE SURFACE VERY LIGHTLY with a fine sanding sponge. Wipe the surface clean with a damp cloth, and then with a clean, dry cloth. Let it dry for 15 minutes.

4. APPLY PRIMER TO ALL THE CABINET surfaces, including drawer fronts and cabinet doors. Follow all the directions on the primer can and anything you learned from the folks at the paint store. You can do the backs of the cabinet doors after the fronts have dried.

5. LET THE PRIMER DRY, according to the directions on the primer can.

TIP: The directions on the sides of primer and paint cans are there for a reason. If you follow them, you will get the best results. But since most of us don't want to wait as long as the directions tell us to, it's a good idea to ask the pros at the paint store how long you really have to wait before applying the next coat, and then do what they say!

6. WHEN THE PRIMER IS DRY, apply your first coat of paint to all the surfaces. Let it dry.

7. MOST PRODUCTS REQUIRE a second coat. Make sure the first coat is dry before applying the second coat. Let it dry.

8. LET THE PAINT DRY FOR AT LEAST 24 hours before reattaching any hardware. If it's a humid time of year, you'll have to wait even longer.

IT HAPPENED TO ME ONCE: I freshened up kitchen cabinets for some delightful customers last summer. The week I chose to do the project, it was unseasonably wet and humid. I had to let the cupboard doors dry for five days before the paint was hard enough so I could reinstall the hardware and put the kitchen back together. If you rush this step, you'll end up with fingerprints and smudges in your paint. It's not worth it. Patience pays.

9. INSTALL THE NEW DOOR HANDLES by holding the handle up to the openings on the door and inserting the screw through the door and into the hole in the back of the handle. Start each screw by hand, and then tighten them with a screwdriver.

NOTE: Sometimes the screws that come with the hardware will not be long enough to go through the drawer fronts, which can be extra thick. If this happens, try using the screws from your old handles: They'll be the right length and will probably work in the new handles. If they don't, you'll have to make a quick trip to the hardware store for longer ones.

10. REINSTALL THE DRAWERS. (This is a great opportunity to clean out those drawers. You may be amazed to find out what is lurking in their depths.)

11. CONGRATULATIONS—you've freshened up the look of your old bathroom vanity for a fraction of the cost of a new one!

FINAL THOUGHTS ON NON-WATER-RELATED BATHROOM PROJECTS

In the big picture of your life, tight towel bars and a new medicine cabinet are probably not high on your priority list of "things that need to be changed so that I'll be happier." But over the years I've discovered that fixing loose towel bars and toilet paper holders, changing vanity hardware, and installing grab bars gives many women a sense of completion and satisfaction. After having read this chapter, you now have the ability to take care of the annoying little problems in your bathroom (and other rooms in your house) that are distracting and frustrating on a daily basis. I hope that successfully completing these projects gives you the same pleasure and peace of mind that it gives me. And if you struggled with any of these projects, remember to have patience with yourself. These are new skills, and they will get easier with repetition.

9.MINOR CARPENTRY JOBS

When I think of carpentry projects, I think of projects involving wood. However, many carpenters today also work with wallboard, tile, windows, and more. Still, if you ask them what they love to do above anything else, it always comes down to working with wood. It's the same for me: There's something about the look, feel, and smell of wood that draws me in. It feels alive and forgiving to me, and some of my best memories of helping my dad in his workshop as a child are associated with the smell of sawdust and wood shavings.

My siblings and I helped my dad build furniture for our dining room and living room when I was in grade school. My favorite projects today are still the ones where I get to use wood as the solution to a problem, or where I get to improve the look of someone's home using wood as the medium.

Most projects that involve wood are best done with the help of power tools, including saws, sanders, and drills. Many women are afraid of power saws; I certainly was, until I learned how to use them safely and correctly. I sincerely hope that after reading this chapter and trying a couple of carpentry projects, you'll feel comfortable and safe using power tools. I also hope that you'll love working with wood just as much as I do.

Most carpentry projects around the house fall into one of three categories: repairing or replacing existing wood, installing a new wood feature, and modifying existing wood. In this chapter we will tackle at least one project in each category. I chose these specific projects for two reasons:

1. THEY ARE WELL WITHIN THE SCOPE of a beginning carpenter. With each of these projects, you'll have a chance to learn and practice basic carpentry skills: project planning, purchasing materials, accurate measuring, cutting, and installing wood vertically and horizontally.

2. THEY WILL ALLOW YOU TO BECOME familiar with a nice range of power tools and will show you what they can do.

The skills used to complete these projects will give you a base of skill and knowledge that you can then use to take on more complex projects around your house. Here are the projects we'll cover in this chapter:

1. INSTALLING NEW WOOD
- ✔ Making a simple shelf
- ✔ Building and installing a new handrail on your stairs

2. REPLACING EXISTING WOOD
- ✔ Upgrading your window or door trim
- ✔ Replacing loose, rotten, or broken stair treads

3. MODIFYING EXISTING WOOD
- ✔ Installing a cat/dog door

Getting Empowered with Power Tools

My ability to complete projects successfully increased dramatically when I learned how to use power tools. Power tools allow me to make more accurate cuts, work more efficiently, and reduce the physical energy I expend. I have the utmost respect for the craftsmen of old who completed amazingly intricate woodworking projects with only hand tools; however, I feel no need to eschew technology in this arena. . . . I embrace it, and I hope you will as well.

At some point you may decide to purchase some of the tools I will describe here, but there is no need to do that until you have decided whether or not you like working with a certain tool. Every tool imaginable is available for rent at your local rental center, and you can always borrow from a friend or family member.

In Chapter 2, I introduced you to a battery-powered drill and a random orbital palm sander. Now I will introduce you to my favorite power saws—circular saws, jigsaws, and compound miter saws—and I'll talk about how to use each one safely.

CIRCULAR SAWS

A circular saw is a handheld saw with a round blade that spins at a high rate of speed. As you firmly push the saw through the wood, the blade makes a cut.

Circular saws are available in battery-powered and electric versions, and they come with different-size saw blades. The most common saw you'll see has a blade that's 7¼ inches in diameter. This

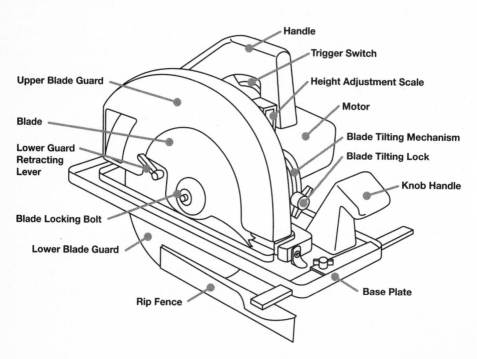

size saw may be too heavy for some women. The smaller saws have a 5¼-inch blade and are lighter, and they're fine for small jobs.

USING A CIRCULAR SAW:

ADJUSTING BLADE DEPTH: Circular saws all have a mechanism that allows you to adjust the amount of blade that shows beneath the plate (the plate is the hard, plastic base of the saw that rests on the wood). Make sure that you only have as much blade showing as you need to cut through your piece of wood. Too much blade is unsafe.

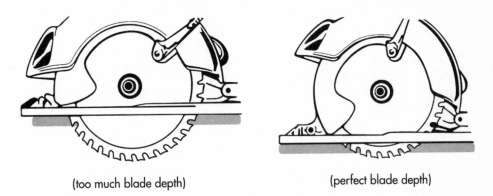

(too much blade depth)   (perfect blade depth)

For example, if you're cutting ¾-inch plywood, you want about 1 inch of blade showing. Once you have adjusted the blade depth, remember to lock the adjustment in place.

ADJUSTING THE BLADE ANGLE: Most circular saws allow you to adjust the blade to make cuts of less than 90 degrees. All of our projects will be completed with the blade at 90 degrees, so always check to see that the blade is in its full upright and locked position at 90 degrees.

GETTING TO KNOW THE TRIGGER: All circular saws have a trigger button, and when you pull it toward you, the saw blade starts to spin. Some saws have a safety trigger release as well, which has to be engaged before the real trigger button will work. If your saw has this second button, you'll have to depress it with your thumb while pulling on the regular trigger with your pointer or middle finger.

HOW TO STAND: Body placement is very important when working with all saws. When you're using a circular saw, it is vital to make sure that your body is well balanced, with your weight settled in your hips and legs. Your body should *never* be directly behind the saw; saw blades occasionally catch, causing the saw to kick back, and if your body is behind the saw, it will kick into you. To prevent that from happening, position your body slightly off to the side.

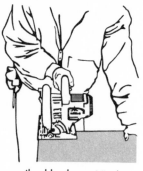

(bad body position)   (good body position)

I'm right-handed, so when I use a circular saw, the saw is always just to the right of my right hip. Whether it's to the left or to the right, always make sure your body is to one side of the saw while the saw is in motion.

PLACEMENT OF THE SAW ON THE WOOD: The large plate (rectangular, not round) at the base of the saw is designed to sit flat on the piece of wood being cut. Many beginning saw users forget this, and they tend to tip the saw slightly left or right or hold it just above the wood surface.

Wrong Ways to Place Saw on Wood

(tipping the base of the saw)   (lifting the base of the saw)

Make sure that the saw plate is always in solid contact with the wood being cut.

SECURING THE WOOD BEING CUT: If both of your hands are on the saw, you have no hands left to hold the piece of wood being cut in place. Use clamps or have someone else hold the wood for you so it doesn't start to move as you begin cutting.

MAKING THE CUT: Each circular saw has some sort of mark on the plate in front of the saw blade; it's there to help you align the saw blade with the mark you have made on the wood indicating where you want to make the cut. Get to know this mark, and learn to trust it.

Make sure the blade is not in contact with the wood when you pull the trigger. Instead, it should be about ½ of an inch from the edge of the wood. If the blade is touching the wood when you turn the saw on, it may damage the wood or jump a bit.

FINISHING THE CUT: Make sure you move the saw all the way through the wood being cut, from the front edge to the far edge. Do not stop pushing the saw forward until the part of the wood you are cutting off falls to the ground. You can set something under this piece of wood to catch it if you like.

PRACTICING: None of what I'm saying will make much sense to you until you put it into action. Pick up some scrap wood of different lengths and widths and make a bunch of practice cuts until you are comfortable with your circular saw.

JIGSAWS

A jigsaw is also a handheld saw, but its blade is small and rectangular, and it has jagged teeth on one side.

The jigsaw blade moves up and down at a high speed and cuts through wood as the saw operator moves the saw forward. The small blade on a jigsaw allows for smaller, more intricate cuts than a circular saw is capable of. A jigsaw puzzle is so named because a jigsaw is used to cut its intricately shaped pieces.

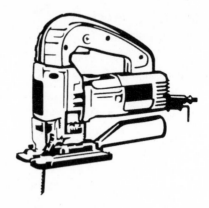

Jigsaws are available in electric and battery-operated styles. Saw blades with lots of little teeth are used for fine cuts, and blades with fewer teeth are used for rough cuts. A jigsaw is one of the easier and least frightening of the power saws, but it takes some practice to learn how to control one.

USING A JIGSAW:

INSTALLING THE BLADE: Each jigsaw has a slightly different mechanism for this process. Usually there's something located on the front of the saw that you either need to lift or pull; while you lift/pull it, insert the blade—with its teeth facing away from the saw—with your other hand. When you release the mechanism, the blade will be locked in place.

SAFETY NOTE: Always unplug the saw when installing a new blade.

GETTING TO KNOW THE TRIGGER: Most jigsaws have only one trigger button. When you pull on the trigger, the blade starts to move up and down. The pressure you put on the trigger determines the speed of the blade movement. It's very similar to stepping on the accelerator in your car.

HOW TO STAND: Make sure you are well balanced and that the area around your feet is clear. Again, the saw should be off to the side of your body, and you should be positioned so that you can see the movement of the blade.

PLACEMENT OF THE SAW ON THE WOOD: The plate on the base of the jigsaw needs to be set down firmly on the surface of the wood being cut.

Keep the plate in contact with the wood surface at all times during the cut. This solid contact will reduce vibrations and ensure a cleaner cut.

SECURE THE WOOD BEING CUT: Use clamps or get a helper to hold the wood in place

MAKING THE CUT: Align the front of the saw blade with your pencil mark, pull the trigger, and move the saw blade into the wood slowly.

You cannot rush this cut. The blade needs to have time to get through the wood in front of it. A steady speed is best, and you'll need to slow down for any cuts that are curved.

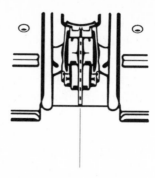

FINISHING THE CUT: Move the saw forward until the blade reaches the end of your pencil line. Then you can turn the saw off and lift the blade away from the wood.

PRACTICING: Jigsaws are fun to use but can be frustrating until you learn how to control them. Get some extra wood, and practice, practice, practice.

COMPOUND MITER SAWS

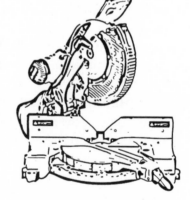

The compound miter saw is the power tool that makes good carpentry work possible for amateurs. This saw replaces the miter box, which is a unique box made of wood or plastic that allows you to cut accurate angles with a special hand saw. The compound miter saw is a stationary saw, so rather than moving the whole saw through the wood (as with the two previous saws), with this saw, the only thing that moves is the blade. Its nickname is the "chop saw" because its blade chops wood in two pieces when you lower the saw down onto it.

The magic of this saw is that it allows you to cut wood at an angle, and to do it accurately. In order to cut wood for window or door trim, chair rails, or picture frames, you need to be able to cut two pieces of wood at a 45-degree angle and then put them together to make a 90-degree corner. Cutting those pieces of wood by hand in a miter box is very challenging, and it takes a lot of practice to do well. Cutting those same pieces of wood with a compound miter saw, however, is simple—once you know how to use the saw. After some practice, you'll get so good at it that you'll be running around your house looking for more places to add wood trim!

USING THE COMPOUND MITER SAW:

SETTING UP THE SAW: Since this is a stationary saw, it needs to be set up in a location where it will be stable and where its parts can move freely. I usually set mine up on a piece of plywood balanced over two sawhorses, on a workbench, or (when I'm feeling lazy) on the floor. The floor works fine, but you have to get down on your knees to make all the cuts. These saws are quite heavy, so you don't want to move it around more than you have to.

ADJUSTING THE SAW ANGLE: Herein lies the magic of this saw. A knob or lever on the front of the saw allows you to move the blade to the left or right. Angle markings on the saw tell you when the blade is at the desired angle, be it 22.5, 35, 45, or any other degree. Once the blade is at the location you want, it can be locked in place. The locking method varies with each saw.

GETTING TO KNOW THE TRIGGER: Your saw may have a trigger button *and* a safety button. If so, you have to depress the safety button for the trigger to work. The speed on a compound miter saw is not variable; it's either on or it's off.

HOW TO STAND: Body placement for this saw is different from that of the circular saw and the jigsaw. Since this saw is stationary and really can't kick or jump, it's safe (and necessary) to put your body directly in front of it. Stand with your weight in your feet and hips, with one hand on the trigger and the other hand holding the wood at a safe distance from the saw blade.

PLACEMENT OF THE SAW ON THE WOOD: In this case you are actually placing the wood on the saw. The wood you're going to cut rests on the large, flat surface beneath the saw blade. Place the wood so that your pencil mark indicating where the cut should happen lies about where you think the saw blade will be. Move the wood around as necessary to line the pencil mark up with the saw blade. Some compound miter saws have a laser light that indicates exactly where the saw blade will fall. I suffer from saw envy every time I see them! If yours doesn't have a laser, lower the saw blade *without* engaging the trigger first to check the location of the blade on the wood. Keep adjusting the wood until you're satisfied that the blade will cut your line.

SECURING THE WOOD BEING CUT: Put one hand on the trigger and use the other hand to hold the wood firmly against the backstop so that it's perfectly square to the saw blade.

MAKING THE CUT: Once the wood is in place and your second hand is well out of range of the saw blade, engage the trigger and *slowly* lower the moving saw blade into the wood. Most beginners using these saws tend to move the blade down too quickly, trying to force it through the wood. This can result in a bad cut and a burned-out saw. Always go slowly.

FINISHING THE CUT: These cuts do not take long, even when you're moving slowly. Take the blade all the way through the wood and then raise it back up. Take your finger off of the trigger and remove the wood.

PRACTICING: As with the other two saws, practice is the only way to get comfortable working with this saw. Extra practice is needed to get used to moving the saw blade and cutting at angles other than 90 degrees.

GENERAL RULES OF SAW USE

I'll talk more about how to use each of these saws in the projects that follow, but I will say a few words here. First: Safety, safety, safety! I'm going to repeat something I said in Chapter 1 about tools: I have never hurt myself while using a power tool, but that's because I am

IT HAPPENED TO ME ONCE: My dad came to visit recently and he worked with me on a big project for one of my clients. While he was working with me, Romeo discovered that the blades in both my compound miter saw and portable table saw were dull. I was given a lecture I had heard many times before about dull saw blades and how they ruin saws. He was right, of course. I tend to get a little lazy about the blades on those saws because they are more time consuming to change than the blades on a circular or jig saw. I learned my lesson (again), though, and I will be sure to change all my saw blades before Romeo comes to visit again. Before he left that last time, he also sharpened all the knives in my kitchen. Aren't dads the best?

hyperaware of the potential damage that they could do. The most important things to remember when using power saws are:

1. ALWAYS wear safety goggles.

2. ALWAYS KNOW EXACTLY where both your hands are, and be sure they are nowhere near the saw blade.

3. KEEP THE AREA AROUND your feet clear. When working with a circular or jigsaw, you don't want to have to look down and check your steps while you are moving the saw.

4. KEEP AN EYE ON THE SAW'S electrical cord, if it has one. Make sure it will be able to move freely through the entire cut. If it gets caught or snagged on something, it will pull against the saw, and you won't be able to complete the cut.

5. BE SURE TO UNPLUG and put all saws away and out of the reach of children after use.

Each of the power tools required to complete the projects in this chapter are available for rent at your local rental center, or you may have a friend who will loan you her tools. If you borrow from a friend, ask her how new the blades are in her saw. If she can't remember, it might be worth it to you to purchase a new saw blade to use for your projects—it's impossible to make good cuts with dull saw blades. Take the saw with you to the hardware store and ask for help in purchasing and replacing the blade. Most places will be happy to help you.

Project Management

When you're planning a carpentry project, the two most important aspects of project management are (1) determining how much and what kind of materials you will need, and (2) figuring out what tools will be required to complete the project.

BUYING WOOD

When purchasing wood for the kinds of projects we'll cover in this chapter, you'll need to know how to calculate the total amount of linear feet you will use. Linear feet are the total amount of wood measured (in feet) that would be used if all the wood were laid out end to end in a long line. For example: I want to install chair rail in a room that is 10ft long by 8ft wide. How much chair rail wood do I purchase?

8 feet x 2 = 16 feet
10 feet x 2 = 20 feet
16 feet + 20 feet = 36 feet

The maximum amount of chair rail trim I would need to use is 36 feet. However, I always purchase at least 10 percent more wood to allow for mistakes.

10% of 36 feet = 3.6 feet (round up to 4 feet)
36 feet + 4 feet = 40 feet

I would purchase 40 linear feet of chair rail trim. Most lumber yards and home centers sell wood in 8-foot, 10-foot or 16-foot lengths. So, for this project, I would either purchase four 10-foot pieces or five 8-foot pieces.

 **SHOPPING TIP:** Most lumber yards or home centers will take returns on unused pieces of wood if they meet a minimum length requirement. That requirement is usually 8 feet. It never hurts to purchase at least one extra 8-foot length of wood to have on hand just in case—you can always return it if you don't end up needing it.

FINISHING WOOD

The final step in most projects involving wood is applying a finish to seal and protect the wood. Even though it's the final step in the building project, it's one of the first steps in the planning process, because the choice of finish will affect your choice of wood. If the wood is going to be finished with oil, stain, and/or polyurethane, then the type and quality of the wood will be visible through the finish. With these finishes, you'll probably want to use a higher-quality wood.

If the wood is going to be painted to match other wood in the room, then a lower-quality wood can be used. When purchasing wood from the lumber yard or home center, tell the person helping you how you plan to finish the wood. This will help them direct you to the appropriate wood choices.

FIGURING OUT WHICH TOOLS YOU WILL NEED

You are going to use tools to transform the wood you purchase into a finished project. In order to determine which tools you will need, you have to figure out what kinds of cuts will be required:

CROSS CUTS are used to shorten the length of a piece of wood. If you purchase a 4-foot-long piece of wood and you want it to be 3 feet long, you need to make a cross cut. Cross cuts can be made with a hand saw, a circular saw, or a miter saw. Miter saws are limited in the width of board they can cross-cut. You'll have to experiment to determine your compound miter saw's width limitation.

RIP CUTS are used to change the width of a piece of wood. If your piece of wood is 8 inches wide and you need it to be 6 inches wide, you'll have to make a cut along the length of the wood to remove 2 inches from its width. Rip cuts are best done with a circular saw or a table saw.

MITER CUTS are used to cut angles in wood. When you purchase wood, the ends are cut at 90 degrees. In order to turn that wood into window or door trim, you'll have to cut some ends at a 45 degree angle. Miter cuts can be made with a handsaw and a miter box, but I recommend a compound miter saw.

MISCELLANEOUS CUTS such as curves and circles are used to make finer decorative cuts in wood. A jigsaw is required to make these odd shapes.

OTHER TOOLS YOU'LL NEED
Once you have completed a few carpentry projects you will begin to see a pattern of tools that are generally needed. Some projects will need additional tools, but these are the basics:

CARPENTER'S TOOL KIT
✔ Saws (circular, jig, compound miter, and handheld
✔ Speed square or straight edge
✔ Steel measuring tape
✔ Pencil
✔ Hammer
✔ Safety goggles
✔ Nailset
✔ Sander (power or hand)
✔ Glue
✔ Wood filler for nail holes
✔ Paint, oil, stain, and/or polyurethane
✔ Paintbrushes (small craft paintbrush and 2½-inch sash brush)
✔ Putty knife
✔ Stud finder

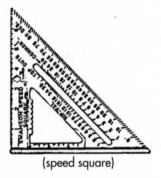
(speed square)

Building a Simple Shelf
PLANNING FOR MATERIALS
We're going to construct our shelf from a piece of ¾-inch-thick birch veneer plywood and a piece of ¾-inch pine trim (to cover the cut

edges). Plywood makes great shelving, because it is strong enough to resist sagging and is relatively inexpensive. The only downside of plywood is that the cut edges are ugly, and the three sides of the shelf that will show will need to be covered. Our shelf is going to be 3 feet long and 10 inches wide before we add the trim. Plywood is usually sold in large sheets, but it's available in most home centers in a smaller, "craft" size.

Determining how much wood to buy for trimming the edges of the plywood requires some simple math. The edge of the shelf that will be against the wall does not require trim, so that leaves the remaining three edges to cover. Since this is a small project, we'll calculate the total number of inches needed and convert that to feet.

36 inches + 10 inches + 10 inches= 56 inches
56 inches divided by 12 inches = 4.67 feet of trim

We should buy 6 feet to ensure that we have enough, but we may have to buy 8 feet if that's the minimum length sold.

BUILDING A SIMPLE SHELF
Materials you will need:
- ✔ A small sheet of ¾-inch birch veneer plywood
- ✔ 6 feet of ¾-inch trim molding
- ✔ 1½-inch finish nails
- ✔ Carpenter's glue
- ✔ Sanding sponges
- ✔ Straight edge
- ✔ Pencil
- ✔ Steel measuring tape

Tools you will need:
In order to determine what tools will be required, we have to think through the steps of the project and make a list of the tools needed for each step.

1. Cut the plywood down to the correct width (make a rip cut):
CIRCULAR SAW

2. Cut the plywood to the correct length (make a cross cut): **CIRCULAR SAW**

3. Cut the trim with miter edges: **COMPOUND MITER SAW**

4. Attach the trim to the plywood: **HAMMER**

5. Bury the nailheads so they can't be seen: **NAILSET**

6. Smooth everything out: **SANDPAPER**

7. Finish up with paint or stain and polyurethane: **PAINTBRUSH**

Hopefully we've thought of everything we will need, but we may discover partway through the project that we forgot something. Don't worry, this happens all the time! It's nothing a quick trip to the hardware store can't fix.

MEASURING, MARKING, AND CUTTING PLYWOOD

1. PUT ON YOUR SAFETY goggles and sharpen your pencil.

2. USE YOUR STEEL TAPE to measure 36 inches down the length of the board at one edge.

3. MAKE A "V" MARK there with your pencil.

A **V** mark makes for a more accurate cut than simple lines (shown on the next page). Pencil lines tend to be crooked, or they end up very wide.

4. REPEAT THE PROCESS along the opposite edge.

5. LAY A STRAIGHT EDGE along the tips of the **V** marks and make a line across the board by resting your pencil against a straight edge. A "straight edge" is anything that you can trust has a truly straight, not warped, edge. I often use my 48-inch level as a straight edge.

6. DOUBLE-CHECK THAT EACH end of the line is 36 inches from the farthest end of the plywood.

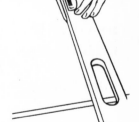

7. MEASURE ACROSS THE PLYWOOD at three different points and make a **V** mark at 10 inches.

8. USE A STRAIGHT EDGE to connect the **V**'s.

9. DOUBLE-CHECK YOUR MEASUREMENTS. You should now have a pencil drawing of a 36- by 10-inch rectangle on your plywood.

10. MAKE ANY adjustments needed.

11. USE THE CIRCULAR SAW to make the rip cut down the length of the board along your 10-inch mark.

12. USE THE CIRCULAR SAW to make the cross cut along the 36-inch mark.

13. YOU SHOULD NOW HAVE a piece of plywood that is 36 inches by 10 inches.

CUTTING THE TRIM MOLDING

1. SET UP THE COMPOUND MITER saw for a 45-degree cut to the right side.

2. PLACE THE PIECE OF PINE TRIM wood on the saw and make the cut near the right end of the wood.

3. THE MITER CUT NOW HAS an inside (or short) edge and a long (or outside) edge. Measure exactly 36 inches over from the inside edge and make a mark there with your pencil.

4. MOVE THE SAW BLADE TO the left and lock it in at 45 degrees.

5. MAKE A CUT JUST TO THE LEFT of your mark, leaving the pencil line visible.

6. SET THE PIECE OF TRIM against the plywood and see if it fits.

7. IF IT IS SLIGHTLY LONG, you can cut a tiny bit off of the left side.

8. REPEAT THE PROCESS FOR THE TWO 10-inch pieces of wood that will be attached to either end of the plywood shelf. These pieces will have a miter edge that meets the trim across the front of the shelf, and a straight edge that lines up with the back of the shelf.

IMPORTANT NOTE: When cutting trim with a miter saw, it's important to make sure the trim is always oriented in the same direction for every cut. I usually put the widest part of the trim on the saw base and cut from the thinnest part into the thickest part. It's easy to get slightly dyslexic when using a miter saw, at least for me!

Always double-check to make sure you are cutting your angle in the correct direction. If you cut the angle the wrong way, that piece of wood will probably have to be tossed out. You can make practice cuts in scrap wood to make sure you have the "right" angle down.

ASSEMBLING THE SHELF

1. USE YOUR SANDING BLOCK to lightly sand the edges of the plywood and the cut ends of the three trim pieces. Don't sand away the sharpness of the edges; just remove any small splinters of wood.

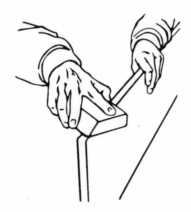

2. PLACE A THIN BEAD OF GLUE on the long cut edge of the plywood. A little glue goes a long way.

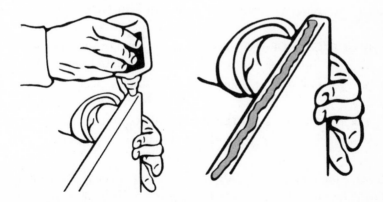

3. SMOOTH OUT THE GLUE WITH A FINGER (my tool of choice, which is why all my work pants are covered in glue, paint, and caulk) or a small craft paintbrush.

4. SET THE LONG PIECE OF TRIM on the plywood edge, making sure the corners meet up nicely.

5. USE YOUR HAMMER AND ABOUT five finish nails to attach the trim to the plywood. Place a nail about 1 inch from each end, one nail in the middle, and the last two nails between the center nail and the end nails.

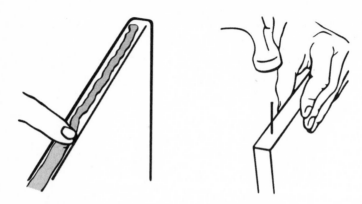

Hammer the nails through the thickest part of the trim, and don't place any nails closer than a full inch from the end. Any closer and you might split the trim. Stop hammering when about $\frac{1}{8}$ of an inch of nailhead remains visible above the wood surface.

6. HOLD THE TIP OF THE NAILSET on the head of the nail. Apply the hammer to the other end of the nailset and slowly drive down the head of the nail until it is just below the surface of the wood.

7. ATTACH THE TWO SHORTER PIECES of trim to the ends of the shelf with the same process, using three nails for each piece.

NOTE: You might be wondering why you're using both glue and nails. The glue will actually be doing the bulk of the work, but the nails will hold the wood until the glue is firmly set. Together they give a better result than just one of them alone can.

FINISHING THE SHELF
1. COVER THE NAILHEADS with a small amount of wood filler. You can use a putty knife for this, but I find (once again) that my finger does a better job.

2. LET THE WOOD filler dry.

3. SAND THE ENTIRE SURFACE of the shelf and all the trim pieces with a fine sanding sponge.

4. REMOVE ALL THE DUST with a vacuum cleaner or soft rag.

5. WHEN THE SHELF IS FREE OF ANY DUST, you can finish it with primer and a couple of coats of paint, or stain and polyurethane. Be sure to repeat steps 3 and 4 after the first coat of primer or polyurethane.

6. HANG THE SHELF ACCORDING the directions for hanging a shelf with brackets in Chapter 3.

7. PAT YOURSELF ON THE BACK! You are now a carpenter.

Installing A New Handrail

A handrail on a stairway is, first and foremost, a safety item. As such, it needs to be made of a sturdy piece of wood and firmly attached to the wall in several places. Some state building codes require that both ends of the handrail include returns. A "return" is the part of the handrail that curves in toward the wall on either end (as seen in the sketch below). Returns prevent things like purses and hanging belts from getting caught on the end of the handrail and causing a fall.

(this is an ornate oak handrail with a curved return)

Our handrail will be of a simple design and will include a 90-degree return.

PLANNING FOR MATERIALS

Our handrail is going to be made of a relatively simple handrail stock. We'll also need hardware to attach the handrail to the wall. The wood will also need to be sealed with primer and paint, or stain and/or polyurethane.

INSTALLING A NEW HANDRAIL

Tools you will need:

All the tools needed to complete this project are included in the carpenter's tool kit list on page 238, with the exception of a power drill and drill bits.

Materials you will need:

✔   1 piece of handrail (needs to be about 2 feet longer than the stairwell)
✔   1½-inch finish nails
✔   Sanding sponge
✔   Paint or stain and polyurethane
✔   Glue
✔   Wood filler
✔   Hardware for attaching the handrail to the wall
✔   Piece of string and 2 tacks
✔   Blue painter's tape

WHERE TO PUT THE HANDRAIL

A handrail should be installed at a height that's comfortable for the people who will be using it. A simple way to determine that height is to stand at the top of the stairs with your arm bent slightly at the elbow. Wherever your hand ends up when you do that is where the top of the handrail should go. Make a pencil mark at this height.

Walk down the stairs and, standing on the bottom step, repeat this process. Make another pencil mark. Connect your two pencil marks with a piece of string and two tacks or nails.

FINDING THE STUDS

It is very important that the hardware you use to attach your handrail to the wall be screwed directly into the wall's studs; it's the safest and sturdiest way to secure the railing to the wall.

1. MOVE YOUR ELECTRONIC STUD finder along the wall, just under your string. Make a pencil mark at both edges of each stud. You won't be using all of the studs for your hardware, but you need to know where each one is so you can determine the best location for your hardware supports.

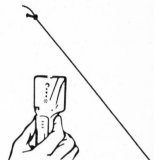

2. MAKE A SPECIAL MARK AT THE STUDS located closest to the two ends of your string. Your top and bottom supports will go here. Additional support hardware will be spread out along the other studs, one every 3 to 4 feet or so. The location of the studs determines the location of the hardware, so it's hard to say precisely where they'll end up. What you want is for the hardware to look as evenly distributed as possible.

INSTALLING THE SUPPORT HARDWARE

For each stud where you have decided to install a hardware support, you'll do the following:

1. HOLD THE PIECE OF HARDWARE against the wall at the location of the stud, with the top of the hardware resting just under the string.

2. MAKE SURE THE HARDWARE IS straight, then use a pencil to mark the screw holes.

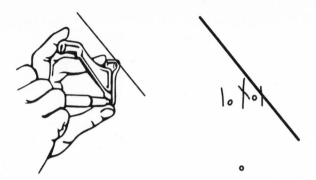

3. USE A DRILL BIT THAT IS SLIGHTLY smaller in diameter than your screws to predrill the marks at each screw hole.

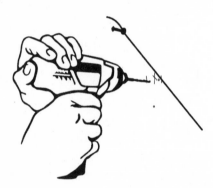

4. REPLACE THE DRILL BIT with a screwdriver bit and screw the hardware into place.

CUTTING THE HANDRAIL TO LENGTH

There is no formula for exactly how long a handrail should be. The most important thing is that you find a handrail when you put your hand down looking for support. If it's too short, it will be uncomfortable and possibly unsafe. One option is to lay your uncut handrail on the supports you have just installed and see where a good starting and ending point seems to be.

1. DETERMINE HOW LONG YOU want your handrail to be, and mark that measurement on your piece of handrail with a pencil.

2. USE YOUR SPEED SQUARE on each end of the handrail to mark opposing 45-degree angles.

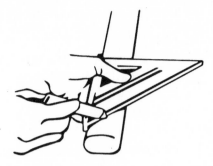

3. DOUBLE-CHECK THAT THE LENGTH of the handrail is still correct if you measure from the outside edge of one angle to the outside edge of the opposing angle.

IMPORTANT NOTE: If you have cut your angles in the wrong direction, the handrail will no longer be the right length. This is a mistake you want to find before you make your cuts!

4. SET THE HANDRAIL UNDER THE COMPOUND miter saw, resting the bottom of the handrail on the bed of the saw. Use your compound miter saw to make your 45-degree cuts on each end of the handrail.

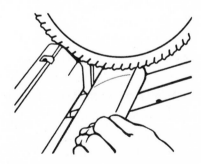

ATTACHING THE HANDRAIL TO THE HARDWARE

It's helpful to have another set of hands for this step, if possible. I've done it alone many times, but it's just easier if you have someone else to hold the handrail in place while you fuss with the hardware.

1. REST THE CUT HANDRAIL ON the hardware that has been attached to the wall, making sure that the bottom of the handrail is resting on the top of the hardware.

2. PLACE THE CURVED PIECE OF hardware over the top of the wall hardware and against the underside of the handrail. Use a pencil to mark the screw holes in the bottom of the handrail. Do this at each hardware location.

3. REMOVE THE HANDRAIL and set it on a flat surface. Predrill at each screw hole you just marked. Be careful to only drill in about ¾ of an inch; *you do not want to drill all the way through the handrail.*

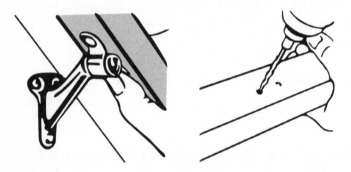

4. PLACE THE HANDRAIL BACK on the support hardware and attach it using the screws and clips provided. Repeat for each set of support hardware. Be patient, and take your time. This sounds really easy, but I find that it is harder than it seems it should be. I think it's because you're working at a difficult angle.

CUTTING AND INSTALLING RETURNS

1. AT THE TOP OF THE HANDRAIL, use your steel tape to measure from the wall to the outside edge of the handrail. This will be the length of your return at its longest point.

2. TRANSFER THIS MEASUREMENT to a piece of the leftover handrail with a pencil, and make sure that your angle is going in the correct direction.

3. CHECK, CHECK AND DOUBLE-CHECK! (You may have guessed by now that I have made this mistake more than once, and that I am trying to save you a return trip to the lumber yard for another piece of handrail stock!)

4. USE YOUR COMPOUND MITER SAW to cut the return to the correct length.

5. REPEAT STEPS 1 THROUGH 4 for the return at the bottom of the stairs.

6. CHECK THE FIT OF YOUR PIECE by setting it in place at the top of the handrail.

7. IF IT'S SLIGHTLY LONG, TAKE THE EXTRA off the straight edge. If it's slightly short, don't sweat it. It will be fine.

8. APPLY AN EVEN LAYER OF WOOD GLUE to the angled, cut surface of the return and place it against the cut edge of the handrail. The two pieces should fit perfectly together.

9. USE SOME BLUE PAINTER'S TAPE to hold the pieces together while the glue dries.

IMPORTANT NOTE: If your return is just a tiny bit short, you can still use it. Place a folded over piece of paper or cardboard to act as a shim between the end of the return and the wall to hold it in place while it dries.

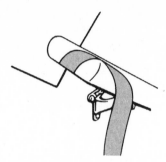

10. ONCE THE GLUE HAS DRIED, predrill a small hole through the handrail into the return, being careful not to drill all the way through the return. Nail a small finish nail into the hole you made with the drill.

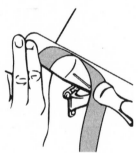

11. TAP IT FURTHER IN WITH a nailset and cover the hole with some wood putty.

FINISHING TOUCHES

You may need to smooth out the joint where the return meets the handrail with a little sandpaper and then touch up your paint or stain and polyurethane finish.

Other than that, you're done—congratulations! Each time you walk up or down your stairs, you will be able to enjoy the comfort given to you by your safe and stable handrail.

IT HAPPENED TO ME ONCE: On more than one occasion, clients have asked me to install additional handrails where one already existed. In one case, I added a second handrail on the opposite side of the stairway, so my client could have both hands on handrails when climbing or descending her stairs. In another situation, I added a second handrail below the existing handrail for a toddler: He was just beginning to use the stairs, and his parents wanted him to have something to hold on to for extra balance. There is no end to the number of places that you can add a handrail if it will bring an added level of safety.

Replacing Existing Trim

The second basic category of carpentry projects that I want to help you with focuses on places in your home where you would like to replace existing wood, either because it's unsafe or because it's outdated or unattractive. A very common repair required in many homes is replacing a tread on a step that has cracked or rotted away. A simple (and relatively inexpensive) way to update your home is to replace your window, door, and baseboard trim. Many builders install the simplest, least expensive, and most generic trim when building homes. It's not necessarily ugly; it just does nothing to make the room special.

REPLACING EXISTING WINDOW OR DOOR TRIM

Tools you will need in addition to the carpenter's tool kit:
- ✔ Six-in-one painter's tool
- ✔ Small pry bar
- ✔ Larger pry bar
- ✔ Utility knife

Replacing interior trim is a great way to practice the basic carpentry skills we have covered so far in this chapter: measuring, making 90-degree and 45-degree cuts, nailing, filling nail holes, and finishing.

But a new skill—demolition—is required for this project. In order to replace the old trim with new trim, you have to remove the old trim first. Let's start there.

REMOVING EXISTING TRIM

No matter what kind of trim you're removing— window, door, or baseboard—the removal process is the same. For this example, we'll be taking off the trim around an interior doorway:

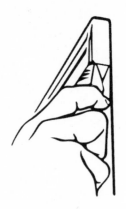

1. USE YOUR UTILITY KNIFE TO SCORE around the outside edge of the trim, where the trim meets the wall. Often this gap has been filled with caulk; the caulk will hold the trim to the wall, making it difficult to remove. Scoring this area will cut the caulk and also the paint, reducing the damage that is sometimes inflicted upon the surrounding paint when woodwork is removed.

2. A FEW INCHES DOWN FROM THE TOP of the door trim, set the flat edge of the six-in-one tool against the seam where the leading edge of the trim meets the door frame. Use your hammer to tap the edge of the tool into the seam, creating a small gap.

3. MOVE 6 TO 10 INCHES DOWN, and repeat step 2, gently opening the space between the trim and the door frame. You're not trying to remove the trim yet, just prying it away a little at a time.

4. NOW MOVE TO THE OUTSIDE EDGE of the trim (where you made the cut with your utility knife). Repeat step 2 again, moving from the bottom of the door all the way up to the top.

5. INSERT YOUR SMALL PRY BAR (or large pry bar, if the space is big enough) into the opening you have created. Push down on the pry bar; the leverage you create should begin to move the trim farther away from the frame.

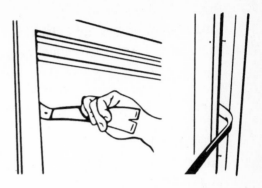

6. BY NOW YOU SHOULD BE ABLE TO SEE all the nails that are holding the trim to the frame. Put the pry bar close to the nails for greatest effect. In some cases, the nails will come out with the trim; in other cases, the trim will pop off and leave the nails behind. Either situation is okay!

7. KEEP WORKING WITH THE PRY BAR until you can pull the piece of trim off the frame.

8. REPEAT ON THE OTHER SIDE and top of the door frame.

9. ONCE ALL PIECES OF TRIM HAVE been removed, use your pry bar or hammer to remove any nails that are left behind. Sometimes it's impossible to get the nails out if their heads have been removed. If that happens, use your hammer to hit the nail farther into the wood until it's not sticking out.

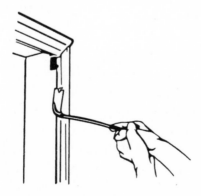

10. DOUBLE-CHECK TO MAKE SURE that all the nails have been removed or hammered in.

PLANNING FOR MATERIALS

Now that the old trim is gone, you can start the process of installing the new trim. Use your steel tape to measure up both sides and across the top of the doorway. Add the three lengths together, and then add a couple of extra feet for cutting purposes.

Tools you will need:

All the tools you need to complete this project are included in the carpenter's tool kit list on page 238, with the exception of a combination square.

SHOPPING TIP: You will have a wide variety of trim options at your local lumber yard or home center. Your choice is only limited by your budget and personal style. My only recommendation is that you learn how to select boards that are straight; many of the pieces of wood available in home centers have been picked over and left behind because they are warped.

When selecting pieces of trim, remove each piece of wood and hold it out in front of you. Look down its entire length while you rotate it in both directions. If it's noticeably warped, don't buy it. Shopping at a lumber yard where you can get help with your selections can sometimes be easier; it doesn't guarantee that you'll get straight wood, but at least you'll have someone helping you assess each piece.

PLACEMENT OF THE NEW TRIM

If the old trim came off without breaking, you can use it as a pattern for the new pieces of wood to be cut. Just lay the old wood on top of the new wood, making sure that the thicker edges of the trim are on the same side, and trace the outline of the cuts from the old wood onto the new wood. If the old wood isn't available to be used as a model, or if it broke during removal, then you'll have to measure and cut the new wood.

THE DEAL WITH REVEALS

If you look closely at existing window and door trim in your house, you'll notice that most of it is installed with about an ⅛ of an inch reveal. Instead of being set flush against the edge of the window frame, window trim is installed so that about ⅛ of an inch of the wood frame shows (is "revealed"). This is a decorative style that has become the norm over time, because it's more interesting than a flush installation.

MEASURING AND MARKING FOR YOUR REVEAL

You can use two different methods to measure and mark a reveal line:

1. SET A COMBINATION SQUARE AT ⅛ OF AN INCH and use it to trace a pencil line along all three sides of the doorway.

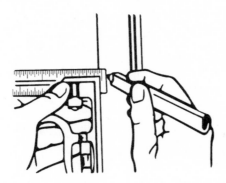

2. MEASURE ⅛ OF AN INCH FROM THE EDGE of the door frame at several locations. Lay a straight edge against your marks and trace a pencil line.

MEASURING AND CUTTING YOUR NEW TRIM

1. USE YOUR MITER SAW TO CUT A LENGTH of trim, making it about 3 inches longer than you will need. Make a straight 90-degree cut, not an angled cut.

2. SET THE PIECE OF TRIM IN PLACE along your reveal line.

3. MAKE A PENCIL MARK WHERE your trim's inside edge crosses the horizontal reveal line along the top of the door (it also helps to make a rough pencil mark at this time that shows you the direction your angle cut should go).

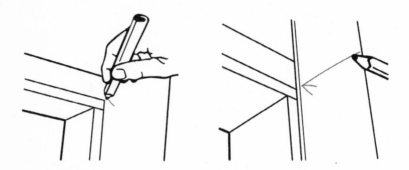

4. USE YOUR COMPOUND MITER SAW to make a 45-degree angle cut at your pencil mark. Your mark is the short end of the cut: You should cut from the short, inside edge of the angle to the long, outside edge of the angle.

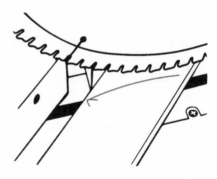

 IT HAPPENED TO ME (MORE THAN) ONCE: I have cut this angle the wrong direction many times. It's not a mistake you can recover from without purchasing more wood. Always double- and triple-check that you're cutting your angle in the right direction before you make the actual cut with the saw.

5. SET YOUR CUT PIECE OF TRIM BACK in place along the reveal line and tack it in place with two finish nails—one near the top, and one near the bottom. Don't hammer the nails all the way in yet.

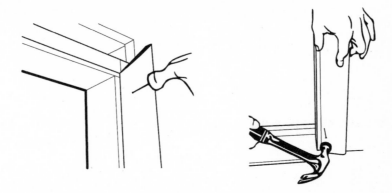

6. REPEAT STEPS 1 THROUGH 5 for the other side of the door frame. Remember that the angle cut will have to go in the opposite direction.

7. CUT A PIECE OF TRIM A FEW INCHES longer than you will need for the top trim piece.

8. LAY THE TRIM PIECE, *UPSIDE DOWN,* across the tops of the two pieces of side trim you have just installed.

9. MAKE A PENCIL MARK UP FROM the outside edge of each vertical trim piece where the horizontal piece crosses it. Now you know how long the top piece needs to be, and you just have to make marks for your miter cuts.

10. IF YOU LOOK AT YOUR TWO LONG side pieces of trim, you can see that the miter cuts on your top piece need to be cut to fit perfectly against your side pieces. Use your compound miter saw to make a 45-degree cut at each end of your top piece at your pencil marks. *Double- and triple-check the angle direction before you make the actual cut with the saw.*

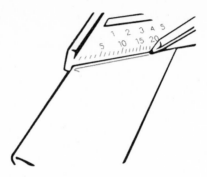

11. SET THE CUT PIECE INTO place and see if it fits.

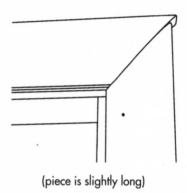

(piece is slightly long)

12. IF IT'S SLIGHTLY LONG, CUT A LITTLE bit off one end until it fits. If it's a tiny bit short, don't worry about it—you can fill it with some caulk later and no one will know any better.

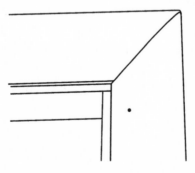

13. TACK THE TOP PIECE INTO place with a couple of finish nails.

14. ONCE YOU'RE HAPPY WITH THE FIT of all three pieces, you can finish nailing them in place. Use about five or six nails along each edge of each trim piece. Place the nails about ¼ of an inch in from the outside edge, and about 1 inch in from either end (to prevent splitting).

15. USE A NAILSET TO embed the heads of the nails.

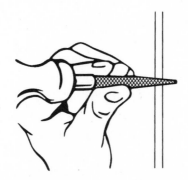

16. COVER THE NAILHEADS with wood filler.

17. LET THE WOOD FILLER DRY, sand it, and then paint or stain the trim.

Replacing a Stair Tread

Materials you will need:

✔ Enough wood or composite product to replace existing tread(s)
✔ 2½-inch long galvanized common nails or deck screws

SOMETHING NEW

All the tools needed for this project are included in the carpenter's tool kit listed on page 238, with the exception of the **CAT'S PAW**. A cat's paw is a specialized pry bar; it got its name because its tip looks like a cat's paw.

The tip is designed to be driven under the head of a nail that's embedded in a piece of wood. Set the tip of the cat's paw just next to the head of a nail, and bang on the back of it several times, hard, with a hammer. Once the tip is under part of the nailhead, pull back on the handle, and the nailhead will lift slightly out of the wood. Repeating this process several times allows you to get nails out of most pieces of wood. However, be warned that—like a real cat's paw—this tool does a lot of damage. It should only be used in demolition projects, when the wood being removed is going to be replaced. You will notice that I did not use a cat's paw on the interior door trim removal project: I was very careful to try to remove that wood with as little damage as possible, because door and window trim can be reinstalled or recycled at a new location. In this case, however, we don't care if the wood we're removing is going to be damaged.

Like the previous project, this one requires removing existing wood before cutting and installing new wood. This stair tread could be part of an interior or exterior stairway. For the purposes of this lesson, I am going to assume that our tread is the bottom step on an exterior stairway.

In the parts of the country that get lots of rain and snow, exterior stair treads receive a great deal of abuse. Replacing rotten or broken treads is a common item on to-do lists in the colder, wetter climates. The bottom tread often needs a cutaway so it fits around the handrail post; you'll have to use a jigsaw to make it. The new tools that you'll get to use for this project are a cat's paw (for removing old nails) and a jigsaw (for making unusual cuts). The skills you will learn on this project will be easily transferable to other projects, including repairing decking and exterior siding.

You're going to want to repair the wood that's damaged with the same kind of wood, if at all possible. The best way to do this is to remove the existing wood and take it with you to the lumber yard. Some stair treads are made of one piece of wood, but they are very often made of two pieces with a small space between them. If only one of the pieces is damaged, you'll only need to replace that one; however, for aesthetic reasons, you may choose to replace both pieces while you're at it.

LET'S RETREAD

1. REMOVE THE EXISTING PIECE of broken or rotten stair tread with a combination of a cat's paw, a hammer, and a regular pry bar. This just takes practice and elbow grease. Place the tip of the cat's paw next to the head of the nail, and bang on the back of the cat's paw with the hammer until the tip of the cat's paw is under the head of the nail.

2. USE THE CAT'S PAW AS a pry bar to start lifting the nail out of the wood.

3. IF THE CAT'S PAW DOESN'T GIVE you enough leverage, replace it with a pry bar. Repeat this process for each nailhead that you see.

4. PLACE THE END OF THE PRY BAR under the lip of the step and bang on it with the hammer. Use leverage to try and lift the old tread up. Once you start, you'll see opportunities to use the different tools as you go. Keep at it until you get the entire step up. It may come up in several pieces.

5. TAKE THE OLD MATERIAL WITH YOU to the lumber yard and buy enough of the same kind of wood to replace it. Exterior treads are often made of cedar or pressure-treated wood. Whatever you get, make sure the new piece is a little bit longer than the old one.

6. IF YOU WERE ABLE TO GET THE OLD tread off in one piece, you can use it as a template for the new piece; just lay it on top of the new wood and trace where to make your cuts.

7. IF THE ORIGINAL PIECE BROKE, you will have to take measurements and transfer them onto the new piece of wood using a speed square and a straight edge.

8. USE YOUR CIRCULAR SAW TO CUT the board to length. Make sure to set the blade depth about ¾-inch deeper than the thickness of the wood. Set the board on a secure surface before you make your cut. Always remember your safety goggles, and take a good, balanced posture.

9. IN ORDER TO MAKE THE CUTS TO allow the board to fit around the post, you'll need to use the jigsaw. Be sure that the flat plate of the jigsaw rests firmly on the wood for the entire cut (it can be tempting to lift it or twist it to either side, but resist the urge). In order to cut out an **L**-shaped piece of wood, you'll need to make four cuts:

- ✔ Cut from the outside edge of the wood all the way to the inside corner of the **L** on one side.
- ✔ Cut from the outside edge of the wood all the way to inside corner of the **L** on the other side.
- ✔ Repeat both cuts on the other end of the tread

10. THE L-SHAPED CUTOUT SHOULD now fit loosely around the base of the post. It's better for it to be slightly loose than really tight or snug. Wood likes to be able to expand and contract, especially outdoors.

11. ONCE THE WOOD IS IN PLACE, use the galvanized nails and your hammer to secure it to the stair stringers below. Two or three nails, spaced evenly into each stringer, should be sufficient. I often find that screws designed for exterior decking do a better job of holding stair treads in place, so be prepared to use either nails or screws, whatever works best for you.

12. CONGRATULATIONS, YOU'RE DONE! Replacing a piece of rotted wood is usually a straightforward job, but not necessarily an easy one.

Installing a Pet Door

Tools you will need:
- ✔ Jigsaw with a sharp blade (a rough-cut wood blade for wooden doors, or a metal blade for metal doors)
- ✔ Drill and ⅛-inch drill bit
- ✔ Steel measuring tape
- ✔ Straight edge
- ✔ Hammer
- ✔ Screwdriver

Materials you will need:
- ✔ Pet door
- ✔ Tape
- ✔ Something to set the door on (like two sawhorses or a couple of trash cans)

One of the more frequent calls I get is a request to install pet doors in a door in someone's house. Perhaps the homeowner wants to put the kitty litter in the basement, or in a closet under the stairs, but a wooden door stands in the way, and they don't know how to go about it.

IT HAPPENED TO ME ONCE: I was called to help a couple who had already tried to do the pet-door installation. When I arrived I discovered that the husband had tried to drill the starter holes through a beautiful old wooden door that was about 1½ inches thick with a screwdriver bit instead of a drill bit! He just didn't know about drill bits, so he used the screwdriver bit that came with the drill.

I think that for most women the scariest part of trying to install a pet door is using a jigsaw to cut a large hole in the door. It is hard to hide a large hole in a door if you make a mistake. It's not like you can hang a picture over it or put a piece of furniture in front of it like you can with a hole in a wall. Before attempting this job—which is more scary than difficult—I strongly recommend that you practice with both your drill and jigsaw on a separate piece of wood. It is important to feel comfortable with both tools before starting on the door itself.

SHOPPING TIP: Jigsaw blades are designed to cut different kinds of materials. You can buy them for fine or rough wood cuts and for metal cuts. If your door is made of wood, as most interior doors are, get a blade designed for rough cuts. If your door is made of metal, which it often will be if it goes outside or into a basement or garage, make sure you get a blade designed for fine metal cuts.

All pet doors you purchase will come with a complete set of directions and a template for the hole you will cut. I will run through a rough set of directions that should supplement the ones that came with the door.

1. DETERMINE WHERE YOU WANT the pet door to be located. There is no right answer. One suggestion is to measure up from the floor to the bottom of your pet's stomach and using that measurement as the bottom of your opening. You can decide based on what you think

IT HAPPENED TO SOMEBODY ONCE (BUT NOT ME, THANKFULLY!): Be sure to make a rough mark, like a big red X on the door to indicate where the pet door will be cut before you remove the door from the hinges. It is remarkably easy to get the top and bottom of the door mixed up once it is off its hinges. More than one person has cut an opening for a cat door in the top of their door! This is not a mistake that is easy to hide!

will look best and what you think will work for your pet. Make a rough mark on the door to indicate the location.

2. THE NEXT THING YOU WILL WANT TO DO is remove the door from its hinges (see Chapter 5 for how to remove a door from its hinges). You don't have to remove the door from its hinges in order to install a pet door, but I find it makes the job much easier.

3. LAY THE DOOR ON YOUR SAWHORSES, trash cans, or a table, making sure that you have access to the area that you marked and that there is nothing under the area you will be cutting and drilling through. Place the template for the pet door opening on the door in the correct location, and use tape to hold it in place. Trace the line of the opening with a pencil and then remove the template, but don't throw it away; it may have directions printed on it that you'll need to refer to later. The safest thing is to hold onto it until the job is done.

4. PLACE A DRILL BIT THAT'S THE SAME size as (or larger than) your saw blade into your drill, and then drill a hole inside each corner of the template. Be sure to keep your drill perpendicular to the door while you're drilling so the hole doesn't go through the door at an angle. You're drilling these holes so you have a starting place for the jigsaw blade.

5. PLACE THE BLADE OF THE JIGSAW into one of the holes and—very carefully and slowly—start cutting along your line until you reach the next hole. The trick to using a jigsaw correctly is keeping its base flat against the surface of the door; this keeps you from lifting or tipping the saw. You also want to go slowly: The saw can only move through the wood as fast as it can cut; don't try to make it go any faster. When you reach a corner, stop.

6. LIFT THE SAW UP AND OUT, face it in the new direction, and then place it back in the hole. It's easier to do this than to try turning the saw. If your pet door has a curve along the top, exaggerate the slowness of the saw. Jigsaws don't like curves, they like straight lines; you have to convince your saw that the curve is just a bunch of small straight lines.

7. REPEAT UNTIL YOU HAVE CUT out all four sides of your opening.

8. THERE ARE TWO SIDES TO A PET DOOR. One side goes into the opening you just cut; the other sits on the surface of the door. The two sides are usually connected with four screws. Set the first side into the opening to see if it fits. If it doesn't, mark the area that needs more cutting with a pencil.

9. CONTINUE CUTTING AWAY WOOD until the pet door fits easily into the hole and the flap can move back and forth without interference.

10. PLACE THE DOOR back on its hinges.

11. FOLLOW THE DIRECTIONS THAT CAME with the pet door regarding screwing it to the larger door. You may need to pre-drill for the screws. On a couple of occasions, I've had difficulty getting all four screws to screw into something. If you have the same problem, don't worry; if at least three of the screws are tight, the door will be fine.

12. NOW THE HARD WORK STARTS—teaching your pet how to use its new door!

FINAL THOUGHTS ON MINOR CARPENTRY JOBS

After having completed this series of carpentry projects, you now have a working knowledge of how to plan a carpentry project. You also have a basic comfort level with some great power tools, including a circular saw, a compound miter saw, a jigsaw, and a handheld sander. With these combined skills, you're ready to take on many of the minor carpentry repair jobs that will be needed around your house. You are also qualified to take on some "beautification" projects involving wood trim. As time goes on, your confidence level will grow, and you may surprise yourself by saying, "I can do that!" to a project that in the past seemed impossible. Remember to keep safety as your first priority, and to have fun!

10. BUT ELECTRICITY SCARES ME

Women are more scared of electricity than anything else in their homes. I also used to be really scared of electricity; now I'm only a *little* scared of it. What happened for me was that I came to understand it a little better, I learned how to work with it safely, and I learned what my limits are with electrical situations. Let's face it: Electricity is different from a piece of wood or a paintbrush. A painting error can only result in an ugly room, while an electrical error could result in an actual injury (to you or your house). When I first started working with electricity in my house, I made a few mistakes. As a result, I experienced a few small shocks. They didn't hurt me, but they were unpleasant, and I became determined to learn enough to protect myself from future incidences.

Working with electricity may not appeal to you. Some readers will skip this chapter entirely, and that's completely okay with me. You shouldn't take on projects around your house that push you so far out of your comfort zone that you're scared. However, there are a lot of women out there who are tired of being scared of electricity and would like to know enough to safely take on small electrical projects in their homes. This chapter is for you. This chapter will not, however, tell you everything you ever needed to know about electricity but were afraid to ask. There are plenty of comprehensive electrical books available (see Resources), and for those of you who want to understand electricity at a deeper level, I strongly encourage you to go get the more detailed information that's available elsewhere.

The goal of this chapter is very simple: I want to treat electrical projects the same as the other home improvement projects I have covered in this book. I'll tell you which tools you'll need and how to complete the project safely, and then I'll go through the project step-by-step.

The Circuit Breaker Box: Where It All Begins

The electricity entering your home from the street comes into your main electrical panel, which is broken up into circuits. A circuit is like a road that travels through a specific area of your house and then returns to the electrical panel. If a thoughtful electrician wired your house, your electrical panel contains a map upon which each circuit (and where it goes) is labeled. If you're like many of us, however, you have inherited an electrical panel that has little or no labels. Before you take on any electrical projects, you need to identify where each circuit in your electrical panel goes, and then label them accordingly.

ELECTRICAL CIRCUIT ROADTRIP

This can actually be fun, and it should take no more than an hour or so. The best way to do it is with a friend and a couple of cell phones. This is what you do:

1. WALK THROUGH YOUR HOUSE and turn on every electrical switch that you find. This should cover most of the lights and fans.

2. NOW GO THROUGH AND TURN ON everything in your house that's plugged into an electrical outlet, including lamps, televisions, radios, and computers (be sure no files or programs are open on the computers).

3. HAVE ONE PERSON (PANEL PERSON) stand at the electrical panel with a notebook and pad. The other person (Moving Person) moves through the house with her own notebook and pad.

4. PANEL PERSON SHUTS OFF THE FIRST circuit breaker in the box and makes a note of which circuit number was shut off in her notebook.

5. MOVING PERSON WALKS AROUND the house and identifies what items lost power when the circuit was shut off, then calls Panel Person on the cell phone and tells her what they are.

6. MOVING PERSON AND PANEL PERSON each make a note identifying what was turned off in their notebooks.

7. THEY REPEAT THE PROCESS WITH the next circuit breaker in the box.

8. THE TWO PEOPLE CONTINUE THE process until each circuit has been shut off and identified.

9. ONCE THEY FEEL THAT THEY HAVE successfully identified all the circuits, Panel Person can begin to turn each circuit back on while Moving Person verifies that the correct items came back to life.

10. A NICE WAY TO FINISH THE PROJECT is to make a map that can be attached to the inside of the electrical panel with details about what items are included on each circuit. Keep a copy of the map somewhere else in the house for your records as well.

TURNING BREAKERS ON AND OFF

When a circuit breaker is in the full "on" position, it's leaning toward the center of the electrical panel. When a circuit breaker is in the "off" position, it will be leaning a little or a lot away from center.

The best way to turn a circuit breaker off is to push it hard to the outside of the box. So for the breakers on the left side of the box, "off" is to the left, and for breakers on the right side of the box, "off" is to the right.

Occasionally breakers will look like they're on when they're not; these are the ones that are only a little bit to the side of center when they're in the "off" position.

The best way to turn a circuit breaker on is to make sure it's all the way off first. Push it hard to the outside, and then push it hard all the way back to the inside. It will not move very easily, but when it does, it should feel like it kind of snaps or locks into place.

WHY SUCH A LONG LESSON ABOUT CIRCUIT BREAKERS?

Occasionally you'll see an electrician replace a ceiling light fixture after only turning off the power at the wall switch. If the pros want to do it that way, that's fine. However, I do not recommend it for the home do-it-yourselfer. The only way to be sure that there is no power going to the outlet, light switch, or light fixture you are working on is to shut off the power for the appropriate circuit at the electrical panel: That's why you went to the trouble of identifying all your circuits. So if you want to replace the light switch in your dining room with a dimmer switch, you can go to the electrical panel and turn off the breaker labeled "Dining Room lights." Then you can go back into the dining room and double-check to see if you can turn on the light. If the light does not come on, then you know you have successfully shut off the power to that circuit.

Doing Your Own Electrical Work

In most states, homeowners are allowed to do some electrical work in their own homes; however, it varies from location to location. The best thing to do is call your building inspector, electrical inspector, or electric company, and tell them what you would like to do. They'll let you know if you can proceed at once, if you need a permit, or if only a licensed electrician can do that particular job.

There are three simple electrical jobs that women ask me about frequently, all of which you can tackle safely (with permission from the proper authorities, of course):

✔ Replacing an outlet
✔ Replacing a light switch with a dimmer switch
✔ Replacing a light fixture

We'll go through each of these jobs step by step, but first let's look at the tools you will need to do basic electrical work. Most of the tools you need are already in your tool kit:

✔ Phillips head screwdriver
✔ Flathead screwdriver
✔ Needlenose pliers
✔ Utility knife

A couple of tools you may want to invest in that will bring you great peace of mind while you're working with electricity are very inexpensive:

✔ **CIRCUIT TESTER** (less than $5)

✔ **OUTLET TESTER** (less than $10)

✔ **BLACK ELECTRICAL TAPE**

With this handful of tools, you can easily take on these three electrical jobs.

Wall Outlets

There are two common reasons for replacing a wall outlet: It doesn't work, or you don't like its color. I have had experiences where I replaced a wall outlet that wasn't working with a new outlet, and when I turned the power back on, the new outlet didn't work either. At that point, I call an electrician; I don't have the skills to diagnose complicated electrical problems, but most of the time a bad outlet is just that—bad—and once it's replaced with a new one, the problem is gone.

IT HAPPENED TO ME ONCE: It's very embarrassing to call an electrician to fix a "broken" outlet that turns out to be wired to a wall switch. I made that mistake in my early days as a homeowner!

Sometimes one outlet in a room is wired to a wall switch, or half of the outlet is. This setup is most common in houses that were built without overhead lighting in the bedrooms; it allows for a lamp to be plugged into the designated outlet and turned on and off from the switch by the door. Before you decide your outlet is broken, make sure that it's not just wired to a nearby wall switch.

REPLACING A WALL OUTLET

1. THE FIRST THING YOU'LL NEED to do is purchase a replacement outlet. They can be found at hardware stores, home centers, and electrical supply houses.

2. TURN OFF THE CIRCUIT BREAKER for the circuit that corresponds to the outlet.

3. PLUG THE CIRCUIT TESTER INTO the outlet to verify that the outlet is not receiving power.

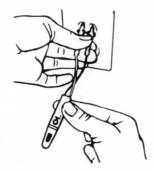

4. REMOVE THE OUTLET COVER with a flathead screwdriver.

5. REMOVE THE TWO SCREWS holding the outlet in place.

6. GENTLY TUG ON THE TWO METAL PIECES at the top and bottom of the outlet and pull it a couple of inches toward you. Don't touch anything behind or to the sides of the outlet.

NOTE: *Is the power really off? Am I really safe? Am I going to get zapped?* If you're still scared and you're asking yourself these questions at this point, you can use your circuit tester to double-check that the outlet is dead and no electricity is traveling through it. Just hold the legs of the circuit tester with one tip on a screw on either side of the outlet. In doing this, you're forming 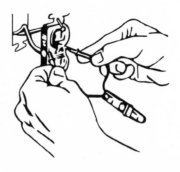 a circuit. If there is still power entering the outlet, the light on the circuit tester will come on. If the circuit is dead and the power is off, the light won't turn on.

7. ONCE YOU'VE VERIFIED THAT there is no power coming to this outlet, pull it farther out of the wall so you'll have better access to the wires.

> **TIP:** Some outlets will only have two wires attached to them, while others can have three, four, or five. If you start the project by unscrewing all the wires from the old outlet, it can be really easy to forget where they were attached to the old outlet, and that makes it very difficult to correctly attach them to the new outlet.
>
> Here are three different ways to keep the wires straight:
>
> a. Mark each wire with a piece of tape and a note like "top wire on right side" or "attached to green screw."
> b. Take a couple of pictures with a digital camera so that you can use them as a reference when reattaching the new outlet.
> c. Or, my favorite (and the system I use), which completely prevents me from making a mistake: As you remove a wire from the old outlet, immediately attach it to the new outlet in the corresponding position.

8. HOLD THE NEW OUTLET UP NEXT to the old one and make sure it's oriented the same way. Some outlets will say "top." For outlets with a hole for a third prong, make sure you keep it in the same position as the opening on the old outlet.

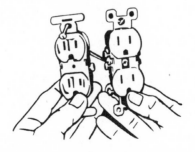

9. LOOSEN A SCREW ON THE SIDE of the old outlet until you can easily pull out the wire it's holding in place.

10. MOVE THAT WIRE TO THE NEW OUTLET and wrap the wire under the corresponding screw on the new outlet. You may need to use the needle-nose pliers to open the little hook in the end of the wire enough to get it off the screw on the old outlet. Once you've placed it around the screw on the new outlet, use the needle-nose pliers to close the opening in the hook back up.

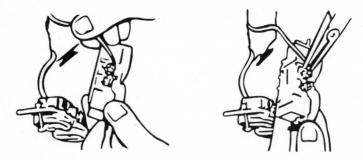

11. TIGHTEN THE SCREW down onto the wire.

12. REPEAT THIS PROCESS for each wire on the old outlet, continuing until they have all been transferred to the new outlet.

13. WRAP BLACK ELECTRICAL TAPE around the sides of the new outlet, covering all the screw heads that are securing wires. This is an extra safety precaution and a good habit to get into.

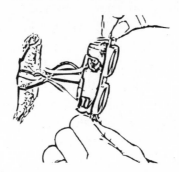

14. GENTLY PUSH THE OUTLET BACK into its box in the wall. You may have some difficulty getting the wires to fold back into place—they're very stiff. I have sometimes used a wooden spoon for help at this point.

15. ONCE THE OUTLET IS BACK in the box, reattach it by tightening the upper and lower screw. You may have to wiggle them around a bit to get them into their holes.

16. REATTACH THE COVER PLATE with a flathead screwdriver.

17. TURN THE CIRCUIT BREAKER back on and test your outlet, either with the circuit tester or by plugging a light into it.

18. CONGRATULATIONS—you did it!

Replacing A Dimmer Switch

Installing a dimmer switch is one of the quickest ways to change the look and feel of a room. It's also a great way to save energy: The dimmer the bulb, the less electricity is being consumed! Traditionally, dimmer switches were round and you had to push them in and turn them to reduce power to a light bulb. Today's dimmer switches are much more attractive and offer lots of different options, including on/off switches and mechanisms that slide up and down.

Whether you want to install a dimmer switch where a regular switch exists or replace an outdated or broken dimmer switch, I think you will be surprised by what a simple job it is.

REPLACING A DIMMER SWITCH

Tools you will need:
- ✔ Flathead screwdriver
- ✔ Needle-nose pliers
- ✔ Circuit tester

Materials you will need:
- ✔ New dimmer switch
- ✔ 3 wire nuts (should be included in the dimmer switch package)

SAFETY FIRST: Before you do anything else, turn off the appropriate circuit breaker at the electrical panel.

1. USE THE FLATHEAD SCREWDRIVER to remove the light switch cover plate.

2. USE THE FLATHEAD SCREWDRIVER to remove the two screws holding the switch to the box.

3. USE THE CIRCUIT TESTER TO verify that power to the switch has been shut off.

4. THERE SHOULD BE THREE WIRES attached to the old switch: a ground wire (either a green or bare copper wire) and two other wires (both black, or one white and one black).

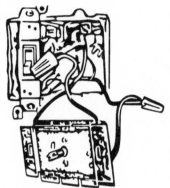

5. USE YOUR FLATHEAD SCREWDRIVER to loosen the three screws holding the wires to the old outlet. Pull the wires off the outlet. Set the outlet aside.

NOTE: *In order to attach the new wires on the dimmer switch to the wires coming from the wall, you may need to learn a new technique.* The wires coming out of the wall need to have a straight, bare wire end that's about ⅜ of an inch long. If the wire is currently bent in a circle, it's easiest to cut that part off with your needle-nose pliers and then strip ⅜ of an inch of the black or white plastic sheathing off the remaining wire with a utility knife. This ⅜-inch piece of bare wire is quite rigid; the bare wire at the ends of

IT HAPPENED TO ME ONCE: When you pull your old switch out of the wall, the wires may not look exactly as I have described them. Don't panic. The best thing to do is take a picture of your wiring with a digital camera or draw a picture of it, and then take it to your local hardware store. There should be someone there to walk you through the parts that are different, and explain how to handle it. The guys at my hardware store have saved my butt on more than one occasion. I take them cookies every year at Christmas just to thank them (and to ensure that they will always be there when I need them!).

the two black wires (or one black and one white wire) coming out of the dimmer switch is made up of little flexible filaments. Hold the flexible filaments of one of the dimmer switch wires up against the rigid part of one of the white or black wires coming out of the wall, and gently twist the flexible wires around the rigid wire. Then twist a wire nut over both wires until it's secure and you can't pull it off.

6. USING A WIRE NUT, ATTACH the green wire from the dimmer switch to the ground wire from the wall. Screw the nut on, clockwise, until it's tight.

7. ORIENT THE DIMMER SWITCH so it's in the correct up/down position. It's easier to do this before all the wires are attached.

8. USING ANOTHER WIRE NUT, attach one of the other two wires from the dimmer switch to one of the wires from the wall.

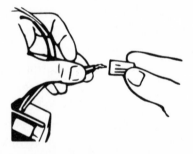

9. ATTACH THE FINAL WIRE FROM the dimmer switch to the final wire from the wall with the last wire nut.

10. DOUBLE-CHECK TO MAKE sure that all the wire nuts are very tight and won't move if you pull on them.

11. GENTLY EASE THE WIRES back into the wall opening, either with your fingers or the end of a wooden spoon.

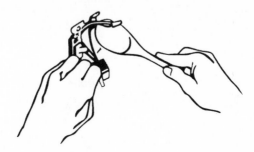

12. SCREW THE DIMMER SWITCH to the wall box with the two remaining screws.

13. ATTACH THE COVER PLATE with a flathead screwdriver.

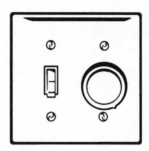

14. TURN THE POWER BACK ON at the main electrical panel.

15. TEST OUT YOUR DIMMER SWITCH, and enjoy the ambiance you've created!

Replacing An Interior Light Fixture

The final electrical project most women would love to be able to do themselves is replacing an outdated/ugly ceiling-or wall-mounted light fixture. This project is one of the more straightforward and (usually) easiest-to-complete electrical projects. The biggest challenge comes if you're replacing a ceiling fixture; it's difficult to do something you have never done before while standing on a ladder with your arms extended above your head. Imagine if the first time you ever changed a diaper, the baby was taped to a ceiling and you were standing on a ladder; or the first time you put hoop earrings in someone else's ears, her head was next to the ceiling (where it was quite dark, because the light fixture needed to be replaced). It's not the job itself that is difficult but its challenging circumstances.

I tell you this in the hopes that you won't get discouraged if it's more difficult than you expected. The instructions you will receive with your new light may or may not be helpful to you, but they certainly will not be sympathetic to the fact that you are doing this for the first time!

INTERIOR LIGHT FIXTURES

If the wiring in your home is currently up to code, you shouldn't run into any ugly surprises when you remove the existing fixture. But if anything looks funky to you when you remove the existing fixture, it's a great time to give yourself permission to call a licensed electrician.

REPLACING AN INTERIOR LIGHT FIXTURE

Tools you will need:
- ✔ Small Phillips head and flathead screwdrivers
- ✔ Needle-nose pliers
- ✔ Utility knife
- ✔ Step stool or ladder

Materials you will need:
- ✔ New light fixture

✔ Electrical tape
✔ Wire nuts (should be included with new fixture)

REMOVE THE EXISTING FIXTURE

All light fixtures are different, so some of what I say here may not apply to your fixture. Just keep going until you find a step that fits.

1. TURN OFF THE POWER TO your light's circuit at the electrical panel.

2. REMOVE the globe(s).

3. UNSCREW the light bulb(s).

4. LOOSEN THE SMALL SCREWS (often decorative) that are holding the light fixture to the wall or ceiling. Be prepared to catch the weight of the light fixture.

5. THE FIXTURE SHOULD NOW BE hanging from two or three wires that are connected to the wires coming from the electrical box in the wall or ceiling with wire nuts.

6. CAREFULLY UNSCREW THE WIRE nuts, holding the black (or black and white) fixture wires in place. *Do not touch any bare wires!*

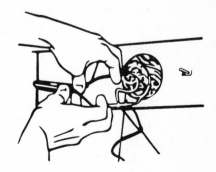

7. USE YOUR CIRCUIT TESTER, held up to the tips of the bare wires, to verify that these wires are no longer live. Once you've done that, you can finish removing the existing fixture by unhooking the wires from one another. Don't forget to unscrew the ground wire, if you have one.

8. MOST FIXTURES HAVE A METAL mounting (or fixture) strap that sits across the face of the electrical box. This strap is what the old fixture was attached to. Remove it by unscrewing the two screws holding it in place.

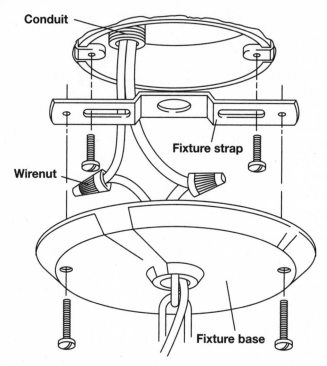

Conduit

Fixture strap

Wirenut

Fixture base

INSTALLING THE NEW FIXTURE

1. TAKE SOME TIME TO READ THE installation directions that came with your new fixture. They may be undecipherable, with bad drawings and very small print; occasionally, they will be well written and have clear images.

2. IF YOU'RE LUCKY, YOUR NEW fixture will reattach in the same way the original was attached. I am rarely this lucky. Before you start attaching wires, play with the new fixture and try to get a sense of how it attaches, what screws go where, and what their purpose is.

I've discovered over time that this step is very useful in helping me get a finished image of the installation. After I have that, I can often work back through the directions and they will make more sense, even if they were initially unclear.

3. ATTACH THE FIXTURE STRAP that came with the new fixture to the electrical box with the two screws provided. Sometimes it's easier to use the two screws that were holding the original fixture strap in place. Check to make sure that the fixture strap is oriented in the correct direction, as shown in the installation instructions.

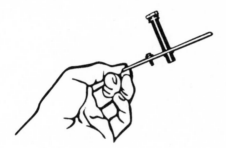

NOTE: The fixture strap may come with a long, threaded tube that goes through its center hole. If you have one of these, then the globe will be held in place with a small finial that threads onto the end of the tube. The length of the threaded tube will have to be adjusted once the fixture is firmly attached to the ceiling. You'll be able to figure out how long it needs to be and adjust it at the end of the installation by placing the globe on the fixture.

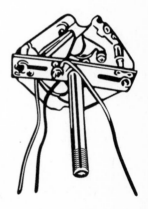

4. ATTACH THE WIRES FROM THE new fixture to the wires coming out of the box, exactly as the old wires were attached. This is the simple mantra to remember: black to black, white to white, and green to ground. Screw a wire nut clockwise, firmly, onto each pair of wires.

5. GENTLY TUCK THE WIRES, wire nuts attached, back into the electrical box.

6. SECURE THE NEW FIXTURE to the box following the installation directions.

7. IF YOUR FIXTURE HAS ONE OF THE long threaded tubes, now might be the time to attach the finial to the end of the tube. You can adjust the length of the threaded tube by screwing or unscrewing it a little bit. You want just enough of its threads showing through the fixture so that the decorative screw or finial will securely snug the fixture up against the wall, like in this diagram.

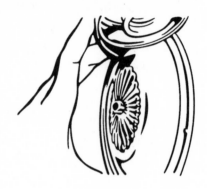

8. INSTALL THE NEW GLOBES and light bulb in the correct order for your fixture.

IT HAPPENED TO ME ONCE: It's easy to get so excited about getting the light bulbs installed that you put them in before you install the globes. I've had to unscrew many a light bulb so that I could go back and install the globe. In fixtures where the globe covers the bulbs completely, however, you're supposed to put the bulbs in before you put the globe on.

9. TURN THE POWER BACK on at the main panel.

10. FLIP THE SWITCH, and enjoy your new light fixture.

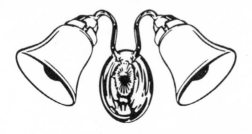

 **IMPORTANT NOTE:** You may have to touch up the wall after installing the new fixture. Use joint compound and a putty knife to fill any small holes or areas that are now visible around the new fixture. Once the compound dries, you can sand it and paint it.

FINAL WORDS ON ELECTRICAL PROJECTS

There is no way I can prepare you for all the little unexpected things that happen when trying to complete electrical projects. What I can tell you is that if something goes wrong, there is a great chance that it's not your fault, and that there is a simple solution to whatever problem you have encountered. If you get stuck at any point in the process, try an Internet search: You will often find a picture that is worth a thousand words (or a thousand words themselves) describing your exact situation.

One of the biggest challenges with installing light fixtures is that each one is just different enough from the last one to make installation frustratingly different. Take the time, before you are on a ladder, to work through all the steps and get familiar with the different parts and pieces and how they go together. This will save you untold frustration and will keep your arms from getting really tired while working over your head. You might want to schedule a massage as a reward for the awkward position you had to operate in while installing your light fixture; you'll be able to afford it with the money you saved by not hiring an electrician!

RESOURCES

1. *HOME IMPROVEMENT 1-2-3: EXPERT ADVICE FROM THE HOME Depot*. This book is available at all Home Depot stores. It covers an extensive array of home improvement projects, and it has great photos.

2. THE HOME DEPOT OFFERS BOOKS THAT GO INTO MUCH GREATER detail than *Home Improvement 1-2-3*. Books on wiring, painting, decorating, plumbing, tiling, and more are available from The Home Depot if you want to delve more deeply into a given area. What I like best about these books is that the projects are broken down into steps, and that they use real photographs.

3. *THE TOMBOY TOOLS GUIDE TO HOME IMPROVEMENT,* BY LYN Herrick. Tomboy Tools is a tool and home improvement company for women. This guide covers many small home maintenance projects that I didn't include in this book. Appliance repair, clogged drains, and winterizing your plumbing are just a few of the projects included in this guide, which was written by women for women. It's available through their website, www.tomboytools.com, where you can also take a look at the line of tools they designed for women.

4. *THE FAMILY HANDYMAN* IS A MONTHLY MAGAZINE FULL OF great tips, techniques, and tool ideas that are useful and fun to read. The last page in each month's issue includes a funny section on goof-ups and mistakes.

5. *THIS OLD HOUSE* MAGAZINE AND WWW.THISOLDHOUSE.COM are both full of great tips from highly skilled professionals who do a good job of making most of the information accessible to do-it-yourselfers.

6. THE INTERNET IS A VAST AND SEEMINGLY INFINITE RESOURCE. Type in "How to replace a toilet," and your search will return multiple websites with step-by-step instructions, many of which will have video clips you can watch. My only frustration with many of the websites I visit is the amount of advertising that I have to wade through. I have found the following websites to be useful:

- ✔ www.diynetwork.com
- ✔ www.doityourself.com
- ✔ www.homedepot.com
- ✔ www.ronhazelton.com
- ✔ www.diyornot.com (This website does a cost comparison between doing the job yourself versus hiring a professional.)

ACKNOWLEDGMENTS

This book wouldn't have been possible without the help of the following people:

Diane Daniel, my own personal angel, who jumpstarted my business with the article she wrote about me in the Boston Globe and who whispered in my ear, "You should write this book."

My women clients, for their trust: They open their homes and their hearts to me. I count many of them as my friends today. Special thanks to Mary Satko for being the first.

Lisa Kolarik, who allowed me to push the boundaries of what I thought I could do each time she said, "Come on Marie, we can do this."

The women who attend my classes and lectures, for giving me the opportunity to teach.

Everyone who read a chapter or two of my work-in-progress and gave me great feedback.

My editor at Seal Press, Krista Lyons, for believing that my passion for teaching women was enough and for holding my hand throughout the process of writing my first book.

My copyeditor Krissa Lagos, designer Tabitha Lahr, illustrator Tim McGrath, and the rest of the staff at Seal Press and Perseus Books, for all your hard work to make this book a success.

The contractors, plumbers, electricians, carpenters, painters, wallpaper hangers, handymen, and helpful neighbors who patiently answered my questions and taught me so much. I am deeply grateful to you all, but special thanks to Gary Whittemore, Tom Greenwood, Bob Lynch, and the guys at MacKay Hardware and Littleton Lumber.

Jo Derr, the best friend a girl could ever have, for sharing the journey with me and reminding me that I can be as big as I dream of being.

Jenni, Lu, Marcia, Sally, and Tamison: the girlfriends I waited for my whole life. You were worth the wait.

My parents: Words can never truly thank you for your neverending love, support, and encouragement.

Renee Baggot, my sister and dearest friend, for believing I could be all that I was scared to dream to be.

My brothers, David and Michael Levesque, for cheering me on and being so proud of me.

My daughters, Renee and Keely: Thank you for believing that Mommy can fix anything, and for sharing my dream with me.

My husband and best friend, Bill Leonard: The biggest thanks of all go to you. My dreams began to come true as soon as you showed up.

INDEX

ABOUT THE AUTHOR

© Deborah Bain

Marie Levesque Leonard first began working on home improvement projects as a child in Albuquerque, New Mexico. During that time her father enlisted her and her three siblings to help him out with the many projects he took on, which ranged from furniture-building to antique car restoration. When the family relocated to northern Vermont in 1971, Marie expanded her repertoire as a "go fer" as her family entered the rental property business. Marie spent many summers helping her parents build and maintain their rental units, but she really became a serious do-it-herselfer when she and her husband bought their first home in 1993. Taking on projects she had no experience with gave her opportunities to expand her range of problem-solving skills.

Before starting Marie's Home Improvement, Marie spent ten years working in corporate America as a financial analyst and human relations generalist, followed by ten years running her first business as a Corporate Trainer, specializing in communication skills and conflict resolution.

Today, Marie lives with her husband, Bill, and her daughters, Renee and Keely, in Westford, Massachusetts. Just like the cobbler's shoeless kids, Marie's home always has a long list of projects waiting for her time. When not working on that list, or helping her clients improve their homes, Marie loves to hang out with her daughters, play golf with her husband, walk her dogs, and watch her favorite Boston sports teams compete.

In addition to running Marie's Home Improvement, Marie finds time to volunteer for the local Habitat for Humanity and regularly speaks to women's groups on her favorite topic: The personal-growth potential for women in taking on home improvement projects. You can find out more about Marie and her current and upcoming projects, read her blog, and find out what her favorite tools are by visiting her website at www.marieshomeimprovement.com.

SELECTED TITLES FROM SEAL PRESS

For more than thirty years, Seal Press has published
groundbreaking books. By women. For women.
Visit our website at www.sealpress.com.
Check out the Seal Press blog at www.sealpress.com/blog.

THE BOSS OF YOU: EVERYTHING A WOMAN NEEDS TO KNOW TO START, RUN, AND MAINTAIN HER OWN BUSINESS, by Emira Mears & Lauren Bacon. $15.95, 1-58005-236-3. Provides women entrepreneurs the advice, guidance, and straightforward how-to's they need to start, run, and maintain a business.

DIRT: THE QUIRKS, HABITS, AND PASSIONS OF KEEPING HOUSE, edited by Mindy Lewis. $15.95, 1-58005-261-4. From grime, to clutter, to spit-clean—writers share their amusing relationships with dirt.

SHE-SMOKE: BBQ BASICS FOR WOMEN, by Julie Reinhardt. $16.95, 1-58005-284-3. The owner of Smokin' Pete's BBQ in Seattle lays down all the delicious facts for women who aspire to be BBQ queens.

OWN IT!: THE UPS AND DOWNS OF HOMEBUYING FOR WOMEN WHO GO IT ALONE, by Jennifer Musselman. $15.95, 1-58005-230-4. This mix of guidebook how-to and personal narrative covers the how-to's and hiccups of homebuying for women braving the process alone.

THE MONEY THERAPIST: A WOMAN'S GUIDE TO CREATING A HEALTHY FINANCIAL LIFE, by Marcia Brixey. $15.95, 1-58005-216-9. Offers women of every financial strata the tools they need to manage their money, set attainable budget goals, get out of debt, and create a healthy financial life.

THE LIST: 100 WAYS TO SHAKE UP YOUR LIFE, by Gail Belsky. $15.95, 1-58005-256-8. Get a tattoo, ride in a fire truck, or use food as foreplay—this collection of 100 ideas will inspire women to shake things up and do something they never dared to consider.

31901046565117